M000197903

Lessons Learned on the Mission Field

Carl Luepnitz

CONTENTS

Copyright © 2018 Carl Luepnitz.

All rights reserved. No part of this book may be used or reproduced by any means, graphic, electronic, or mechanical, including photocopying, recording, taping or by any information storage retrieval system without the written permission of the author except in the case of brief quotations embodied in critical articles and reviews.

Author permits copying of Appendices A, B and C for personal use only.

Scripture quotations marked (NIV) are taken from the Holy Bible, New International Version®, NIV®. Copyright © 1973, 1978, 1984, 2011 by Biblica, Inc.™ Used by permission of Zondervan. All rights reserved worldwide. HYPERLINK "http://www.zondervan.com/" www.zondervan.com The "NIV" and "New International Version" are trademarks registered in the United States Patent and Trademark Office by Biblica, Inc.

Unless otherwise specified, all scriptures are quoted
from the King James Version of the Bible.

LifeRich Publishing is a registered trademark of The Reader's Digest Association, Inc.

LifeRich Publishing books may be ordered through booksellers or by contacting:

LifeRich Publishing
1663 Liberty Drive
Bloomington, IN 47403
www.liferichpublishing.com
1 (888) 238-8637

Because of the dynamic nature of the Internet, any web addresses or links contained in this book may have changed since publication and may no longer be valid. The views expressed in this work are solely those of the author and do not necessarily reflect the views of the publisher, and the publisher hereby disclaims any responsibility for them.

Any people depicted in stock imagery provided by Getty Images are models, and such images are being used for illustrative purposes only. Certain stock imagery © Getty Images.

ISBN: 978-1-4897-1978-2 (sc)
ISBN: 978-1-4897-1977-5 (hc)
ISBN: 978-1-4897-1976-8 (e)

Library of Congress Control Number: 2018911371

Print information available on the last page.

LifeRich Publishing rev. date: 11/05/2018

Foreword and Endorsements

I have been a very small part of my Brother Carl's Ministry for around 20 years and I thank him for writing this "How To" book for missionaries. I was blessed to be taught the things of the Spirit by Carl Luepnitz before this book.

I remember observing his life, being this freshly Holy Spirit baptized young man that had no teaching on the things of the Spirit. Carl's daily walk was being led by the Spirit in everything he did and it made a great impression on my life. He stopped and prayed about everything, even while he drove. He prayed about what day, what hour and what place, he took nothing for granted. Carl always followed the Holy Spirit and we did nothing until we had direction from the Holy Spirit. God used Carl to groom me in preparation for my future missionary ministry years. The way this book is written it is very straight forward and no nonsense, just the way he follows the Holy Spirit in his own life.

Before I met Carl and Helen I had never seen a miracle, but in Eternal Love Ministries, we saw miracles, deliverances and healings every day. I saw one miracle where God re-created a lady's foot after it had been ran over by an eighteen wheel truck. It looked like a swimming fin. We prayed and I could hear the bones popping as God made her foot normal again. There were seven men who would never come into the church, but after seeing this miracle they came running forward to be saved. Another time, when we were flagged down by a man, he wanted us to pray for his daughter. She looked gray and clammy when we prayed for her. I didn't understand what was being said, but after several minutes she sat up and said we should have a service. During the service, we had several men come forward to be saved. It was normal after some notable miracle that there were always groups of people who wanted to be saved. After the service, I talked with our interpreter who said, she was told, that the daughter had been dead for nine hours. I believe God kept me in the dark because I don't know if I had the faith to pray for raising the dead. We have seen hundreds of miracles while working with Eternal Love Ministries. Even when Carl sent us out without him we saw miracles, deliverances and healing in every service, because we prayed the prayers he told us to pray and followed his directions, we got the same results as Carl did through the Holy Spirit.

I recommend this book to people that have the call to be missionaries or for anyone that wants a closer walk with the Lord. The principles taught in this book will work anywhere for any one; all you have to do is apply them to your life.

Dr. T. Jerry Caver, Dean of Citadel Bible College

Carl & Helen Luepnitz are amazing people of faith with an abiding presence of the Holy Spirit in their lives.

As I read the stories of faith, the challenges and great victories, I remember back, with great joy, twenty-nine years ago when Carl invited us to come and work with Eternal Love Ministries. It was an education in missions.

Watching Carl and Helen follow the Lord Jesus, obeying the Holy Spirit and ministering to pastors and hurting oppressed people developed in us a deeper hunger for people of all nations.

Carl teaches with profound revelation and signs following the Word of God. "Lessons Learned on the Mission Field" will inspire your faith and give you a personal look into the heart of a "General". -

Thank you Carl and Helen for your amazing love for the Master.

Norman & Carol Jacobs
Pastors of Trinity Family Church, Columbia, TN

Carl Luepnitz had a long career in the United States Army which prepared him with the discipline, commitment to detail and an affinity for strategy that has helped him to be a success on the mission field.

All ministry is actually a military mission, a very real warfare against the ultimate evil enemy!

God's strategies, revealed in His Word, enable us to overcome in spiritual conflict.

Listen and learn from this seasoned warrior and servant of God. Carl will help guide you to victory on the battlefield of gospel ministry!

David Brown
Pastor, Victory Church, Amarillo, TX

This mighty Christian warrior challenges today's Christian to wake up and heed God's Word. Using true life experiences from his military years, his work on the mission field and his revelation from the Word of God, Carl Luepnitz reminds us that there is a great spiritual war we face today and satan is deceiving Christians and destroying lives. We need to find our purpose for reaching this lost world, always relying on the power of the Holy Spirit. The fields are ripe for the harvest and the lessons learned by this mighty missionary can save us from many years of ineffective ministry.

Steve Gryseels

I first met Carl and Helen Luepnitz in the fall of 1991 while on a short-term mission trip to their Saltillo base. They had just completed the purchase of the school in Puerto Escondido, Oaxaca.

While talking with me he was describing the need for labor to help at both bases, which amazingly I had experience in almost every area of need.

I spent most of 1992 working with Eternal Love Ministries. I can only describe that time in my life as the most exciting, rewarding time in my life. As a worker and often times traveling companion to Carl the time was truly an adventure in God. I watched him take the time to pray about the seemingly insignificant things before getting direction from God and then it was full speed ahead accomplishing more than any man half his age.

Because of his military background, the story of the centurion in Matt. 8:5-10 describes Carl to me. Especially verse 9:"For I also am a man under authority, having soldiers under me, and I say to this one, 'Go' and he goes; and to another, 'come' and he comes; and to my servant 'do this,' and he does it"

Following Carl around was like living out a modern day version of the book of Acts to me. The whole Luepnitz family took me in and treated me as a member of the family. When I was in the Saltillo base Helen fed me at their table and fussed over me like one of their own. I am about the same age as Carl Jr. and he and Marina took me in also. This family will always hold a special place in my heart.

Allen Kinney

I first met Carl and Helen Luepnitz in 1988 after a friend had spoken of them. Carl was (and is) a retired military officer, who dedicated his life to ministry, when his service to our country was fulfilled.

Carl and Helen traveled extensively in the ministry and had their main focus on the Nation of Mexico. He and Helen would enter into the country and minister the Lord to many who had either never heard the message or given their lives to Jesus. They were totally sold out to the carrying of the message to many.

We heard glowing reports of miracles and healing of many kinds. We invited Carl and Helen to come speak at our church in the Austin, Texas area the next time that they would be in Texas. I'll never forget that first night. Our church was full. The Holy Spirit was at work drawing more people into our meeting than we usually saw. We could tell that God was up to something special. Carl & Helen brought something refreshing with them. One women, who went on to be a member of our church, had been addicted to cigarettes for many years and had a strong desire to overcome this habit. She told us later that, from the time Carl laid hands on her, all desire and need for cigarettes left, and stayed gone for the rest of her life. She has been free for close to 40 years.

The main thing though that I remembered about them, was their tireless efforts to carry the Gospel to as many as possible. They gladly spent and were spent to carry the message of hope with joy, dedication and determination. Many times they sacrificed greatly to do so.

I saw them in various cities and towns in Mexico such as, Saltillo, Monterrey, Ciudad Victoria, and others. They just kept going, healings, miracles, helps. They always traveled with joy and the presence of God and power. This book will bless and excite you as you hear of their wonderful journeys through life!

Pastor Don Aldridge

PREFACE

When the Lord told me to write this book and gave me the title "Lessons Learned on the Mission Field," I was surprised as the first book had been in print less than two months. I thought to myself, this will be easy and quickly wrote what readily came to my mind, while remembering it is a sequel to the first book. I tried to avoid subjects that would be offensive to any reader as I had done in the first book. It became obvious that this was not what the Lord required; and everything changed. One comment from the Lord reminded me I was writing to please Him, not man. In addition I became acutely aware that this book was not my book but the Lord's and He knew how He would use it. Settling on the content and tone took me some time as the intent was to shake and invigorate the millions of people who appeared to be drifting in complacency, without fear of God and under false impressions.

I have included many scriptures (God's Word) and examples how we, His children, are ignoring God's Word to our eternal detriment. God wants us to be part of His End Time Army; as soldiers who know His voice and obey Him. We must seek His presence, put Him first in our lives, fast, pray and read the Word. As we seek His presence, we will be getting rid of the perversions and corruption (sins) that so easily interfere or block our relationship with our Heavenly Father, the Lord Jesus and the Holy Spirit.

Because this book is a wakeup call, I would like to clarify to the reader that we are not saved by works. We are called to live a changed life and this is not in conflict with the incredible grace that God has provided for us. If the fruits of the Spirit are not taking hold in one's life and the tendency to sin is not diminishing in that life, there is a great problem that needs to be dealt with.

The purpose of the first book was to bring people who had fallen by the wayside back to the Lord. We know Jesus is the Way, the Truth and the Life. Diligently seek Him. The need is greater now than it was when I started writing the first book; as we are approaching catastrophic times in which only the Father, Jesus and the Holy Spirit can provide what is needed. His security, safety, sustenance, guidance/direction, joy, peace and harmony are and will continue to be desperately needed. We must reach Him now while He is knocking at our door.

CHAPTER 1

Introduction

DOING THE WILL OF GOD:

The wonders and joys on the mission field never ceased as God fulfilled our schedule each day with His glorious presence, and the needs of the people were graciously met. It was truly a joy, an inner and outer elation, to see God's miraculous power manifested in the healings and in the words of comfort that were applied as appropriate. Such elation is beyond measure or price just to experience it and to know that Almighty God would use us as His instruments of love to touch people who felt forsaken and sometimes even worthless. Nothing on this earth is comparable to the feeling of God's deep love and compassion for all people, created by Him in His image and for fellowship with Him. Oh, that all mankind would turn to the one who created them and realize His divine love and plans he has for them – heaven on earth. We are his children to whom He extends His love beyond measure, but we must accept His love. He sacrificed His son Jesus on the cross for our sins; that all who believe, accept and confess His sacrifice for us, might be rid of the burdens of sin and free to fellowship with God our Father. These lessons learned are to help prepare the readers for work of the ministry that we all encounter and are called to do as we follow the Shepard down the path he has chosen for us.

When my book "A Challenge to Live" had been published about a month and a half, the Lord said to write a sequel to it titled "Lessons learned on the Mission Field". The dictionary states a sequel is a logical consequence, a literary work continuing a story begun in a preceding one. It is by its name to address lessons which I learned on the mission field.

Helen and I spent 26 years in the US Army (much of it overseas), and we continued living in foreign countries about 40 more years as missionaries; with God, Jesus and the Holy Spirit in charge. Obviously, I had opportunity for many learning experiences, and we were privileged for Jesus to trust us with some of His authority and power, which on occasion was not easy for the human mind to comprehend.

We soon learned at a basic Christian level how He wanted us to minister salvation, healing to the sick, deliverance to demonically controlled people and help in the resolution of people problems. The Lord had us operate in most of the nine Gifts of the Holy Spirit, with the nine Fruit of the Holy Spirit as a guiding presence in our lives. Over time we were confronted and sometimes baffled by the multitude and complexity of problems people were experiencing that were rooted in the spiritual issues.

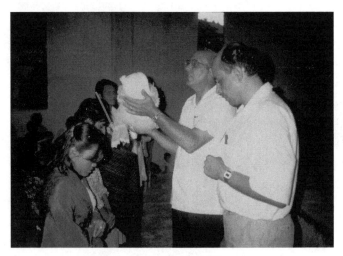

Dedication of Babies, Guerrero

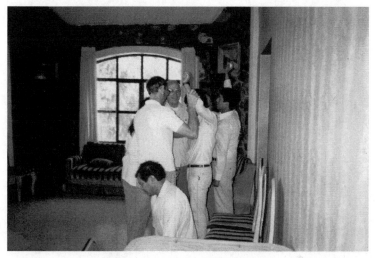

Praying for Baptism of Holy Spirit, Saltillo, Coahuila

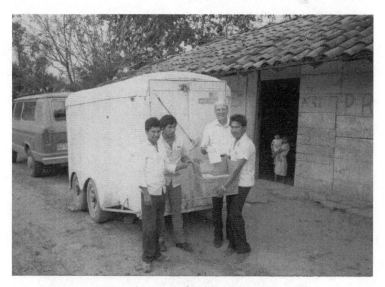

Distribution of Bibles, Veracruz

Projecting Movies, Monterrey, Nuevo Leon

I spoke forcefully to myself to keep doubt out that God would heal when I pushed my hand into a leg full of puss that was scheduled for amputation the next day. I had to tell myself, "Just speak the Word in Jesus name," when I was facing a man with gnarled fingers, hands and arms; or people with a white eye, or leprosy, or multiple sclerosis or Crohn's disease or lupus disease. The Lord has spoken to me on several occasions, "Carl, don't doubt, only believe."

Praying for the Sick in Oaxaca

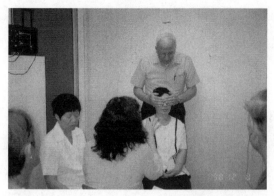

Praying for Blind Lady in Singapore, Asia

Visiting Pastors Praying for Sick in Saltillo, Coahuila

Praying for Men in Saltillo Auditorium

This man brought his son for prayer to the Puerto Escondido Base

USE GOD'S AUTHORITY:

God created mankind in His image to be in a loving relationship with Him. Mankind was to have dominion over the earth. A delegated authority, not God's supreme and absolute authority but a jurisdictional limited authority. Because of mankind's sin (disobedience) they were unable to fulfill God's purposes and plans for their lives, and rule over the world was given to satan.

When Jesus came to earth, He carried God's authority. "And Jesus came and spake unto them, saying, All power is given unto me in heaven and in earth." (Matthew 28:18 KJV)

"But Jesus called them unto him, and said, Ye know that the princes of the Gentiles exercise dominion over them, and they that are great exercise authority upon them. But it shall not be so among you: but whosoever will be great among you, let him be your minister; And whosoever will be chief among you, let him be your servant: Even as the Son of man came not to be ministered unto, but to minister, and to give his life a ransom for many." (Matthew 20:25-28 KJV)

As Christians we are to use any authority we have, within our areas of influence, under the authority of Jesus and the direction of His Spirit.

BREAKING BARRIERS:

Before the start of our ministry in Mexico the Lord sent a man to me that gave me the ideas for two prayers. They inspired me to write what is now Appendices A and B in the book "A Challenge to Live" and in this book. Appendix A covers getting rid of certain curses and demonic influence. Appendix B is to get rid of any unforgiveness. I used these two prayers almost every time I ministered to a group of people and as needed with individuals.

Per request by several people who are using the book "A Challenge to Live" in their daily ministry, I am including Appendices A and B in Lessons Learned on the Mission Field. Healing Scriptures which I used over the years, is also added as Appendix 3.

Even after going through those two prayers and commanding the sickness, demons, etc. to leave in Jesus name, some people were not healed or delivered. Obviously, there were other complications in their lives that needed to be taken care of before God's healing power was automatically received. Their complications (barriers) needed to be addressed and eliminated before they were free to discover and explore their true identity in Christ. The barriers in any given individual may be many in number and variety, and may involve sins of ancestors from many generations.

The obstacles that hold people in bondage for the most part are clearly stated in the Bible; however, they aren't taken seriously by the people affected (which is nearly everyone). The chapters in this book "Lessons Learned on the Mission Field" address many of these obstacles. These obstacles/barriers/problems are there because the person did not repent of every sin. The person did not recognize what they were doing as sin or they had no fear that God's Word was true and that there was a consequence for their action as clearly stated in God's Word.

SOME EXAMPLES OF THE SIN IGNORED:

Millions of people are under God's curse because they have unforgiveness in their heart.

Jesus stated in Mark 11:26, (KJV) "But if ye do not forgive, neither will your Father which is in heaven forgive your trespasses." About 1/3 of the people in regular churches in the 1980s had unforgiveness. I believe it is over 50 percent now. People who don't repent, ask the Lord's forgiveness, and forgive everyone all offenses, will end up in the lake of fire.

Idolatry is another prime example:

This occurs when people place religious beliefs, time, people, activities, how you vote, thoughts, decisions, objects etc. ahead of God. This is occurring even though the Word clearly states in many scriptures that those who practice idolatry and have not repented will not enter the kingdom of God but spend eternity in torment (in the lake of fire).

"But the fearful and unbelieving and the abominable, and murderers, and whore mongers, and sorcerers and idolaters and all liars shall have their part in the lake which burneth with fire and brimstone." (Rev. 21:8 KJV)

—"Be not deceived, neither fornicators, nor idolaters, nor adulterers,"—"shall inherit the kingdom of God." (I Cor. 6:9-10 KJV)

GOD'S BLESSINGS AND CURSES:

Many people suffer disease, sickness, infirmities, problems, etc. needlessly because they ignore God's word on blessings and curses. Deuteronomy 28:1-68 is an example: Verses 1 through 14 are blessings of obedience. Verses 15 through 68 are curses because of disobedience. Disobedience must be repented for, as with any curse. Blessings and curses are mentioned over 600 times in scripture.

Calling good evil and evil good, and blaspheming God for the evil, certainly falls in the cursed category. "For without are" — "and idolaters and whosoever loveth and maketh a lie" (Rev. 22:65 KJV)

"If my people, which are called by my name, shall humble themselves, and pray and seek my face, and turn from their wicked ways: then I will hear from heaven, and I will forgive their sins, and heal their land." (II Chronicles 7:14 KJV)

It is my hope, prayers, and expectations that millions of people will, as they read this book and realize their fallen state, repent and receive the Lord Jesus.

As each of the chapters were being written for this book, it was obvious that life is a learning process that never stops. The lessons learned therefore include refinements that are the result of hindsight understanding of revealing scriptures.

CHAPTER 2

Anointed Environment For Ministry

GOD'S PRESENCE

A lesson learned on the mission field was that you must maintain an anointed environment for your ministry. As a missionary for the most High God, your environment should be so filled with God's anointing that any legitimate visitor will know they have entered into God's presence. What the visitor senses when the entrance door opens may set the stage for everything else that is to happen while they are with you, then and in the future.

They will be more receptive to the Word of God; and their turmoil, if any, will subside as they are touched by God's peace. Concurrently, an offer, in love, of coffee and American cake, along with a smile, is never refused. As they bathe in the anointing it seems like heaven–on-earth to them, and your ministry will usually be a pleasant and profitable experience. If other people arrive, invite them to sit and rest while they, if appropriate, watch the ministry. Many are saved, healed and delivered before you minister directly to them.

"It came even to pass, as the trumpeters and singers were as one, to make one sound to be heard in praising and thanking the Lord; and when they lifted up their voice with the trumpets and cymbals and instruments of music and praised the Lord, saying, for He is good; for His mercy endureth forever, that then the house was filled with a cloud, even the house of the Lord. So that the priests could not stand to minister by reason of the cloud for the glory of God had filled the house of God." (2 Chronicles 5:13-14 KJV)

"And it came to pass, when the priests were come out of the holy place, that the cloud filled the house of the Lord so that the priests could not stand to minister because of the cloud." (I Kings 8:10-11a KJV)

We see in the above scriptures the things that led up to and maintained the anointed cloud. We see the musicians with their instruments praising and thanking the Lord. When they lifted up their voices, accompanying the instruments, and praised the Lord saying, "For He is good and His mercies endure forever"; then the house was filled with the glory of the Lord.

Here the musical instruments played a big part: however, if you have no musicians, a similar effort can be achieved by prayer or using CD's or other music sources, or just singing and praying in tongues. Obviously, the hearts of everyone were ready (prepared, holy and in unity) to thank the Lord for all He had done, to continue praising Him; and thanking Him for His goodness and mercy that endure forever. Missionaries can enhance the anointed condition with a repentant, thankful/grateful heart that is full of the fruit of the Spirit.

"And beside this, giving all diligence, add to your faith virtue; and to virtue knowledge; And to knowledge temperance; and to temperance patience; and to patience godliness; And to godliness brotherly kindness; and to brotherly kindness charity. For if these things be in you, and abound, they make you that ye shall neither be barren nor unfruitful in the knowledge of our Lord Jesus Christ. But he that lacketh these things is blind, and cannot see afar off, and hath forgotten that he was purged from his old sins. Wherefore the rather, brethren, give diligence to make your calling and election sure: for if ye do these things, ye shall never fall: For so an entrance shall be ministered unto you abundantly into the everlasting kingdom of our Lord and Saviour Jesus Christ." (II Peter 1:5-11 KJV)

SPIRITUAL CLEANSING OF PROPERTY:

After obtaining a facility it needs to be delivered of all demonic spirits and filled with the Spirit of God, an anointed environment. Our bases in Saltillo and Francisco Madero, Mexico were no exception. Prior to our purchase every building and yard had been used for some type of demonic activity and the residual demonic spirits had to be literally driven off the property by the Word of God and with the authority God gave us. In some cases where we needed help, the Lord sent teams from the U.S. to help. One team consisting of a pilot, an aircraft and several greatly anointed people who spent two or three days in intense deliverance. Another team consisted of American pastors who delivered a home of a suicide demon that had been tormenting children at night but hadn't left earlier when commanded to do so.

Any sign of demons attempting to return needs to be countered immediately and forcefully. Occasionally, even after several years, a former demon resident will pass through the facility, apparently checking to see if it is still off limits to him. If it passed by you, for that instant, you may experience nausea.

MAINTAINING THE CLEANSING:

You need to be alert for any demonic spirits entering with visiting groups who are returning to your facility after ministering in the surrounding area. The groups need to command in Jesus Name every demonic spirit to drop off of them and their vehicle before they leave the ministry site. This needs to be a mandatory standard procedure.

SENT SPIRITS:

People full of evil spirits (or with associate demons) will be sent against the missionary and his environment (facilities, vehicles, workers, etc.) by warlocks, witches, covens and other satanic groups. They will use any tactic they think will work. A favorite is blackmail, as the missionaries may be forced to work in a hostile country where much of what he does is illegal; such as the felony of preaching, leading the people in salvation, etc. Another scheme is to offer tainted money to people in the ministry. This is money that is cursed to cause destruction to the receiver. Stealing items and putting curses on the owner; and planting curses on the property (as demonic symbols) are common. Most of them come with a plan to kill, steal or destroy based on a perceived weakness or opening in the ministry such as sickness.

When it is ascertained that a demonic person is in your anointed environment, I suggest he be detained until he gives you the names and addresses of the satanic group that sent him and exactly what his mission was supposed to accomplish. Before you release him plant whatever seeds of salvation you can in him; and bind him and his senders inoperative in doing more harm in your ministry.

UNEXPECTED AMERICAN VISITORS:

Sometimes in a foreign mission, Americans appear at your door unexpectedly. Most will need help for a legitimate situation such as money for gasoline to get to the U.S. border. They may have had a vehicle accident or someone is terribly ill, injured or dead. In most cases your help is absolutely necessary.

A few Americans will be running from relatives, police or other government authorities. They will not tell the truth, as they are con men, full of corruption and with the intent to rob you in any way they can. They are polluting your environment with evil and should be made to leave before nightfall. If you let them stay, you will need to watch them 24 hours a day for as many days, weeks or months they are there. Perhaps money is all that is needed to get an

American con man to move out; however, if he likes your facility, force will probably be necessary. You must initiate expulsion quickly or suffer great damage to your ministry.

It is good to have a friendly relationship with the local police unless they are part of the problem or relations between the U. S. and the mission country are not cordial.

PERSONAL DISCIPLINE AND THE ANOINTED ENVIRONMENT:

To maintain the desired anointed environment, I found that study of the Word, anointed worship, prayers and periodic fasting were necessary; along with the immediate resolution of any conflicts. Work distribution for the day was addressed in prayer for the Lord's direction and proper allocation of resources. If possible, this was done in the early morning hours because the days were normally more hectic as the hours passed. People who were waiting when we got out of bed or arrived during prayer would join us or wait. Many made exclamations such as, "They are praying for us and we don't even pray for ourselves." It is easy to become so busy that the time of Bible study, prayer and worship is skipped; much to everyone's detriment as some of the problems that confront the day may turn into frustrations.

On occasions, the Lord would alert us to pray all the way to the destination of a scheduled service. This was usually a half hour to six hours travel time (up to 15 hours in Southern Mexico) of exposing and destroying the enemy's plans to disrupt the service or destroy the transport vehicle or other equipment. This prayer was also effective in maintaining the harmony between ourselves and the village inhabitants. Any word of caution from the Lord could mean the difference between life and death; and whether expensive vehicles and other equipment were spared from destruction.

Note: Unusual equipment and vehicle problems on the mission field can be caused by demons that have entered the area with people and their vehicle; however, the demons didn't leave with the people. In many parts of the world witchcraft, divination, levitation and other satanic rituals are taught and practiced in public schools. Children may suddenly appear around your facilities or vehicles to practice the devil's homework. Every time you pray or use scripture (English, local language or tongues), you are reinforcing your anointed environment.

THE GREAT ENHANCER – THE FRUIT OF THE SPIRIT

I cannot stress too highly the needs to operate every day with the Fruit of the Holy Spirit in evidence in everything you say and do. Your words are a constant infusion of God's authority and power: and the unlimited resources of heaven, into the environment. Do your talking, thinking and actions have a positive impact; addressing the solutions or magnifying the problem?

"We are His workmanship, created in Christ Jesus for good work which God prepared beforehand so that we could walk in them." (Ephesians 2:10 KJV)

"While we have opportunity, let us do good to all men - - - -." (Galatians 6:10 KJV)

"So as those who have been chosen of God, holy and beloved, put on a heart of compassion, kindness, humility, gentleness and patience, bearing with one another, and forgiving each other. Whoever has a complaint against anyone, just as the Lord forgave you, so also should you." (Colossians 3:12-13 KJV)

Speak into your atmosphere. Do not allow anything to stop you. The devil, the prince of the power of the air, lives in the atmosphere.

You can take him out with the fruit of the Holy Spirit as you pursue heaven–on–earth. While you use the Fruit of the Spirit, light comes into the devil's darkness and the darkness leaves. You designate which Fruit of the Spirit you apply to the situation until the atmosphere changes.

"Thanks be to God who always leads us in triumph in Christ." II Corinthians 2:14 KJV)

God does not allow a negative in your life without a provision and a promise. The bigger the negative the bigger the provision. Make no allowance for losing as we already have the victory.

"Whatever is born of God overcomes the world and this is the victory that overcomes the world, even our faith." (I John 5:4 KJV)

"In this world you will have tribulations, but cheer up I've overcome the world." (John 16:33 KJV)

(I Thessalonians 5:16-18 KJV) "Rejoice evermore. Pray without ceasing. In everything give thanks: for this is the will of God in Christ Jesus concerning you."

EVERY SOUL IS PRECIOUS

Missionaries need to be alert to the fact that every person is precious in God's sight and that none should perish. God's help for visitors will probably come through you regardless of who they are, where they come from or whatever they need. We must minister in honesty, purity, unity and holiness; with no display of ungodly anger, alcohol or corruption. As much as possible be punctual, enthusiastic in helping others and inspirationally passionate in the Lord's work.

OTHER KEYS TO SUCCESS

Maintain your concentration on Jesus and His solution, not the problem.

Use the prayers, scriptures, booklets, etc. that the Lord specifically tells you to use.

Don't ever use a booklet, tract, CD, DVD, or anything else that the Lord said to burn.

Everything we say reflects on the spiritual environment, good or bad.

Give out handouts that people can take home to bless the rest of the family.

Periodically pray over the facilities to prevent demonic attachment.

Only leave facilities in the hands of an anointed person who will drive demons out if any are detected.

Place posters on the wall that enhance the anointed environment. Especially the Nine Fruit of the Spirit (Galatians 5:22-23), the Ten Commandments, (Exodus 20:3-17) and the Nine Gifts of the Holy Spirit (I Corinthians 12:8-12).

OTHER CONSIDERATIONS THAT AFFECT A MISSIONARIES ENVIRONMENT:

BRIBES

In several countries bribes were expected by people who provide any service to include border officials, police, administrative processing, drivers licenses and other permits; and utilities as telephone, electricity, and water. Bribes were sometimes paid to avoid harassment, continuing delay, abuse, or to obtain any service at all. The Lord did not permit me to pay bribes unless He said to do it. He stated to me once, "Let me do it my way."

CORRUPTION

Money is god in certain professions in some countries. That includes politicians, bankers, lawyers, insurance agents, judges, and police. I needed to be vigilant at all times. Examples: All reference to a building, and a plot of land were left out of legal papers by a lawyer, vehicle insurance coverage had zeros in all spaces reflecting the insurance company's liability. A legal dollar banking account (for purchasing a home in Mexico) was arbitrarily converted to pesos and the peso depreciated over a few months to almost nothing before releasing the tiny remaining balance to me.

GOVERNMENT TO GOVERNMENT ANIMOSITY

The prevailing official government attitude towards missionaries was projected in newspapers, magazines, radio, television, official documents, business negotiations, etc. Sometimes borders were closed. Government directed hatred toward the U.S. or its citizens were painted on roadway walls with graphic expressions. Local conflicts between government institutions and private individuals were daily. Christian individuals were driven from their villages under threat of death. A Christian man I knew had his hand cut off while he and his family were being forced from their home in a communist controlled village.

CONTROLLED AND MONITORED

In some countries government surveillance of foreigners (including missionaries) was continuous; with periodic identity checks of living quarters, passports and visas. In one country everything electric (telephone, fax, computer) had monitoring devices attached by wires in the government controlled basement. Editing of all incoming and outgoing mail was evident. In another city the legitimate mass distribution of Christian flyers, mailed to pastors, evangelists and other workers were given to the local bishop who had them destroyed.

UNDESIRED PUBLICITY

A local newspaper included ads that blamed all the problems of alcohol, drugs, prostitution, divorce, illicit sex, bad weather, kidnapping children for body parts, corruption of all types, etc. on protestant missionaries, Fortunately most people in that area of the country knew better; however, some became violent. The Lord told me, "Just keep your eyes on Jesus, not what is going on around you."

When a prisoner escaped from the local prison the pastors and missionaries who held services for prisoners were blamed and penalized. (To the extent that most terminated their mission work there.)

FIGHTING AMONG THE CLERGY

Certain elements of the local clergy, some under denominational control; exhibited jealousy, greed and destructive competitive practices toward each other. Visiting Americans (there to teach, etc.) and missionaries could easily get sucked into this unchristian under-current. The need for me to hear the Holy Spirit and practice vigilance never ceased.

PROMISES BROKEN

Sometimes American visitors would be so overcome with compassion that they felt an uncontrollable need to help local pastors; especially the local younger men who were wanting to establish a congregation and build a church. The Americans would commit to help, usually by a monthly donation they could provide through me. This was a great blessing for many; however, in some cases we never heard again from the individual making the promise and they made themselves unavailable. This was a great embarrassment to me, as an intermediary, and I finally would not promise a local pastor anything for them, from anyone, until the funds were in my hand.

DELIVERANCE

In the early missionary years, deliverance of people from demonic spirits was a daily occurrence, sometimes several cases throughout the day or several at once. It was an interruption that impacted our environment and we needed to make sure evil spirits left our environment. Over time, as the local pastors and other Christians received the Holy Spirit, they realized that the evil spirits would leave at their command in the name of Jesus, and the deliverance work load for me in that specific village decreased. Deliverance is very time consuming as each person delivered must be instructed to renounce, repent, receive Jesus, ask for the Holy Spirit and taught how to keep the deliverance. Deliverance was an interruption that had to be tolerated and disposed of as soon as possible; if not it would continue to consume our energy at some other inconvenient time. On occasion when I was very tired, I ministered deliverance while sitting on the front pew or chair and the people who needed deliverance came to me. However, I do not recommend delivering people when you are exhausted physically or spiritually.

CHAPTER 3

God's Lovingkindness

KNOWING GOD

How can human words describe a loving kind God who cares for us so much that He allowed His Son Jesus to be brutally abused and nailed to a tree to die for us? For Him to endure terrible shame and humiliation that we might be free of our sins. Not His sins but our sins. Can we grasp the magnitude of His sacrifice? What would it be like to see your own son suffer terribly for the sins of others, to let him endure the horrible agony that Jesus suffered for us.

Oh that we might know Him, the eternal loving God that created the universe and mankind. A God who wants to be in innermost fellowship with us, His creation. A God who wants to share His love with us, a love that appears to be beyond our imagination or comprehension; but which is already ours and is free to those who diligently seek Him.

ETERNAL LIFE

1. Eternal Life is knowing the Father God and the Son Jesus. Jesus lifted up His eyes to heaven, and said: "Father, the hour has come. Glorify Your Son, that Your Son also may glorify You, as You have given Him authority over all flesh, that He should give eternal life to as many as You have given Him. And this is eternal life, that they may know You, the only true God, and Jesus Christ whom You have sent. I have glorified You on the earth. I have finished the work which

You have given Me to do. And now, O Father, glorify Me together with Yourself, with the glory which I had with You before the world was." (John 17:1-5 NKJV)

2. He gives Eternal Life to those who hear His voice and follow Him. (John 10:27-38)

3. You must come to Him to get Eternal Life. (John 5:39-40)

4. It is not a doctrine; it is a person. Jesus is the resurrection and the life. (John 11:25-26)

5. Paul gave up all to know Jesus. (Philippians 3:7-14)

6. If you know Him you will keep His commandments. (1 John 2:3-5)

7. Loving others is evidence we know God. (1 John 4:7-8)

8. Jesus helps us know God. (1 John 5:20)

9. Jesus is able to save completely those who come to God through Him (Hebrews 7:23)

10. Jesus in John 17:6-20, prays for His disciples. Put your name in place of the disciple and you will see what Jesus is praying for you.

11. We are to know Father God like Jesus knows Him as experienced in John 17:21-22 and John 10:27-30.

12. God is conforming us to the image of Jesus, that we will ·know God and Jesus. (Romans 8:29 and John 17:3)

13. God told me on the mission field, "I have put a desire in every human being to know me." That means to me that nothing else will satisfy you; not money, alcohol, drugs, seeing places, sex, knowledge, religion or works; only knowing Jesus and God can satisfy your need.

14. Jesus said unto him, I am the way, the truth and the life; no man cometh unto the Father, but by me. (John 14:6 KJV)

15. In Hong Kong when pastors were praying around a casket of a lady evangelist for her to come back to life, the Lord spoke to me, "Nothing moves unless I, (Jesus), touch it."

I think often of the times that I or my loved ones would have died if God had not intervened with His loving kindness, even when we were in disobedience to Him:

- Of an angel holding my briefcase as my mangled body climbed out of the wrecked van on the mountainside in Mexico.
- Of the hundreds of derogatory incidents that could have occurred among the 1200 soldiers that were under my command in the 169th Maintenance Battalion. As the Lord said to me "You had fewer incidents in two years than most of the commanders had in their battalions in any given day."
- Saved from death when I woke up to find the vehicle driver asleep at the wheel, heading for a concrete and steel bridge abutment and a raging river.
- When I awoke to a large engine roar, jumped out of the tent in time to pull the driver from his sleeping bag before the large fuel truck backed over the tent.
- When the Lord kept Helen and I away from Luby's Restaurant as the customers were being shot.
- As Helen and I prayed for my brother Al that his life be spared and that he be committed to do anything God wanted him to do.
- As I heard air leaking from a tire over the noise of the vehicle on a dangerous mountain road.
- As I received a warning to speed up and leave the area where two robbers were about to kill, saving the life of a Mexican pastor and myself.
- When my right leg was caught between two logs which came within a second of ripping my right leg off.
- When God warned me that satan would try to kill Helen and I on the road that day and how He picked up a full grown cow only a second before we would have hit it.

This list could be much longer as the Lord saved me from injury, sickness or death many times.

Gods loving kindness are shown in the following examples:

HELEN'S CANCER REMOVAL AND GOD'S INTERVENTION:

I arrived back to Helen's and my home in Saltillo, Mexico from one of many six-week trips which I made to Indian and African Mexican villages in Southern Mexico. As usual, after these six-week trips my stomach was greatly upset and I was happy to be back with Helen and American type food.

As I opened the front door my nostrils reacted in shock to an intense smell, like real bad body odor. I thought this couldn't be from Helen, she is a very clean person. She was in bed for the night and wasn't aware of the odor which was coming from her. I suspected it was from cancer and I knew I had to get Helen to a U.S. doctor quickly.

The next day we left Saltillo and arrived that evening in Temple, Texas. The succeeding day Helen telephoned Darnell Amy Hospital at Fort Hood, Texas and for two weeks Helen's time was spent with appointments, tests and more tests. Then; finally, an appointment to discuss the results and make decisions. On our way to the appointment time we drove past Luby's restaurant and we agreed to stop there for lunch, after Helen's appointments were over. Helen's tests revealed there was cancer of the uterus and arrangements were made for almost immediate surgery with an outstanding doctor at Brooke Army Medical Center in San Antonio, Texas. When everything was done at Darnell we started to leave; however, a nurse came directly to us and said for us to wait until she specifically released us. We thought this is strange but we sat and waited for what seemed to be a long time before she came back and said, "You can go now." We had noted a flurry of activity right before we left of several people arriving on stretchers.

We were informed that a man with a gun had driven a truck through the front wall of the Luby's Restaurant and shot many people in the restaurant. It was the restaurant we would have been in if Helen had been released from Darnell when her appointment was over. Devine intervention was obvious to Helen and I. At the time the nurse had told us to wait, the shooter had not yet entered the restaurant.

During our time of waiting at Darnell I received confirmation from the Lord that Helen was not to accept chemotherapy after her surgery. In our initial visit with the surgeon we insisted Helen would not accept chemotherapy and I also mentioned that my brother had told me that if Helen had chemotherapy it would kill part of the colon and that in a few years she would require another surgery to remove the dead part of the colon. The doctor stated this was true and he didn't mention chemotherapy again.

SAVED FROM CARBON MONOXIDE DEATH:

Helen and I had ministered most of the afternoon, the evening and half the night in a Mexican village which in a few years would be within the borders of the quickly expanding city of Saltillo, Coahuila. Outdoor services with 16mm films, a brief message, deliverance and healing had been scheduled weeks in advance. Before we realized that at the mountain elevations around Saltillo it could be freezing temperatures that time of year.

These services in the streets and vacant lots were normal for us. Almost everyone needed to invite Jesus into their hearts. Most required God's touch for healing or other problems. Several individuals were controlled by demonic spirits and had to be set free. In spite of the cold weather the people needed help and we were there to help them as God moved through us.

With stiff fingers and toes and shaking from the cold we returned to our upstairs apartment. It was almost the same temperature as outside, the water pipes leading to the apartment were all frozen. The only heaters were wall type gas which I lit to take the chill off the apartment, knowing it could be death to fall asleep with them lit. We left our long johns and our outer clothes on and slipped under the blankets, hoping to warm up and that I would stay awake to shut the heaters off when the vapors from the heaters was noted. Sometime later, perhaps an hour, something woke me up. The apartment was full of the overpowering smell of gas, my head felt like it was drugged and splitting with pain. I shook Helen violently and hollered at her as I stumbled my way to an exterior door. The icy cold air felt fresh; and I was about to return for Helen as she groggily appeared at my side. It was another close call with death.

Something had shaken me awake and was telling me to get up while I could hardly breathe or think. I had a near panic feeling to get an outside door open and to get Helen to the door: all the while wondering if she was still alive.

I know a loving, kind God awakened me and kept Helen and I from death that night.

GOD'S LOVING-KINDNESS IN ALABAMA AND TENNESSEE REHABILATATION FARMS:

In the mid-1980s, as opportunities for me to minister in the U.S. presented themselves, I accepted invites in Alabama and Tennessee to inmate rehabilitation farms. These experiences were a great delight to me and to the recipients. Not because of me but because God always had a plan and He always knew how to minister through me to any recipient and on any subject He knew was needed. I always finished my visits with a sense of great elation.

At that time, some U.S. states still had Christian farms where judges could sentence people for rehabilitation work, classes, etc. as needed. These people (inmates) had been involved in every type of corruption imaginable and most had spent time in prison; however, they had convinced a judge that they were willing to discipline themselves and were sentenced to a Christian farm for rehabilitation and ultimate return to productive society.

On a farm in Alabama, twenty-seven of the residents came to my teaching session. The supervisors and owners of the farm were all present. I didn't know what to start with, so I just started to speak about one type of corruption and continue with other corruptions until the Lord had me stop.

I led everyone collectively through the prayers for unforgiveness and to break demonic influences and curses. Then the people who wanted individual ministry came forward one at a time and I ministered to their specific problems until they were confessing they were free. As whatever words, scripture, etc.; (that were needed by them for their salvation, repentance, forgiveness, healing, deliverance or whatever else), were applied to each individual the joy and peace of the Lord was evident in their demeanor.

The owners and people that operated the facility were elated and indicated that in my initial presentation I mentioned every one of the problems of the twenty-seven inmates. An indication the Holy Spirit was in control. I was greatly pleased that the Lord had used me in such a wonderful way.

God's ministry at a restoration farm in Tennessee, at a different time was equally effective; however, I do not remember the specific details, only that I and responsible people were greatly elated by the way God demonstrated His loving kindness to every person who came forward to receive ministry and to later testify of their new found freedom.

God's loving kindness never ends.

THE PRODIGAL SON: (Luke 15:11-24)

As Jesus tells the story, the Loving Kindness of God is clearly portrayed by the father of the prodigal son.

When he saw his son coming a long distance away he was filled with love and compassion; and he ran to his son, embraced and kissed him, and had the finest robe in the house put on him. A ring was put on his finger and sandals on his feet. A celebration feast was planned.

The father did these things for a son that felt he was unworthy of his father's love. To know God we must learn to receive His love, to say yes to His offer. We must stop feeling unworthy and receive. It is God's nature to love and He chooses to love us as He loves Jesus.

As I projected 16mm films of the Prodigal Son in a prison in Mexico, some of the hardened criminals wept at the realization that God loved them in spite of what they had done. They repented and they asked Jesus to come into their hearts.

Paul's word for you:

> "And you hath he quickened, who were dead in trespasses and sins; Wherein in time past ye walked according to the course of this world, according to the prince of the power of the air, the spirit that now worketh in the children of disobedience: Among

whom also we all had our conversation in times past in the lusts of our flesh, fulfilling the desires of the flesh and of the mind; and were by nature the children of wrath, even as others. But God, who is rich in mercy, for his great love wherewith he loved us, Even when we were dead in sins, hath quickened us together with Christ, (by grace ye are saved;) And hath raised us up together, and made us sit together in heavenly places in Christ Jesus: That in the ages to come he might shew the exceeding riches of his grace in his kindness toward us through Christ Jesus. For by grace are ye saved through faith; and that not of yourselves: it is the gift of God: Not of works, lest any man should boast. For we are his workmanship, created in Christ Jesus unto good works, which God hath before ordained that we should walk in them." (Ephesians 2:1-10 KJV)

ABBA FATHER:

About five years before I left the U.S. Army, I had an experience which I believe demonstrated God's Loving Kindness. I sought the Baptism of the Holy Spirit with evidence of speaking in tongues and I received a beautiful flowing language. I was elated and after work each day I prayed in this new language; however, in about a week, I had a vision of a short piece of pipe in the trunk of my car and the tongues stopped. I instantly knew what the problem was. I had accepted this piece of pipe as a substitute for a piece I owned that was to hard to be threaded. The pipe in my trunk was not mine, it was government property; and I was compelled to return it to the plumber who handed it to me and to repent to the Lord for having accepted it.

A week later I sought the Baptism of the Holy Spirit again and received an extremely different language. The language include a clicking of the tongue against the top of my throat which was peculiar to an African Tribe. Since then my prayer language has changed several times. It was during this time period of repentance that the word "Abba" came into my speech, along with the word"Father." I found the words "Abba Father" three times in the King James version of the New Testament. (Mark 14:36, Romans 8:15 and Galatians 4:6) The dictionary "Finding meaning in God's Words" from Thomas Nelson Publisher indicates that Abba means Daddy or Papa; an affectionate term for father. It shows how privileged we are, because of Jesus, to be able to approach the God of Creation and call Him Daddy with childlike trust. God's loving-kindness takes on many forms.

THE BETHESDA POOL EXPERIENCE

When Jesus saw him lying there and learned that he had been in this condition for a long time, he asked him, "Do you want to get well?" "Sir," the invalid replied, "I have no one to help me into the pool when the water is stirred. While I am trying to get in, someone else goes down ahead of me." Then Jesus said to him, "Get up! Pick up your mat and walk." (John 5:6-8 NIV)

Here we see Jesus extend God's Loving-kindness to a disabled individual who didn't appear to know God as he was putting his faith in a ripple-of-water rather than God. In verse 14, John relates to us; "Later Jesus found him at the temple and said to him, "See, you are well again. Stop sinning or something worse may happen to you." (John 5:14 NIV) This scripture reminds me of many terrible experiences observed on the mission field where people sought solutions to their problems from sources that were not God.

Sometimes the people in an entire village have been taken over by witches and demons that the deceived people blindly follow because of spiritual ignorance. I am including here several such cases where through God's loving-kindness the people were set free.

THE MATRIARCHS' DILEMA

In one of my early years in Mexico, a man came to ask me to go with him to a village a considerable distance into the mountain ranges, which was populated by the descendants of a man and his wife. Their 23 children were all grown along with several generations of descendants. The father had died and the wife was now 93 years old. She was sick and not expected to live much longer. She had sent the man to bring me to her and I felt the need to do so.

Just thinking of this trip excites me. It was mainly through unpopulated terrain, beautiful to the eye and rugged in all aspects. It took us two days and one night on a one lane dirt road and then on human and horse trails. Driving was intense to go around obstacles of all natural types to include mountain slopes, flowing rivers, boulders, trees, bushes and thorny plants. Finally, as we came up a slope from a river we had just crossed, my guide pointed and said, "There is her house."

Lying on a rustic homemade bed, (as was all of the furniture), was an elegant, dignified lady; the one I call the Matriarch. Her every gesture, word, look and smile seemed to demand respect. Yes, she was sick, feeble and wrinkled; and those who entered showed great concern for her.

After prayer and the pain left her body, she confided in me that there was another problem of greater concern to her. A problem that involved everyone in the valley and was the real reason she sent for me.

The people of the Valley, her descendants, were rapidly changing. The virtues of hard work; an industrious, energetic mindset, and the spark of the spirited, lively, neat and orderly Christian society were being shattered.

Many of the people appeared to be in a stupor; a daze, apathetic, lethargic, lazy and not concerned with anything of personal or spiritual value to themselves or others.

I could only stay for a few days, to show Christian films and minister to and observe the people. What I found out shocked me. Five or six months earlier two strangers came to the valley posing as religious, upright people. They however were workers for Satan, teaching witchcraft and ungodly living. In addition, they injected fear into the people by telling them that everything they had built or created for themselves in the valley community would probably be lost to unscrupulous politicians or bureaucrats. They indicated that almost everything belongs to the government; Such as the land, water, trees etc. The government was socialist and not capitalist private enterprise. The people in this valley didn't have permits to live on the land and use its resources nor permits to cut trees, use the water, etc. Horrible samples of what the government had done to some others were cited.

Witchcraft and fear were literally destroying many of the people in the valley. I provided the Spanish Bibles I had with me and several dozen copies of the prayers I used for deliverance, breaking curses, forgiveness and the Baptism of the Holy Spirit. Several of the men and the matriarch were excited and continuously doing ministry with the material I left with them and they had plans to cover the entire valley. Liaison with appropriate government officials was being initiated to legalize their status.

I was very pleased with seeing the people that love God to again take their rightful place. Thanks be to God's loving kindness.

MEXICAN HUSBAND IN A STUPOR:

Not many days after I had been to the matriarch's valley, I met a couple in a market area of Saltillo. The American wife was outgoing and she wanted to talk. Her Mexican husband's manner was like that of the men I saw in the stupor in the matriarch's valley. She saw me looking at him and told me that when he was a small child, his mother started passing eggs over him. He became very passive in the years under his mother's control and was unable to change. She told of the numerous times they visited specialists but to no avail. I offered to help him, but she had lost all interest in trying to change him. I never saw them again.

WITCHCRAFT IN THE VILLAGE OF ESTADOS UNIDOS:

A Mexican evangelist, (Juan), and I were returning from a distant village where we had been ministering and were passing through the village of Estados Unidos. It was a village we both knew very well and had been there many times. The people saw us and initiated a church service. They had a communication system of bells that reached the surrounding farm areas and the people assembled in the church.

Juan and I watched from the elevated area behind the pulpit. We noted the people were not acting normal. They were in a stupor that made them act like zombies. A quick check revealed they were all under witchcraft control. Someone had taught the women how to pass eggs over their children and in a short time that included everybody. We conducted a mass deliverance and watched as demons left, and people resumed to their normal self. It was a shock to me to realize these Christians fell so easily for a demonic scheme.

SOUTHERN MEXICAN VALLEY UNDER ATTACK

A group of men came to our Puerto Escondido base asking for help. They needed healing and deliverance. They were part of a Central American denomination I've never heard of (which was true of most churches in South Mexico). An evangelist from the denomination had prayed for them but they still needed deliverance and healing.

I took them through the prayers the Lord had me write a few years before to renounce Satan, break curses and get rid of un-forgiveness. They all vomited up demons and claimed they were healed.

They then asked me to come to their village church, about three hours away at a specified date and time. I accepted and the service was routine for me; however almost everyone vomited demons when I laid heads on them.

They asked me to come for another service and I set the time early in the day so Helen and I would be able to return to our base in the daylight. They were apprehensive that denominational officials might come, but expressed satisfaction when told they would not be there. Apparently the denomination believed a Christian cannot have a demon and that if once saved they were always saved.

Helen and I prayed much of the way to the church binding demons from interfering with the service. We hoped to return to our base early, but that was not to be. It seemed everyone needed to vomit and some of the deliverances took extra time. Everyone claimed they were healed or delivered and as Helen and I were ready to leave, they insisted we needed to pray for some people in their homes. The first family was a father and mother and seven children. They were healed of minor afflictions and had me take their picture as a family. We were then led to another house, that of a 105 year old man with arthritis or rheumatism. When he indicated he was free, we proceeded to another house where they also wanted a photo. The father looked like the man from the earlier family. He was, he had two families in the same village.

We now went to our van, expecting to leave but we could not. The narrow one lane dirt road was full of people on mattresses, pads, sheets, cots, in chairs, etc. They were sick people, laid there by friends who stood by them for at least a quarter mile. They were desperate for a touch from God. Some hours later we reached the last person who explained that only about half of the people went to the church. She also stated and confirmed with the egg setting on the seat with her, that she and many other people were practicing witchcraft.

GOD'S CALLING AND FAVOR

While I was in grade school a Lutheran pastor offered catechism classes after school to anyone who wanted to attend. I attended along with my younger sister. Classes were more interesting than I thought they would be; and I felt the presence of the Holy Spirit for the first time. Since then, when I did something that wasn't right, I felt a conviction in my spirit and off-color jokes and lewd behavior irritated me. The calling of God on me was noticeable enough that my father and other people made comment of it. I also believe that with the calling of God came God's favor. Perhaps it was my guardian angel watching over me as most of the many thorns I experienced ultimately resulted in beautiful roses. It is my testimony of a loving, kind Heavenly Father who cares for His children. An example was my life with a terrible kindergarten and first grade and my graduation from high school as the Valedictorian.

ARMY ASSIGNMENTS AND GOD'S TIMING

Commissioned as a Second Lieutenant in the U.S. Army Ordnance Corps; I along with many other new Lieutenants reported to the Ordnance school at Aberdeen Proving Ground in Maryland for training. We were required to prioritize all the Ordnance School courses in accordance with our personal preferences. This I did and I put the Ammunition Supply course last on my list. When I received my orders they stated I was to attend the Ammunition Supply course. I didn't want that course and thought I will appeal it; however, a strong desire came on me to leave it alone, perhaps it was God, a supernatural intervention in my behalf and I did not question it further. I took the course and had the MOS, (Military Occupational Specialty), entered on my records.

About ten years later, (and after several assignments), I was alerted with a tentative date for a hardship assignment to South Korea without my family. This was bad news for all of the family. Carl Alan was a baby and I didn't have a place off base for Helen and the five boys to live. Suddenly orders were received and to our great elation, they assigned me to Taiwan with my family. The Department of Army had received an emergency request for an ammunition supply officer for Taiwan as they were getting ready to cut my orders for South Korea. It was a great day for us as we prepared for Taiwan. Taiwan was the best army assignment we ever had and the only time in my 26 years of service that I used the Ammunition Supply MOS. There is no doubt in Helen or my minds that the Holy Spirit orchestrated the whole assignment. We have never stopped thanking the Lord for divine intervention.

MISSIONARY PREPARATION

A. When I look back, I can see that the Lord was preparing me for the Missionary work in many different ways without

Him telling me what He was doing. Life was exciting but I didn't know what would happen next. He had baptized me in the Holy Spirit with the evidence of speaking in tongues, and I was realizing more and more that God was a loving God who wants fellowship with His creation, (mankind), but that we must diligently seek and obey Him.

B. It is clear to me that man opens the door to demonic influence and that the curses of God automatically apply. Even ancestor's un-repented sin needs to be repented of and forgiveness received.

C. In Copperas Cove, Texas I felt the need to cleanse my house of Asian wooden carved gods by burning then in the home fireplace. Five years later, in Temple, Texas, before going to Guadalajara, God identified and I destroyed everything in my house that had been or was still worshipped by people somewhere in the world. When anything is placed ahead of God, it is considered to be idolatry.

D. After a lady told me of her husband's impacted tooth, the Holy Spirit said "All you have to do is pray." When several of us laid hands on him and prayed the swollen jaw receded to normal and he never saw a dentist.

E. Another person I prayed for was a lady with swollen legs the size of her hips all the way to her ankles. It was an infirmity the doctors had been trying to resolve for two years. Within two days after prayer the swelling totally disappeared.

F. Some of us military and Youth with a Mission planned and conducted a Victory in Jesus Rally at Fort Hood's Pritchard Stadium for several days. God responded mightily by healing everyone who came to worship and desired prayer. It was a great elation for the several hundred people who participated. The Lord let us know that the rally effectively opened a great door for Him to move.

G. During this period of time some of us started a Full Gospel Business Men's Fellowship International chapter for Killeen and Fort Hood. With Helen and I in Mexico on the mission field and military deployments depleting the chapter officials, the chapter ultimately terminated.

MOVE TO TEMPLE, TEXAS

One day in prayer I was told to move to Temple, Texas. Helen and I drove to Temple in one of our two worn out, gas guzzling cars and entered the city on West Adams Avenue. As we passed an old building that didn't look like a church; we noticed a sign on the building which read Trinity Church. The Holy spirit said that is where you are to attend. We drove further straight into Temple until the Holy Spirit said turn right, (on Blackfoot), then right on Antelope Trail. There near the mail box for 3602 Antelope Trail, was a for sale sign with a phone number. The Holy Spirit said "This is your house." After a phone call the sales agent arrived quickly, opened the door and let us in. I saw all of our furniture in place except for a very ornate globe bar which we later disposed of. The sales agent told me the asking price and it was the exact figure the Holy Spirit had said to pay. We agreed and set up a time to meet and transfer papers.

In Copperas Cove, I had already met with a sales agent for the sale of our home there. He had placed a "For Sale" sign in the front yard, but nothing else was done except in prayer. I told the Lord I needed to sell our two gas guzzling cars and the home. Two separate individuals came to my office; each wanted to buy one of the cars and accepted my price. The Lord gave me a price to sell the home for and indicated the home would be sold the day the little barrel cactus in the front yard bloomed. I asked the Lord what vehicles I should buy to replace the old ones and I received GLC and LUV. When I contacted dealers, I found out the GLC was a small Mazda sedan, which was a new make in the U.S. and LUV was a small Chevrolet Pickup also new to the U.S. I found a Mazda dealer in Temple,

Texas who had GLCs at hail damage prices of $3,000 dollars each. Two dealers in Bell County had LUVs, with each vehicle a different color. I had asked Helen what color LUV she would like me to buy and she said, "Anything except the red one, I don't like red trucks." I checked every one of the LUVs at the two dealers and all had a major defect in the dash cover except for the red one. I had enough money for one LUV and one and a half GLCs for all the drivers in the family. Glen had $1,500 saved for college and he used it to pay the balance for the second GLC. Both GLCs had over 200,000 miles when they were disposed of several years later. The LUV pickup was traded in after several years, not because of the overly high mileage, but because of its life spent on Mexican roads and having been under water on two occasions.

One morning as I left for work at daybreak, I noted the barrel cactus were in bloom. Joy encompassed me as I knew the Copperas Cove house would be sold that day. I was in the General's conference room until noon then I went to my office. There were notes waiting that said someone wanted to buy the house. I contacted him and arranged to meet him at the house. I asked $1,200 more than what the Lord told me the home would sell for. When I mentioned my price, he asked how much would I knock off if he paid cash for my equity. I said $1,000. He agreed, laid the cash on the table and we closed the sale. Some days later the office that handled the old home transfer called me to state there was a problem and for the buyer and I to meet at his office later in the day. He informed us that the bank was charging $400 to transfer the mortgage as a new legal requirement. The buyer turned to me and suggested we split it. That took the $200 that was over what the Lord had told me. It sold on the exact day and price that the Lord had told me.

The home in Temple was only five years old when I purchased it, but needed more foundation support on the chimney end of the house. This I observed when I purchased it; however, with a Dallas foundation company doing the outside work, and doing the inside work myself, this problem was quickly solved.

Another problem I noted was the pecan trees that surrounded the house were full of worms. I mentioned it at a prayer meeting with Bill and Imogene Wallace and Imogene said to walk around the yard praying Psalm 91:10 and Malachi 3:11 while commanding the worms to leave. The next morning not one worm was left in the trees.

BEGINNING THE MISSIONARY JOURNEYS

On the first of January 1980, Helen and I crossed the U.S. border into Mexico on our way to a Guadalajara language school. We were excited every mile of the way as God displayed His presence to us in various manifestations; Such as triple half rainbows near Saltillo and the other half near San Luis Potosi. As we prayed, the rain ceased for us while we drove through dangerous sections of road and as we read messages in the clouds.

On arrival at the school in Guadalajara, the clerk looked at Helen (47 years old) and myself (50 years old) and acted shocked to see us and indicated they didn't accept students who were over 32 years of age. I had four or five one hundred dollar bills displayed to pay tuition in my hand and she suddenly took the money and registered us. We found a duplex not far away and I paid for an apartment. The first week I spent many hours scrubbing the apartment while we started classes. We were overjoyed to be doing the Lord's desire and almost skipped on the way to classes. The classroom temperature was basically the outdoor temperature which is the best in the world; however, the classroom was cold in the winter and hot in the summer. They had kerosene heaters, but never any kerosene. The wood chairs we used with much caution as they frequently projected slivers into whatever part of the body they contacted. After a couple of days we realized, as did the teacher, that we could not do the full curriculum and we soon had our own teacher and the young students had their own teachers.

Most evenings we took a short break and went for a walk before the sun set. It was pleasant, in a good part of the city and we enjoyed ourselves; that is except for one problem, a sneaky dog. The dog was always lying in a yard with the gate open. The dog acted like it was ignoring us until we passed. Then it very rapidly sneaked out and bit Helen in the buttocks. Not enough to draw blood, but to give her a good scare while the dog quickly returned to the yard apparently enjoying a good laugh. We learned to carry a stick and watch the dog.

One day I noted a cup left on the step to the duplex where we lived. It looked like those that came with the apartments, but it was in front of the other apartment. I knew the occupant, an airline stewardess, who was on a flight to the U.S. and wouldn't be back for a few days. I picked up the cup and put it down on my side of the steps thinking I will check this later. In the early evening I was rearranging some furniture in the back room of the apartment and Helen was in the kitchen near the front door. The doorbell rang; Helen opened the door and she screamed "Carl" with fear in her voice. I immediately walked to the hallway which led to the front door and observed two men. The first with a gun in his left hand standing in the apartment in front of the open door. Because of their close haircuts, I thought they were off duty policemen or military. The Holy Spirit said "I didn't bring you here to get you shot, the gun will not fire" and I briskly kept walking down the hall toward the gunmen. As the man raised the gun with his left hand and braced it with his right hand, I knew he was a trained gun user and the words came out of my mouth, "You stupid fool, what do you think you are doing?" I put my hand on his chest and pushed the two out the doorway and swung the door to shut it. It closed across the wrist of his left hand with the gun. I released the door sufficiently for him to pull hand and gun out. I shut and locked the door and dropped myself to the floor. As I looked up at Helen, staring at me, frozen in shock and with her mouth wide open; I hadn't felt anything. It was like this is something I do every day. However, it was something very important; we were just starting on the mission field and the Lord demonstrated His love and protection for us.

Early the next day I told the owner all of the details of what happened, even about the cup on the step and my having left it on my side. As the blood drained from his face, he turned absolutely white and fear came on him. He excused himself, ran to his truck, returned with more tools and entered into the stewardess's apartment. For a day and a night he was in her apartment working feverishly as he ripped out panels from the walls, etc.

I also reported the attempted robbery to the police, who on several occasions brought people by for us to identify as the robbers. None of them were. About eight months after the attempted robbery, two policemen were convicted of another robbery and confessed to being the men who entered our apartment. They had been caught off duty attempting another robbery. I suspected that someone had placed the cup on the stewardess's step for the robbers to identify the apartment. I had intervened by moving it to my step. I never saw the stewardess after the robbery. When I mentioned the attempted robbery to the student body at the school, someone commented, "You could have been shot." I thought, not with Jesus in charge.

A MISSIONARIES HOME

After about three weeks in Guadalajara, the Lord told me to offer to stay in a missionary's house. I knew about this missionary, but was hesitant to tell a stranger that I wanted to stay in his house. The next day Helen said, "Carl, I believe we are to offer to stay in that missionary's house. I said OK Lord and went to see him at his address. His family was having an emergency and he needed someone to live and watch his house while they were in the U.S for three months. We offered to pay our usual rent and moved in as they moved out. The wife felt she was going insane and was having symptoms similar to her mother and sister who were in some type of institution in the U.S. I perceived that it was 6 demons affecting the wife and she needed deliverance: which she received while in the U.S. I have included her case here to stress that missionaries are susceptible to demons like everyone else except they are often the point of multiple demons attacking at once to create a behavior that is perplexing, complicated, strange and confusing. The afflicted person is usually embarrassed, lonely, ashamed and doesn't want anyone to see them in such an abnormal state.

The Guadalajara missionary's home was a new experience for Helen and I; although it was common to the area. The water supply consisted of a huge concrete tank under the garage floor which periodically received water from a city water line. The city line was dependent on water from Lake Chapala, which in turn was dependent on seasonal rainfall that left the lake dry part of the year.

An in-home pump was necessary to take the water from the reservoir under the garage and push it up the distance of two and a half floors to a tank on the roof where a valve shut the pump off when the roof tank was full. From the roof tank the water flowed slowly by gravity through pipe to the designated locations in the home. The system worked, but was prone to malfunction at inappropriate times.

The level of the water in Lake Chapala also controlled the generation of electricity which was rationed on a variable schedule such as two days per week. To keep items refrigerated or frozen more than a short time required a propane operated refrigerator.

Testify of What Jesus has Done

A BLESSING TO EVERYONE:

One of the most rewarding things, to me and to others, on the mission field was to tell people who have a need what Jesus has done for me and for others, (often with the same or similar need).

Testimonies of what Jesus has done, builds faith and opens them up to receive their miracle, healing or other blessing that they need. It is giving them confidence that what Jesus did for others, He will also do for them. It gives them the faith that Jesus wants to solve their problem and He will do it if they will believe.

Luke 24:48 (Jesus speaking to the apostles before going to heaven.)"and you are witnesses of these things."

Hebrews 3:1 "Wherefore, holy brethren, partakers of the heavenly calling, consider the Apostle and High Priest of our profession (confession), Christ Jesus."

Revelations 12:11 "They overcame the devil by the blood of Jesus and the word of their testimony".

From these scriptures we see the importance Jesus placed on testifying of Him. This includes all communication to include verbal, written, facial, hand and all other expressions.

HOW JESUS MET A TRAGIC NEED:

One year after my battalion executive officer Major Braley, had a change of station to Germany (a 3 year assignment) his wife called our home in Copperas Cove, Texas to state they were back in the U.S. and needed to see us that night. My wife, Helen, answered the phone and sensed that this was very important. She said yes and called me at work. I also sensed that it was very important that we see them.

That evening they explained that Major Braley was returned to the U.S. as he had two diseased kidneys and was to go on a dialysis machine in El Paso, Texas, pending imminent death. For four hours I told Major Braley, his wife and children what we had seen Jesus do in the year they were in Germany; to include the healing of my spine and several of the hundreds of people we saw healed at Kathryn Kuhlman services.

They were personally aware of my spinal defects from birth, damage when assigned to two paratrooper divisions and as a passenger in a vehicle accident in Taiwan. Specifically, a paralyzed left leg, dragging foot, constant pain, a steel back brace and crutches. We shared our experiences about God's reality, how Jesus suffered and died for us and that by his stripes we are healed, if we can only believe. We told them, and they saw how our lives were changed.

JESUS PRESENCE:

After they left that evening I went to the bedroom and prepared for bed; thinking about the evening and talking to the Lord. The words I spoke as I laid down were "Lord should I have told them all those things, they may think I have gone crazy?" An audible voice answered me "You did what you are supposed to do!" I opened my eyes and standing near me on my side of the bed was a figure in a white robe. I started to get up but the figure touched me on the chest and I fell back in a deep and incredible peaceful sleep. Later in prayer I was told the figure was Jesus.

In a letter that accompanied Major Braley's death announcement, Mrs. Braley indicated as a result of our testimony, all of the family received Jesus and she knew her husband was in heaven. She also felt that many relatives and friends came to know the Lord as a result of their conversion. My mind was flooded with a multitude of scripturally supported testimonies of Jesus that have helped me to reach people with every type of problem.

You did what you are supposed to do! What had I done? I had testified of Jesus. Thirty years later when I asked the Lord what I was to speak on in five Hong Kong services, He said "Tell them what I have done." To testify of Jesus brings His presence, healing, deliverance, miracles and tremendous peace to troubled souls.

When Helen and I arrived at the last of five locations in Hong Kong where we ministered we were already exhausted. I mentioned to the pastor that we needed a short rest before tackling a church full of people on stretchers and in wheel chairs. He put us in his office from which we could see and hear the service. For forty five minutes or so he had people who had been healed in our prior services give their testimonies. It put the fire of anticipation into those waiting for healing and reinvigorated Helen and I. The miracles flowed. "Give thanks to the Lord, call on his name; make known among the nations what he has done. Sing to him, sing praise to him; tell of his wonderful acts. Remember the wonders he has done, his miracles, and the judgments he pronounced." (I Chronicles 16:8, 9, 12 NIV)

A MIRACLE CONVERTS A BUDDHIST TO CHRIST:

In the Hong Kong services I was greatly blessed when a Buddhist man in a wheel chair came up for healing. His legs had been crushed between a dock and a large truck. Pins stuck out of his legs. As we prayed for him he jumped up and stepped out of the wheel chair, all the while hollering "I am healed".

A Buddhist woman stepped up and said it felt like a knife was sticking into her head. I commanded the demon to get off of her in Jesus name and it left. She danced around for several minutes hollering "it's gone". Both the Buddhist man and Buddhist woman renounced Buddhism, received Jesus, and were at the last report full time workers for Jesus.

CHRISTIANS DELIVERED:

On a different trip to Hong Kong, and in a church on Hong Kong Island, I spent the better part of a day ministering deliverance to Christian workers (pastors, missionaries, evangelists and worship leaders). Every person we ministered to vomited up demons. One lady evangelist, full of bitterness, vomited for forty five minutes. I was not surprised at the large number of worship leaders that needed deliverance.

Jesus did not let him stay, but said, "Go home to your family and tell them how much the Lord has done for you, and how he has had mercy on you." (Mark 5:19 NIV)

Carl Speaking to Students in a Chinese University

YOUTH TESTIFYING FOR JESUS:

On an extended stay in Hong Kong I ministered in seven churches that were part of Pastor Lamb's group. My message was to stimulate the youth to continually testify of what Jesus had done in their lives. It made them realize they all had a testimony to tell and they were excited about telling the huge number of non-Christians in Hong Kong. They were spirit filled and wanted to pray for the sick, etc.

One of the seven pastors in the Lamb Group also taught music to youth in a private school. His contract specifically prevented him from telling the students about the Holy Spirit. When I talked about testifying about Jesus to these students they were puzzled, none of them had the baptism of the Holy Spirit and they had constant problems. My heart was grieved for them but I was not allowed to violate the contract the pastor had with their school. What a big difference the Holy Spirit makes. By now I believe the Lamb's group youth have probably reached out to them.

"You will be his witnesses to all men of what you have seen and heard." (Acts 22:15 NIV)

TESTIMONIES FASCINATE STUDENTS:

The pastor of a large Alabama church asked me to speak to the students from their school (kindergarten through twelfth grade). At the end of each hour the bell rang and each time the teacher in charge said, "Continue", from 8:00am through 1:30pm. The students and teachers were captivated. Near the end the Lord told the pastor in his office, "Now is the time to deliver those students who need it". When the pastor entered the auditorium the anointing nearly knocked him down. Then he called by name those students who needed deliverance and he delivered them. Needless to say, the teachers and I were amazed and ecstatic. God is marvelous beyond description.

FIRST HEALING IN SALTILLO:

Shortly after moving into the apartment in Saltillo, Mexico the first person to visit us for healing was a young lady. She lived in a small cinderblock building, without water or sewer, in the first stage of developing another section of the city. She had a pastor, who had a vacant lot to construct a church; he only had a few cinderblocks that he laid planks on for pews.

This young lady was a vivacious girl who suffered from a female problem that gave her pain and stifled her life. She cried out to God for help and He told her to go to my street and house number, go to the second floor and ask for Carlos (my name in Spanish). When she arrived she told us what the Lord had told her and what her problem was. We led her through prayers to break curses and demonic influence, and to get rid of un-forgiveness. We then laid hands on her and commanded in Jesus name that the sickness be healed. This was only the beginning of her life. She testified of God's healing to everyone and of our ministry. Soon we were occupied with people from all over Saltillo who heard her testimony. We met her pastor and his wife who became good friends with us, and where we held many services.

THE BLIND SEE AND THE DUMB SPEAK:

Saltillo was growing very rapidly in all directions and God was raising up young men to start churches in all directions. In some areas demonic forces seemed to have strong holds on the people which needed to be broken off for the churches to thrive.

One small church was built in the midst of much satanic activity and everyone seemed to need deliverance. I was scheduled there for five days to teach on the Holy Spirit and handle whatever else arose. After teaching, it seemed I then spent hours of deliverance along with healing. Some of the things I remember were: the first day a woman who had been blind for years was delivered, healed and seeing with perfect vision. A photo of all of us with her revealed she was the only one who didn't need glasses. The second day twin nine year old boys who had never spoken, received their voices. The third day they spent knocking on doors and jabbering at the residents. I expected the church would be packed the third evening; and it was with more people that needed deliverance. This need continued for the fourth and fifth days to include five cases of stomach epilepsy, (the doctor's name for a jumping demon that readily left when told in Jesus name to leave). I don't remember what other type of demons were there, only that there were lots of them and some of them had strange manifestations such as a tongue hanging out eight inches. These areas needed lots of intercessory prayer before we ministered in them.

A PRECIOUS GIRL EMERGED:

A young lady was brought to our ministry in Saltillo by her aunt. She was the youngest of twelve children, looked down upon by her siblings, considered of no value, a nothing, the blunt of jokes and sarcasm, and thought of herself as nothing; so downcast she could not lift her face until I forcefully pushed her head up.

I spent most of the day with her, telling her she was unique, a special creation of God and the only person like her in the world. I had her read a list of about 300 scriptures that told her who she was in Christ. I told her of several people whom I observed changed when they accepted Jesus as their Lord and Savior. She forgave everyone who tormented her, accepted Jesus as her Lord and Savior and received the Baptism of the Holy Spirit. Her face radiated a joy and peace she had never known before. Her aunt returned and was amazed. She was a different person. She looked different, talked different and projected herself in confidence. Helen and I now looked at a beautiful young lady, beaming with joy and enthusiasm. What a wonderful God we serve.

A MIRACLE IN THE MAKING:

In Hugo's church during the time of praying for the sick, a young man and girl requested prayer against an eye infirmity which was obvious. I prayed for them and received a word they were healed; however, it was not evident at the moment. I asked if they could come back the next day. They indicated no because they needed to return to their home in the mountains above Saltillo. I knew the area and a young man who wanted to establish a church there. They also knew him and his building. I told them to meet me there the next day at a specified time for more prayer. I was waiting for them when they arrived; however, they were totally healed during the night and their parents and siblings were with them. The pastor was there and he received them all as the start of the church he wanted to establish in this mountain area.

I ministered there many times over the next few years and watched significant workers for the Lord develop there. One was a man who had been a Catholic policeman until he was ordered to arrest his priest for the rape of a young girl. Twelve years after he arrested the priest, he was jogging past the new mountain church; he heard me speaking, entered and gave his heart to the Lord. He became a very active evangelist in the western states of Mexico. God was always doing things that amazed Helen and I. God is so good.

FULL GOSPEL BUSINESS MEN'S FELLOWSHIP INTERNATIONAL (FGBMFI):

This organization that sponsored business men to give testimonies of how God moved in their lives was expanding with new chapters during our early ministry.

After the Victory in Jesus rallies in Pritchard Stadium at Fort Hood, Texas, several of us military members established a Killeen and Fort Hood Chapter which functioned during the early years that Helen and I were on the mission field.

In Mexico City a national chapter was established about the same time as the chapter in Saltillo. Both provided an excellent place for testimonies of what God was doing and brought many business men into the local churches. I understand the FGBMFI is still active in several areas of the world.

A DYING PASTOR HEALED:

The Missions Director in a church in Alabama asked me to pray for a Baptist pastor who was dying of cancer. On my arrival at his house I interviewed him (one third of his body was full of cancer) and I analyzed the demonic atmosphere of the house. Demonic spirits were present in an adult son's room, where witchcraft and other demonic items were displayed openly. The pastor's bedroom had demons hanging from the ceiling over his bed and above the door (evident as black clouds). They would drop on people who entered the room or when they left.

It was obvious that the adult son was harboring demonic things, and to be practicing witchcraft or other demonic activity. The son needed to get rid of all demonic stuff, repent for his sin and receive forgiveness from his Dad; or move out of the house with his stuff, he chose to move out. We then cleaned house; commanding all demonic spirits to leave in the name of Jesus as we went through every room, closet or hallway, anointing with oil as we went.

The pastor went through a prayer of forgiving his son and anyone else, of repentance to the Lord for the sin of allowing demonic items in his house and to forgive himself. As the pastor repeated the two prayers a fairly large black snake unwound from his body, headed for an exterior wall, turned, looked back and then proceeded to leave through the wall. He was totally delivered, healed and spent years traveling and testifying in Baptist churches of how God healed him.

WOMAN'S CANCER AND DEAF BOY HEALED:

I was notified a woman was dying of cancer in an African Mexican village. She was the mother of a well-known black evangelist/pastor who was a graduate of our bible school and worked closely with me. He was a blessing to everyone and he was an open door to many people in Southern Mexico. Her healing therefore was important and urgent in several ways.

We started out early, driving a couple of hours, then across a lake in a rented boat, and then a walk to her house where she lay on a cot. Several other women and some children were there. I thought, this is a good opportunity to teach many people on healing. Everyone listened intently and I knew I had an audience anxious to hear the Word and to see the cancer disappear.

I led her through two prayers, (Appendix A and B), laid hands on the cancer area and in Jesus name commanded the cancer to be gone. It disappeared! Several people had to verify with their hands that it was gone. The mother of a six year old boy asked me to pray for his hearing. I put hands over his ears and commanded in Jesus name they be opened. The Lord said to me, it is done. The boy didn't confess his healing; however, and when he was facing away from me I called his name. He instantly turned and looked at me. He was hearing!

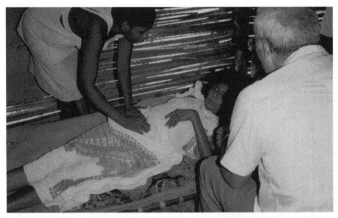

Innocencio's Mother Dying of Cancer. Carl taught two hours to her and a dozen other women on healing. When hands were laid on her, the cancer disappeared, never to return.

One of many African Mexican Churches on the West Coast of South Mexico where Carl Ministered.

An Outdoor Service on the Beach of El Azufre. Many services are conducted in the open where storms ravish the area.

An African Mexican Church and an American Visitor.

A WORD FROM GOD DOES MIRACLES:

While doing outreaches from the village of Tamalacacingo to surrounding villages, I finished my message to a group of assembled men of a village and made an invite for salvation. No one moved. The Lord said that boy has a named physical problem. I spoke this to him. He appeared shocked. Then the Lord spoke of another specific problem with a different boy. I spoke it and commanded "come up here now and the Lord will heal you". They both came forward and received their healing, thus another village was opened to the gospel. I didn't know it then but it would be my only visit to this village.

A SHOCKING SERVICE:

A pastor asked me to teach in his large church in Pinotepa National, Guerrero. I used scripture after scripture that spoke of sins that open the door to the devil. Then I led them through a forgiveness prayer, a prayer to renounce satan and break curses; and then an invite to come forward if they felt they still needed prayer. To my astonishment, almost everyone wanted personal prayer, which took a long time to address the literally hundreds of sins and problems they had. It was a many hour long service but very satisfying. All things are possible with God.

FIVE HUNDRED YOUTH FOR JESUS:

One of our Bible school graduates organized a gathering of 500 Indian youth in South Mexico. I was to speak the first two full days and one evening. These youth arrived from many villages over a large area with no roads. Many of them walked cross country to include mountain ranges, rivers, etc. The gathering village was at high altitude, which in January was cold during the day and freezing at night. We had to break the ice for water baptism.

As I spoke what the Lord wanted, the Holy Spirit was working on the youth. A group of youth would vomit demons then another until all were free. Some cried out to Jesus for forgiveness or whatever. The presence of the Holy Spirit was strong and repentance was flowing. The results were spectacular over the next few years with youth that participated in this gathering entering and graduating from our

Bible school. Students from different tribes that historically hated each other would repent for their tribe and weep over each other. God was doing amazing things. Many of these former youth are now pastors of their own churches in villages throughout a vast area.

A Youth Meeting in a Church without a Roof.

People Gathered on the Street for a Church
Service, Healing and Deliverance.

NOTHING MOVES UNLESS I TOUCH IT:

Arriving back in Hong Kong after renewing my China visa in the U.S.; I was met by a driver who took me to Pastor Lamb's church in Hong Kong instead of my quarters. I knew something very significant was going on that the people wanted me involved in. At the church I saw a coffin with Pastor Lamb's sister in it. She had been renowned as an evangelist who displayed considerable talent while operating in the Gifts of the Holy Spirit. The casket was surrounded by the pastors who had churches within Pastor Lamb's group. They were earnestly praying for the sister to rise from the dead. I entered into prayer also but to seek the Lords guidance. After several minutes the Lord said to me; "Nothing moves unless I touch it." This indicated to me that she would not rise from the dead as the pastors thought. Only Jesus the Lord could do that. After some more time passed the Lord again spoke; "She is with me." I felt the Lord Jesus was saying that nothing these pastors said was going to bring her back to life. I became keenly aware that Jesus is the source of life.

ASLEEP AT THE WHEEL:

A youthful experience occurred when I woke up in the back seat of a Model A Ford and found everyone in the car asleep including the driver. The car was on the left shoulder of the road and heading for a huge abutment. I quickly grabbed the steering wheel and firmly steered the vehicle back onto the road, barely missing the abutment. Then I woke the driver. We barely missed death from impact, from vehicle tumbling and or drowning in the swift river current. I believe the Lord woke me up, not a second too soon.

"For unto you is born this day in the city of David a savior which is Christ the Lord. (Luke 2:11 KJV)

Jesus is savior in more than one way.

LOGGING – A NEAR DEATH EXPERIENCE:

Another of my youthful experiences was harvesting logs for timbers and boards. My brother August was operating a large winch that was pulling full tree length logs from the low level river bank to a much higher level for cutting, loading and hauling. I was at the lower level watching, with a cant hook in hand, to make sure the tree being skidded didn't lodge itself against a tree trunk, earthen bank or any other solid obstruction that could cause the large tow cable, which was under considerable tension, to break. If it broke it would fly back through the air at considerable speed and cut anything it touched into two pieces. It was a dangerous place to work as my brother could not see me and modern communication means had not been invented.

The log being pulled slid sideways against another huge felled and trimmed tree. I jumped upon the two logs with the cant hook to try to prevent snagging each other. My right leg slipped between the two logs and I could not pull my leg out. As I was being turned by the moving log, I hopped in a continuous moving circle. I cried; "Jesus" and the two logs separated enough for me to pull my foot out. What a relief. I was within seconds of having my leg ripped off and of bleeding to death. Thank you Lord Jesus for watching over me, you are my Lord.

". . . and I thank Jesus Christ our Lord." (I Timothy 1:12 KJV)

ALMOST SKEWERED:

This near death incident occurred while I was working on a big farm wagonload of hay. My job was to place the huge tines of a hay fork in the hay on the wagon, extend the catches on the tines so as to grab the hay, and to signal the horse driver to pull the load up into the hay mow (done by a large rope and several pulleys). When the load was over the proper mow location I would pull a small rope attached to the catches, trip them and the load would drop into the mow. I then had to pull the tines back over the wagon and down for another load. This meant pulling the heavy rope along the ground and back through the pulleys. A hard extended pull on my part was normally necessary. This time, however, when I pulled the rope there was no resistance and the huge tines came instantly over the wagon and fell straight down to it. I was standing directly where the tines were to fall, in the split second I only had time to make a few inch jumps with my toes. One of the tines caught the back of my shirt and ripped it off of me and imbedded itself in the wagon floor. The worker in the mow had decided to help me and he had pulled the big rope back into the mow without my knowledge, thus it had no resistance to my pull and moved instantly down into the wagon. By the grace of God I was alive and I did a short jig on the bare part of the wagon floor.

I thanked the Lord. ". . . but the gift of God is eternal life through Jesus Christ our Lord" (Romans 6:23 KJV)

SPOOKED HORSES AND A CRAZY BULL:

I was a spectator of the following horse experience. Twice in my years on the farm a black bear appeared within the vision of the horses which were harnessed and pulling a farm machine. The horses instantly spooked and ran wildly back to the barn (once about 2 miles and once about 1 mile), dragging the man with the lines until he released them. On one occasion when the horses spooked, the driver fell down and was run over by the cast iron wheel of the wagon we were using to haul stones. On newly cleared land a poisonous weed sometimes grew, and if eaten by an animal, the animal went crazy (like a rabid animal) and died. I remember one occasion when a bull dropped dead when his horns were inches of dad's chest.

MOUNTAIN TRAVELS IN MEXICO:

While on the mission field in Mexico I had a few close calls with death involving vehicles, some of them are eluded to here.

After extensive rain fall the dirt in the mountains becomes saturated with water. Any movement such as heavy winds, vehicle traffic, hurricanes, or earthquakes can give enough vibration for the earth to move and disappear from under your vehicle, or from in front, or from behind you. If you are in the mountains under such circumstances, you can lose your vehicle with the dirt. Washouts can leave you stranded without bridges, without a vehicle, without a turn-a-round and without any reasonable way to leave the area. I have crossed rivers, driving with my wheels on the bridge beams (without planking, it is scary for me to think about it). You just have to do it if it is the only way out. I have followed donkey paths over the mountain peaks, driven across rivers, through woods, over beach sand and through water that was up to the vehicle bumper. I have had to exit vehicles through the windows when caught in instant flooding. Vehicles have been pulled out of bad circumstances by horses, tractors, winches and man power. I have tried to sleep in the back seat of a van when the vehicle could not get enough traction to pull itself up a slight slimy slope (I also had the tormenting nightmares that went with such circumstances while I waited for help). I was normally able to avoid these circumstances; however, I didn't always know what weather I would encounter; and pastors who were anxious to get back to their families in the mountains weren't always forth-right in their guidance as I would have liked. I never lost a vehicle because of weather and geographic circumstances; however, the vehicle twisting caused radiators to leak and oil loss from the differential, transmission and brakes. There were minor problems like the horn blowing by itself.

On trips between Saltillo, Coahuila and Puerto Escondido, Oaxaca (our two large bases) we almost always pulled a trailer loaded with supplies and equipment when going south. Before the super highways were built, every trip was a trying experience with broken trailer axles, broken trailer springs, spring shackles ripped out and blown tires.

The V8 and V10 gasoline engines in the towing vehicles all ultimately knocked which was a prelude to a blown engine. Over time some vans used three engines. I started purchasing vehicles with diesel engines which were a blessing when going over the mountain ranges. On one occasion I drove a diesel van a thousand miles without shutting off the engine as a part was broken. The Saltillo mechanic said it was impossible, but with God all things are possible.

DRUMS AND SMOKE SIGNALS:

On the way to an Indian village in south Mexico, I was driving and a Mexican pastor was with me. We were about to pass two people walking on the road to the village when the Lord spoke; "Speed up." I applied the gas and arrived at the village soon thereafter. As I talked with the pastor and others in the village I noted men were mounting their horses and carrying what weapons they might have. The pastor inquired what was happening and was told that two men walking on the road to the village had been killed about the time we arrived at the village. Their bodies were at the point on the road where the Lord told us to; "Speed Up." They had been robbed and the village men were forming a posse to look for the killers. Shortly after our arrival I had noted Jesus walking among the people and looking at them. I knew it was Jesus because it was something I noticed in other villages. I don't believe the people could see Him and I seldom mentioned it. This time the people were busy sending up smoke signals and the tom toms were going. They were still sending smoke signals and beating the drums three days later when I left. People in the other village read the signals, knew about the killings, and were watching for the killers. It was an education for me to see how the people responded to the drums and smoke signals to communicate in an emergency.

Blood on the Road where Robbers Killed Two Men

Drunk and Demon Controlled People
Parade between Religious Shrines

Typical Mountain Village

CHILDREN BITTEN BY A RABID DOG:

Upon arrival in an African Mexican village where I had ministered before, a tall stately black lady came running toward me, she was frantically calling for me. I recognized her as being a member of the local church and wondered what was going on. She proceeded to state that her children were bitten by a rabid dog, please come with her and pray for them. I went with her to the hut they called home all the while thinking they need rabies shots. I had never prayed against rabies before but I knew it was deadly. As I was commanding in Jesus name, that the rabies leave the children, word came that the dog had died. The mother calmed down by then and was thanking the Lord for the children's healing. She explained it was impossible for them to get rabies shots as they were the lowest priority to get a doctor or any medication under the Mexican medical system. They relied on the Lord and she had been praying for me to come. Over the years, I stopped at the village several times and I had the privilege to see her children grow up into fine Christian adults. There were hundreds of other villages I could have been at that critical day.

Children Healed of Rabies

SHE RECEIVED WHAT SHE ASKED FOR:

At the start of the evening service in a Saltillo church the Lord said; "I will heal everyone here." Later in the evening I noticed a lady with one leg much longer and larger than the other. I asked her if she had been through the healing line earlier and she said she only mentioned a pain in her neck which was healed. We became good friends and her leg was prayed for at various times without any change. The leg had stopped growing at 11 years of age when she received the polio shot in the hip. If she had mentioned the small leg, I believe it would have been healed. During my friendship with her family, I learned a lot about Mexican society. Her youngest son, Carlos, was picked up by the police and charged with drug possession (which was not true) and the police demanded a million pesos for his release. We had extensive intercessory prayer for him and he was finally released. I was shocked at how brazen the police were to make such a charge and demand payoff. I stopped at her home one day with a group of American visitors when a Mexican car drove up looking for me. They had a two year old child whose legs hadn't grown since birth. I mentioned this to the Americans: but, before anyone else prayed one of the Americans jumped up grabbed the child's feet and commanded in Jesus name that the legs grow and they were instantly normal.

FUEL TANKERS BACKS OVER TENT:

An incident in Germany occurred during the time I was an umpire in an armored division training test. Testing had finished for the day and my driver and I retired to our sleeping bags in a small two man tent. I was awakened by a loud roaring noise as I tried to ascertain what kind of vehicle made the roar. I didn't recognize what it was; however, the noise became louder and louder. I jumped out of my sleeping bag and out of the tent, into the snow. Just in time as a huge fuel truck started backing over our tent. I yanked the driver out only a second before the tanker backed completely over the tent with its huge tires. I had thought our tent location was in a safe place; however, to back up to refuel a combat tank, the semi-trailer tanker needs lots of space (in the woods, in the dark and snow, all without a guide). It was nice to be alive and not squashed like a bug. Thank you Lord.

A DEMON OF SUFFOCATION:

One night in bed I instantly felt like an elephant had laid on me. I couldn't breathe and I was trying to call out Jesus. The thought came to me "force it." The sound; "Jesus" finally came out and the weight on me left. Over the years in the mission field, I met several people who had the same experience. I also knew of several men who had died in bed in their forties and wondered about the heart attack diagnosis.

WHAT DID YOU SAY?

Sometimes in the early years of the ministry I have had trouble ascertaining what a Spanish speaking patient's problem was. I received a phone call to please go to Hospital 1 in Saltillo and pray for a specific pastor's wife with a problem I couldn't ascertain over the phone. John Osteen's secretary was visiting me at the time so we went there together, found the wife but still could not understand what the problem was. Words that neither one of us knew were being used. The wife quickly pulled up her gown; there was a semi-circle cut from hip to hip across her abdomen and blood was leaking from the cut in several places. We instantly knew the problem. A caesarean section was not healing as it should. Within a few seconds the blood leaks stopped once we understood what to pray for.

In a prayer line in a village church a lady tried to tell me her problem. Finally in exasperation she grabbed my hand and placed it on her crotch and said; "Pray." I turned red and prayed.

Many times Mexican Spanish has several words for the same thing and the language structure varies. Indian words from dialects are in common use. When available, I preferred to use an interpreter.

YELLOW JAUNDICE:

On several different occasions I was asked to pray for children who were in comas in the Children's Hospital, Saltillo, Mexico. They each had turned yellow and were in comas. In every case they came out of the comas, changed back to normal color and were discharged.

CAN'T STAND STILL:

In a service in El Calvario Church in Monterrey, Mexico a lady came forward for prayer. I was trying to find what her problem was but she kept moving all the while. I asked her to stand still and tell me what her problem was. She said that's the problem; "I cannot stand still." I sensed she had a demon attached to the back of her head and in Jesus name commanded it to disengage and leave her. She stopped moving. I told her how to keep the demon off of her. Then she said; "My brother and sister have the same problem."

CURED:

In Albuquerque, N.M. we prayed for a woman with pain in the upper chest area. I felt she was healed and after she arrived home that evening she vomited up a cancer.

HOSPITAL MIRACLES:

For a few years a nurse and I visited Hospital Number 2 in Saltillo, Mexico nearly every Tuesday morning. We saw every patient and visitor we could. It was a blessed time as every sickness was healed except two demon possessed cases which we were not permitted to pursue. Most cases were released the next day and some doctors started to devote their free time to working with Eternal Love Ministries.

Over time several people were shot and in the hospital. One had a bullet lodged in an inoperable part of the brain. The hospital kept him for several days even though the bullet had disappeared when he was prayed for.

Another unusual case was a man bloated with cancer who received instant healing. He and his wife were rejoicing when another woman arrived, she also was his wife. The nurse and I quickly left to see a different patient.

An eighteen month old boy was in a coma and appeared to be dying in the Saltillo Children's Hospital. A man picked me up in his car to go pray for him. The Lord said; "Don't pray for him" and we returned to my home. The parents had been told to go to a certain city and do some work for the Lord. Instead they went to Saltillo, and the boy became very sick. When the parents decided to do what the Lord asked and prepared to leave, the sickness left their son.

A LEG SAVED:

After a church service with many healings, a lady asked me to go to her home and pray for her mother who was scheduled to have a leg removed. She had an infection for two years and it was full of puss. I put my hand in the puss and commanded all infection to die in the name of Jesus. As I recall it took 5 ½ weeks to heal over with new flesh and skin. The women later died of a heart attack, a problem she had not told us about.

STROKE PARALYSIS:

In a Baptist church a women who had a stroke was bought in for healing of paralysis of one side of her body. After prayer she could walk slowly, use her arms and speak. I instructed her how to keep her healing; however, I had apprehensions she would lose it. I encouraged her to be in every church service and I offered to come by and pray more for her. Her parents took her on a trip for a month during which time she lost the healing.

REMOVE SATAN AND ASK FORGIVENESS:

In Waco, Texas a healing service was going slow. I knew what the problem was and led everyone in a prayer to break un-forgiveness. As I started the service again the first person was a lady on crutches. When I commanded healing in the name of Jesus she threw the crutches down and started dancing and saying; "I am healed, I am healed." The rest of the healings were as quick as I could touch them and say; "In the name of Jesus be healed."

FISSURES:

I have had several surgeries since 1966. Four of the conditions needing surgery would have ended in death without God's intervention. A lesser surgery, with a tinge of humor, was for fissures. During a medical physical a doctor indicated he knew how to remove fissures such as I had. I was elated. He was the only Army doctor who indicated he could do this surgery. I had been suffering seven to eight years with fissures which developed during my time in the Infantry in Germany. Most mornings and part of the afternoons the company was on maneuvers, in movement with defend and attack, etc.. My normal bathroom time, which was early in the A.M., was interrupted with training for combat and I needed to wait about nine hours each day before a bathroom time was available. It became a painful condition.

The surgery was delightfully successful and a great boost to my spirit. Because I had never had prior surgery, I experienced several embarrassing incidents, which in retrospect are laughable. After being assigned a room in the hospital, a man arrived with a can of shaving cream and a razor. He told me to get cross ways of the bed, on my knees, and my butt facing an open door to a wide busy hallway. It was embarrassing but what could I do – I covered my head with my arms while he joked with a female nurse. I was then given several containers of water (it looked like a gallon but it must have been less). I obediently drank it all. When I regained consciousness after the surgery the doctor told me I needed to urinate within a specified time or he would use a tube on me. He said that turning a tap on slightly in the restroom wash basin and leaving it run, would stimulate me if I needed it, and he left me with a horrible thought of a tube being inserted.

I waited and waited for the urge which didn't come and my time for the tube was getting closer. To turn the water on looked like a necessity. I slipped out of bed and headed for the bathroom door. Then I noticed a tube, dragging on the floor behind me and a mess was following it. Oh, Oh, what have I done, as my head was starting to spin and I stepped quickly into the bathroom. I saw an EMERGENCY button on the wall above the toilet and as I fell, I pushed it, passed out and the nurse that woke me was not happy; in fact she seemed very upset, she talked very loud and as she put me back in bed she kept pointing to a red button on the wall over the bed. She then told me very emphatically that there was a urinal in the night stand and to use it; but not to get out of bed. I obediently said; "OK" and she left the room.

In a short time I believed the urge was coming on me, and it was. I quickly searched the nightstand, it was empty except for a small flat kidney-shaped dish. I thought, this is a stupid looking urinal. As I started to flow I pushed the red button, the nurse was back in a hurry and hollering. She saw the dish but couldn't find anything else. She ran out the door, making funny noises and soon someone appeared with a real urinal. In a few minutes I noted that one urinal was not going to be adequate and pushed the emergency button again. She appeared quickly, got another urinal and left, still pretending to be upset. In a few minutes it was obvious that a third urinal was needed. I was apprehensive of pushing the red button again but what else could I do, I wondered, how will she react? Will she laugh or cry? Fortunately, she laughed. I titled this; "My first hospital stay" while hoping it would be my last. Some blessings come with a price and humor.

. . . Grace, mercy, and peace from God the Father and the Lord Jesus Christ our savior. (Titus 1:4 KJV)

KIDNEY STONES:

While in the Army, and during the early years on the mission field, I passed many kidney stones from my right kidney. These stones were like a ball of sharp and pointed crystal blades that pointed in all directions, causing intense pain all the way to the bladder (they were a real pain in you know what). The doctors didn't show any mercy. They would not give me any pain medication until they were absolutely sure what was causing the pain. It always took four hours for the doctor to decide it was a kidney stone. I believe in every case of right side stones the doctor arrived with a pain pill shortly after the stone passed. The one exception was when I passed a stone in Vietnam. I was in my assigned location outside my boss's office when a man spoke my name. It was the full colonel in my chain of command, two levels above me. As I stood up to speak, I turned white, perspiration popped out of my face and I doubled over in intense pain. The Colonel said this is not a good time to talk. I went to the aid station and continued in pain. No one was interested in kidney stones except to write it in my record. There were too many soldiers who needed immediate care. The stone finally passed. What is interesting is that the Colonel wanted me to go to the Delta to pay several manufacturers for specialized delta boats they made for the South Vietnamese forces. They were paid in cash. A large amount that I wouldn't want to carry anywhere in Vietnam. It would have been very dangerous. Because of a kidney stone, I didn't receive that assignment, a real blessing in disguise.

In Mexico and after several years the stones on the right side stopped and they started on the left side. The stones on the left side were totally different from the right. They were sediment stones, reflecting the contours in the bottom of the kidney, fairly flat (not round) and in their flatness were much larger. They were erratic in passing and often seemed to stop along the route for hours, days or months before entering the bladder. One stone was very large and could not enter the bladder. One of the native Bible Class students made herbal tea and indicated the stone would pass with it. It did not work with me. I walked the floor all night (twelfth night) in intense pain, only stopping to vomit. I told Helen I could not take another night like that and we went to see the only type of doctor in the area, a baby doctor. He gave me a morphine shot that didn't even touch the pain. We went to the second baby doctor who looked fearfully at the scan of a huge mass. He gave me five doses of morphine and watched to make sure I got on an airplane to the U.S. I arrived at a hospital at Fort Sam Houston in San Antonio, Texas. It was late Friday and no doctor would come to work until Monday. My son Glen arrived to see me and took me to a hospital in Austin, Texas that specialized in stone removal. It was the largest kidney stone that they had worked on. Removal was by pincers inserted in the urethra and through the prostate and bladder. The pincers broke the stone into pieces (sand) to be flushed out. They told me that because of the stone size it never would have passed. The scan mass the Mexican doctors saw was inflamed flesh that they probably thought was cancer. The process of stone removal worked well; however, it resulted in damage to the urethra which over the years resulted in blockage to urine flow and severe infection. The result was grand mal seizures and another surgery to save my life (covered under Bladder Infection in this Chapter).

FUSION OF THE SPINAL JOINTS:

I was born with some missing cushions between spinal vertebra and suffered some pain most of my life. I went to chiropractors where I received some relief when they stretched me out on a table, taking pressure off my spine. Their x-rays are the ones that revealed the missing cushions, two vertebra fused together by themselves and others that were inflamed. My prime care VA doctor had x-rays that showed the infection but he was unable to get the Orthopedic Department to take any action.

I found a doctor in Longview, Texas who specialized in neck spinal problems. He had x-rays taken from different angles that reflected a bad infection in one joint; and in another joint, two vertebrae that had already fused together. His surgery was a great success and a tremendous relief from neck pain. In later life; however, two accidents created new upper spine problems. A beam that fell on my left shoulder and the removal of a rib during right lung cancer surgery left a damaged spine. (See sub paragraph Cancer in this chapter.) For pain of the spine, the sciatic nerve and a paralyzed leg I was hospitalized twice. Now I am very careful what I do. I get off my feet frequently and stretch myself out flat for periodic relief.

SKULL AND BRAIN INFECTION:

In the early ministry in Southern Mexico, in an African Mexican village in the State of Guererro, a pastor's wife gave me some tropical plums. To get the little edible flesh off the pit, I scraped them by biting with my molars. A pit slipped and I cracked teeth down through the roots. The dentist thought I was fine; however, over about 12 years an infection was growing in my jaws, skull and brain. A doctor in China said I could have a very serious problem. He was correct. My brain didn't seem to function and on the next trip back to the U.S. from China I developed a bad tooth ache. A dental x-ray revealed a very serious problem and he sent me to a high level specialist. This was May 2004. I underwent two surgeries and was given strong antibiotics for 3 months. The strange feeling disappeared after 2 ½ months. My ability to think has come back to a degree; however, I believe the Lord had me write two books to recapture some of my memory, etc., a process that is still continuing to this day.

…"Verily, Verily I say unto you; what so ever you shall ask the Father in my name, He will give it to you." (John 16:23 KJV)

BLADDER INFECTION:

During surgery in 1999 to remove an impacted kidney stone the urethra was damaged causing a restricted urinary flow. Years later, this was a great hindrance to ministry in China to be constantly looking for and running to a restroom. I suffered Grand Mal seizures but didn't know what they were called. I didn't know I had a massive bladder infection. On the long flight from Hong Kong, China to Vancouver, Canada I needed the restroom every 10 to 15 minutes; however, the aircraft restrooms had a problem and some restrooms were closed. I spent much of my time waiting in line to the one functioning restroom, along with many other people. All of which were standing in a puddle, it was a truly miserable trip. I had a change of clothing in my carry-on luggage and a delay before the Vancouver to Dallas flight. I used the terminal restroom to bathe and change clothes. A few days after my arrival in Temple, Texas I had a terrible experience, a Grand Mal seizure with continual convulsions of every muscle in my body. Constant flailing like a fish out of water and with terrible pain the ambulance took me to King's Daughters Hospital. It was an experience I don't want to describe. After the infection was controlled I went under TURP surgery in Scott and White Hospital.

LUNG CANCER:

An x-ray at the V.A. indicated I had a mass in my right lung, frequent scans indicated it was a very fast growing type. My son Glen who was part of Austin based Lone Star Oncology was in a meeting with other doctors in Baltimore when he had a dream. In the dream a doctor said to him, "I am sorry to hear of your Dad's death." Glen replied; "My Dad isn't dead." Another doctor came to him in the dream and said the same thing. When Glen returned to Austin he noted my wife Helen had sent him an email that stated a mass was discovered in my right lung. He came to Temple to see me, it was the day I was scheduled to see the V.A. cancer doctor. The doctor came to the waiting room an hour and ten minutes late (after the normal hospital duty hours were past). He appeared to be exhausted or sick and didn't know why I was there. I reminded him I was his cancer patient and that he had scheduled this appointment. In his office he told me what he would do over the next several months, mainly to continue to scan each week or so. I indicated it looked like he would not get to do the surgery until October. He responded, the V.A. could not promise me surgery. That he didn't even know where the funds would come from. He gave me the phone number to keep him informed. I indicated no one ever answered that phone. He said; "You are right," and gave me the name Peggy and her number to keep him informed.

After Glen and I returned to my home, Glen told me of his dream and that is why he had come to see me. He stated he could make all the arrangements for my surgery to include the hospital, surgeon, cancer doctor, etc. and have me back home in ten days. I said; "do it." When Glen gave me the applicable data for surgery I notified the V.A. doctor. He responded; "What took you so long?" His answer indicated to me that it was what he wanted me to do but didn't tell me.

As I promised I called Peggy at each step of the way (6 calls) and I asked her to please tell the doctor each time. Her response to every call was; "I don't know why the doctor is having me do this, it isn't in my job description." She did promise to tell him each time I called. Everything went as Glen scheduled it and I was back home in ten days. God had prevailed in many ways and I was very thankful.

Seek ye first the kingdom of God and his righteous and all these things shall be added onto you. (Matthew 6:33 KJV)

GOD OF MIRACLES:

Today I am 89 years old. THE LORD IS NOT THROUGH WITH ME YET.

CHAPTER 5

Obey the Lord Explicitly

A NEAR DEATH EXPERIENCE:

Another lesson learned on the mission field was to obey the Lord explicitly. That is; exactly, specifically, precisely, distinctly and clearly. Obedience takes precedence over reasoning, rationalizing, persuasion from others, how things appear, what the enemy may be telling you, defective theology, pressure from relatives or any other excuse for disobedience.

My sheep know my voice and I know them, and they follow me and I give unto them eternal life and they shall never perish, neither shall any man pluck them out of my hand. (John 10:27-28 KJV)

We are familiar with David's love of God and his earnest desire to **obey** Him. Psalm 23, written by David, expresses many of the blessings of God that David experienced in obedience.

1. The Lord is my Shepard, I shall not want. Comment: The Lord will lead me and provide abundant life.
2. He makes me to lie down in green pastures: He leads me beside the still waters. Comment: I will have a good resting place and water to refresh me.
3. He restoreth my soul: He leads me in the paths of righteousness for His name's sake. Comment: My soul is whole. He guides me on the right path with no cause to stumble, no falling or going astray.
4. Though I walk thru the valley of the shadows of death. I will fear no evil, for He is with me: His Word will comfort me. Comment:

He will give me safe passage through the valley of the shadow of death-the deep, waterless, gloomy, wild beast infected, rocky, dangerous, death lurking ravine common in Palestine.

5. He prepares a table before me in the presence of my enemies: He anoints my head with oil: my cup runs over. Comment: He prepares a feast for me and I will fear no evil because of His constant companionship, watch, and protection. Before the feast my head will be anointed with perfumed oil. Not only plenty of food but plenty of wholesome drink.

6. Surely goodness and mercy shall follow me all the days of my life and I will dwell in the house of the Lord forever. Comment: Confidence that goodness and mercy will follow me to the end of my life. Faith in life after death in God's house forever. No fear of the future.

Disobedience, even if only one word, can mean life or death, a healthy body or a battered body full of broken bones and mangled organs. It also means the difference between a beautiful 15 passenger four wheel drive van (loaded with tools and equipment for a new mission base), now turned into a pile of scrap metal and the tools and equipment scattered down a mountain side for 1/3 of a mile.

Carl was in the Passenger Seat as the Van
Tumbled down the Mountain

The Holy Spirit had said "No" in a clear soft voice to not allow the other man to drive. Several hours later my reasoning had turned the No into a Yes. Everything appeared okay. I had been driving seven hours, it was a good blacktop road, the man claimed he had driven 26 years in California and I reasoned "why not let him drive?" The result was very costly: spiritually I felt terrible for having disobeyed the Holy Spirit, the time of several precious people was lost, medically my body would never be the same, fractured bones, and ribs ripped off my spine and sternum would take months to heal, and critical funds for the new base and van were needlessly consumed. After the accident while in the Mexican hospital, I noted the man's driver's license required he wear glasses, which he did not have. I have lost count of how many times the Lord has saved my life. He had saved it again in this accident; however, I paid a dear price for my disobedience.

— Obey my voice, and I will be your God and you shall be my people: and walk in the ways I have commanded you, that it may go well unto you. (Jeremiah 7:23 KJV)

An intelligent God wants to speak with mankind, all of us. He knows every language. Those of us who speak English, He will speak to us in English. He wants a conversational relationship which Jesus has restored to us. All believers can do this and they must.

OBEY FOR PROSPERITY:

While praying in my second year on the mission field the Lord said, "Prosperity is knowing the will of God and doing it." Prosperity is what we need and want, especially on the mission field.

We may <u>hear</u> God's voice, we may <u>see</u> God's voice in visions or dreams and we may <u>feel</u> God's voice through our senses.

And thine ears shall hear a word behind thee, saying, This is the way, walk ye in it... (Isaiah 30:21 KJV)

Samuel, Learning to hear and recognize God's voice. (1 Samuel 3:2-10)

And the word of the LORD was precious in those days; there was no open vision. (1 Samuel 3:1) Note the words, word and vision, both are about hearing God.

Jeremiah still prophesied by faith even though he had been a prophet many years. It was not a certainty or it would not be faith. See Jeremiah 32:8

Each missionary must know the will of God for themselves; therefore they must recognize and receive His communications.

Some of the ways He, (God, Jesus, and the Holy Spirit) has communicated with me are:

1. Hearing His voice <u>audibly</u> 1 Samuel 3:10, Acts 9:3-7,
   Examples: "You are healed.", "Get out of here quickly", "The devil wants to kill you on the highway today."
2. Hearing His clear soft voice <u>in our spirit</u>. 1 Kings 19:12, John 14:26
   Examples: "All you have to do is pray.", "Do what is in your heart."
3. <u>Dreams</u> (Asleep or about to wake up) Genesis 15:1, 20:3, 28:12, 31:10, 31:24, 37:5-10, Daniel 2, Matthew 1:20
4. Visions
   A. <u>Internal Visions</u>: John 5:19-20, 8:38, 40
      Examples: Word of knowledge or wisdom, seeing His words in our spirit.

B. <u>External Visions</u>: Exodus 3:2-17, Josh 5:13-15, Acts 9:3-7

Examples: The persons spirit goes someplace, (heaven, etc.) and returns to the body.

5. Praying in the Spirit <u>with interpretations</u>. 1 Corinthians 14:5-6, 13-15, 26, Romans 8:26-27, 1 Jude 20 Example: Holy Spirit <u>intercedes</u> for us.

6. Discernment, Knowledge, Wisdom. 1 Corinthians 12:7-11, Hebrews 3:14

7. Deeper understanding of a scripture: Psalms:119:1-5 Examples: While reading the Word, Bible verses leap off the page.

8. Personal Prophecy. 1 Corinthians 12:7-11

9. Experiencing another's emotions and/or physical feelings. 1 Corinthians 12:7-11

10. By a poem, song, exhortation, etc. in me or somebody else.

11. A sense of knowing. Examples: Caution, yes, no, wait, speed up, danger, lack of peace, peace, apprehension, evil, etc.

12. By a gift with a purpose or a message in itself.

13. By orchestrated circumstances. (happening) Example: Multiple comments from people on a specific subject such as writing a book.

14. Sending an angel to speak to me. For example; An angel specifically approached me while I was standing in line at the Veteran's Administration. He questioned, "What are you doing here?"

Hindrances to hearing God's voice:

- The ungodly beliefs of unworthiness, fear, failure, defeat, hopelessness and helplessness.
- Sin. Keeps you bound in guilt and shame.
- Demons that block spiritual eyes and ears.

In addition to receiving communications from God, Jesus or the Holy Spirit we need to understand what each communication is trying to tell us, its scope, what it entails, where, when, how, necessary facilities, etc. The Lord may use many people to give you details that need to be written down, a journal for repeated reference and staying on track. He may tell you only once. A journal also shows honor and respect for His voice, His connections with you.

The next step is to do what is "His will for you." You need to flow with the Spirit of God as only He knows everything. Your job is to obey in spite of numerous overwhelming obstacles, complicated problems, government interference, demonized people, false prophets, acts of nature and satanic deception. Satan will attempt to destroy everything God gives to you to do. I repeat, satan will attempt to destroy by any means possible everything God gives you to do.

BIND THE ENEMY AND YOUR OWN FLESH:

Every time on the mission field when we were looking for the location the Lord wanted for us to live or work we received false locations from the enemy. Ultimately, before asking the Lord a question, I bound the enemy from speaking to me and I asked God to bind my flesh from speaking to me. Basically, this is what I said: "In the name of Jesus I bind you satan, every fallen angel, principalities, powers, rulers of darkness, demonic forces of any kind; silent and inoperative, you will not speak to me or influence me in any way; and Father, I ask you in Jesus name to bind my own desires, my own mind, my own soul from speaking to me. I only hear your voice, Father, Jesus, the Holy Spirit or any angel you send to me; and I thank you for your answer." Then I ask my question.

Behold, I set before you this day a blessing and a curse. A blessing if you obey the commandments of the Lord: your God - - - and a curse if you will not obey the commandments of the Lord your God - - - (Deuteronomy 11: 26-27a KJV)

If your workload is consistently heavy, I suggest you take two or three days a month alone with the Lord: fasting, studying the Word, praying; and seeking, loving, thanking and communion with Jesus. It will refresh you.

As you seek the Lord, a demonic spirit will often respond, entering with a noise like a diesel train or other fanciful sounds; pretending to be God. Order him to leave in the name of Jesus and to take all his workers and lies with him. Be patient and the Lord, in His timing, will communicate with you but it may be the third day. This was usually an opportunity for the Lord to speak to me about whatever Fruit of the Spirit He wanted me to concentrate on at that time in my life.

I observed a few cases where people, who received a healing and deliverance, lost it about three months later because of their disobedience. In all but a few cases, I warned them emphatically, with God's word and examples on how to keep their healing or deliverance. Most people carefully obeyed and they stayed free.

Those few who disobeyed, reopened the door to demonic forces by their words and actions; or the words and actions of individuals responsible for them. In some cases, when youth were released from a hospital, they were returned to the parents who were witches. Within a short time the demonic spirits were back in them and ultimately their sickness returned and they died.

"For the time is come that judgment must begin at the house of God; and if it first begin with us, what shall be the end of them that obey not the gospel of God." (I Peter 4:17 KJV)

Some specific comments for me to obey that I received from the Lord over time:

1. Tell her to thank me for her healing:
   In the first months of ministry in the Saltillo area I prayed for an elderly lady who was in bed. I specifically commanded in Jesus name that each of her afflictions leave; but nothing appeared to happen and I asked for the Lord's guidance. He said, "Tell her to thank me for her healings." I told her and as she thanked Him for each healing the sickness left. I believe the Lord was in effect telling me to have everyone thank Him for their healing, etc.; as an element of each ministry. This stressed the points that Jesus is the healer and that God wants us to thank Him.

   "But thanks be to God which giveth us the victory through our Lord Jesus Christ." (I Corinthians 15:57 KJV)

2. I don't hear you:
   I had been praying in my mind on various things and when I started on demonic forces the Lord spoke; "I don't hear you." To rebuke demonic forces, I believe we must speak out loud. I don't believe demonic forces can hear our thoughts.

3. A lesson learned is a lesson lived:
   We haven't learned a lesson until we practice it in our daily walk.

4. Corruption is evil:
   I asked the Lord what He wanted me to speak on at a missions conference. He said; "Corruption is evil." As missionaries we see corruption wherever the Lord sends us. We must keep in mind that all corruption is evil and not to yield to anything tainted with corruption. The enemy is always seeking leverage to control you. All corruption is

of the devil; do not open yourself up to him in any way. If you should sin, repent immediately to keep the enemy out.

"According as His divine power has given unto us all things that pertain unto life and godliness, through the knowledge of Him that hath called us to glory and virtue. Whereby are given unto us exceeding great and precious promises: that by these you might be partakers of the divine nature, having escaped the corruption that is in the world through lust. (II Peter 1:3-4 KJV)

5. Fear is not of the Lord:
   Early in the ministry a woman came to see me who was in constant and intense fear. The Lord said; "Fear is not of God." Fear is a demonic spirit that enters a person during a traumatic experience such as damage from a stroke, a horror movie, a treasonous relationship, a Halloween prank, divorce, a youth pregnancy, an accident, extended use of medication or other drugs, or some other trauma. The demonic spirit of fear, along with any other evil spirits it has invited in, needs to be commanded to leave in Jesus name and replaced with faith that Jesus will heal them.

6. You get what you speak with your mouth:
   The Lord's words; "What you speak over yourself, in the area that you give credit to satan, you give him an open door to do it. This makes a mockery of the covering I gave you through the blood of Jesus."

   "And they overcame him (satan) by the blood of the Lamb and the word of their testimony…" (Deuteronomy 12:11 KJV)

   Life and death are in the tongue…(Proverbs 18:21)

Put on the whole armor of God that you may be able to stand against the wiles of the devil. (Ephesians 6:11 KJV)

Jesus gave his disciples..."power and authority over all the devils"... (Luke 9:1 KJV)

7. Obedience is better than witchcraft, which you practice when you speak evil of someone.
   These were words spoken to me by the Lord in reference to a jealous worker's comments about another worker. Comments which were based on his cultural habits and not God's word. A jealous person, especially a person of prominence, can be very dangerous, . . . the works of the flesh are . . . witchcraft . . . they which do such things shall not inherit the kingdom of God. (Galatians 5:19-21 KJV)

8. Love the Lord:
   The words to me as I sought the Lord in prayer were; "Love the Lord with all your heart, soul, strength and mind; and your neighbor as yourself." (Luke 10:27, Mark 12:30, Matthew 22:37-39 KJV)

9. Don't borrow money:
   "I do not want you to borrow money" were the Lords comments to me on my way home after borrowing money to purchase a 15 passenger van for the ministry in Mexico. I have not borrowed money since; except credit that is paid in full each billing.

10. Tracts not of the Lord:
    "Do not use them, burn them" was the Lord's reply to me reference the tracts "Once Saved, Always Saved" and "Speaking in tongues is of the devil."

"Though He were a son, yet learned He obedience by the things He suffered: And being made perfect, He became the author of eternal salvation unto all them that obey Him." (Hebrews 5:8-9 KJV)

CHAPTER 6

False Doctrines and Deceived People

It was noted on the mission field that many people have been overwhelmed with false doctrines that were promulgated as God's Word; doctrines that originated with satan, written by man and carry the curse of God. These doctrines leave many people, to include Christians, insensible, apathetic and deceived, resulting in a proliferation of cults and occult activities to satan's delight. People are grasping at any religious belief that seems attractive to them such as: reincarnation, Jesus died in India and was buried there, all religions lead to heaven, that Ouija boards and tarot cards are only games, statues of pagan gods are ok in your home if you don't worship them, you can participate in secret organizations, good luck charms are ok, etc. This list could be expanded by the thousands of beliefs that are abominations to God (sin) and separate people from a loving heavenly Father who created them and desires their fellowship.

I cannot cover in detail in this book the multitude of false beliefs I have encountered; however I am including here items that were not covered in my book "A Challenge to Live" and some items that God has specifically included.

MOVIE MINISTRY FILMS:

When compiling a list of three hundred films that would be suitable for missions work, the Lord specified two films that I was not to use. These two films each used a theme of fear to bring people to the Lord. A missionary who had a movie ministry for many years told me that people who came to the Lord through fear did not stay in fellowship very long.

SALVATION AND OTHER TRACTS:

Before we developed our own Spanish Tracts, I used material from many denominations and groups. As I prayed over one batch of tracts, the Lord identified two tracts that I was not to use. I said, "Lord, can I keep one copy of each to show people what I cannot use?" He said very emphatically, "Burn them." These two tracts were titled. "Once Saved, Always Saved" and "Speaking in Tongues is of the Devil." Both of these tracts expound a demon inspired doctrine that man has propagated as Bible doctrine.

As I was writing the book, "A Challenge to Live," a pastor, who I had never met and didn't know I was writing a book, said, "The book you are writing is to bring people back to the Lord who have fallen by the wayside." Occasionally, as I met or heard someone, the Holy Spirit Would indicate, "They need your book." These were people who were no longer serving the Lord with all their heart in some significant area of their life such as; occupation, religion, having unforgiveness/bitterness, self-condemnation, etc.

The subjects of once saved always saved and speaking in tongues are covered in depth later in this chapter.

IDOLATRY:

God's 4 am wakeup call on idols in my home is covered in the book "A Challenge to Live." Only a short comment here to stress that the symbolic items I had to throw in the garbage were only a substitute for the True Living God. They still had to go in the garbage. Since that day, he has shown me a multitude of things that people put ahead of God in their lives that He considers Idolatry. If we expect God's provision for our lives, we need to seek Him first in everything we permit in our lives: What we think, what we say and what we do. God must be first or it is idolatry with God's penalties attached, until it is repented of and forgiven.

BIBLES:

On the mission field I was exposed to the paraphrased version of the Bible, and I asked the Lord about it. He said, "Read it." I felt He was saying any translation was ok that truly helps spread His Word. I already knew of Bibles that had portions deleted and other doctrines inserted to justify a cultic or occultist practice were not acceptable to use. An example is the Jehovah's Bible. Some groups may use a standard bible; however, their interpretation may be occultic.

I have also noted that Bibles that have been used as part of satanic rituals will radiate a demonic force, attract demonic spirits, and cause sickness and other problems to the owners.

CULT AND OCCULT BOOKS, LITERATURE AND PARAPHERNALIA:

Includes instructions on how to do anything of a cult/occult or other demonic/satanic nature. Some subjects are witchcraft, casting spells, divination, palm reading, voodoo, trances, sorcery, séances, levitation, incantations, conjuring demons, curandero instructions, clairvoyance, simulated deliverance and anything else of a demonic nature such as a book on modern slang. All such literature and related paraphernalia should be burnt in fire.

UN-FORGIVENESS:

In 1983, while teaching on the subject of forgiveness/unforgiveness, an old friend became upset. She did not reconcile the forgiveness scriptures which state unless you forgive, your Heavenly Father cannot forgive you (resulting in no salvation) with the scriptures that state believe in your heart and confess with your mouth for salvation. I sought the Lord for an answer. Some weeks later as I was preparing notes for that evening service in an Indian village in South Mexico, the Holy Spirit spoke the words to me, "Unforgiveness will give you a life of misery, lead to an early grave, and put you in the lake of fire." I said, "Ok Lord, I will teach it."

THE SALVATION SCRIPTURES:

Rom 10:9-10 (KJV) That if thou shalt confess with thy mouth the Lord Jesus, and shalt believe in thine heart that God hath raised him from the dead, thou shalt be saved. For with the heart man believeth unto righteousness; and with the mouth confession is made unto salvation.

John 3:16 (KJV) For God so loved the world, that he gave his only begotten Son, that whosoever believeth in him should not perish, but have everlasting life.

THE UNFORGIVENESS SCRIPTURES:

Matthew 6:12,14-15 (KJV) And forgive us our debts, as we forgive our debtors. For if ye forgive men their trespasses, your heavenly Father will also forgive you: But if ye forgive not men their trespasses, neither will your Father forgive your trespasses.

Mark 11:25-26 (KJV) And when ye stand praying, forgive, if ye have ought against any: that your Father also which is in heaven may forgive you your trespasses. But if ye do not forgive, neither will your Father which is in heaven forgive your trespasses.

Luke 6:37 (KJV) Judge not, and ye shall not be judged: condemn not, and ye shall not be condemned: forgive, and ye shall be forgiven:

Other Scriptures: Ephesians 4:32, Colossians 3:13, Matthew 18:21-22, 2 Corinthians 2:10-11, 1 John 1:9, Luke 17:3-4, Luke 11:4, Isaiah 55:7, 1 John 2:9-12, 1 John 3:14-15, 1 John 4:21

ONCE SAVED ALWAYS SAVED – A FALSE DOCTRINE:

First, I want to mention that I do not want anyone's blood on my hands because I didn't obey God and tell the truth. Read Ezekiel 33:1-20. I also want to show myself approved unto God as a workman that needs not be ashamed; rightly dividing the Word of Truth. Read 2 Timothy 2:15 and Proverbs 25:2.

The author of what we now call Calvinism was John Calvin. He was a French theologian during the Protestant Reformation, born July 10, 1509 and died May 27, 1564. He wrote five principles, one of which is referred to as "Perseverance of the Saints" and from which the expression "Once Saved Always Saved" is derived.

CALVIN'S BELIEF – CHRISTIANS CANNOT SIN:

1 John 3:9 is used to justify Calvin's belief that Christians cannot sin. "Whosoever is born of God doth not commit sin; for his seed remaineth in him: and he cannot sin, because he is born of God." (KJV)

We must look at the words "commit" and "cannot" in the original language of Greek to see the true meaning. Commit is from the Greek word POIEO. This word refers to what one does repeatedly, habitually. It does not mean that a person does not occasionally sin, but will not make a constant practice of it. Cannot is from the Greek word OUDUNAMAI. This means morally unable and that which is physically impossible. The word "cannot" does not imply that the child of God has come to the place where he is physically unable to do anything wrong, but that he is morally restrained from it. The Greek word literally means "cannot continue to practice sin."

1 John 2:1-2 indicates Christians do sin. "My little children, these things write I unto you, that ye sin not. And if any man sin, we have an advocate with the Father, Jesus Christ the righteous: And he is the propitiation for our sins: and not for ours only, but also for the sins of the whole world." (KJV)

Therefore the scripture 1 John 3:9 is saying a Christian cannot habitually practice sin and be consistent with Christ.

Calvin's belief: People who fall away were never saved. A hundred or more scriptures warn <u>Christians</u> to be careful they don't fall. Along with applicable scriptures, I am attaching a list of people mentioned in the Bible who fell away, to include many who worked with Jesus and with the Apostles.

FALLING AWAY:

In writing this book I have been very concerned about the large number of people in the U.S. and elsewhere who received Jesus years ago, but who now harbor unforgiveness and live under its curse. In effect they have lost their salvation, but don't seem to realize it. My heart yearns to bring them back to the reality of their situation. The following scriptures address this condition.

For if after they have escaped the pollutions of the world through the knowledge of the Lord and Savior Jesus Christ, they are again entangled therein, and overcome, the latter end is worse with them than the beginning. For it had been better for them not to have known the way of righteousness, than, after they have known it, to turn from the holy commandment delivered unto them. 2 Peter 2:20-21 (KJV)

For it is impossible for those who were once enlightened, and have tasted of the heavenly gift, and were made partakers of the Holy Ghost, And have tasted the good word of God, and the powers of the world to come, If they shall fall away, to renew them again unto repentance; seeing they crucify to themselves the Son of God afresh, and put him to an open shame. Hebrews 6:4-6 (KJV)

For if we sin willfully after that we have received the knowledge of the truth, there remaineth no more sacrifice for sins, but a certain fearful expectation of judgment and fiery indignation, which shall devour the adversaries. He that despised Moses' law died without mercy under two or three witnesses: Of how much sorer punishment, suppose ye, shall he be thought worthy, who hath trodden underfoot the Son of God, and hath counted the blood of the covenant, wherewith he was sanctified, an unholy thing, and hath done despite unto the Spirit of grace? Hebrews 10:26-29 (KJV)

Behold, the Lord's hand is not shortened, that it cannot save; neither his ear heavy, that it cannot hear: But your iniquities have separated between you and your God, and your sins have hid his face from you, that he will not hear. Isaiah 59:1-2 (KJV)

For I am the Lord, I change not; therefore ye sons of Jacob are not consumed. Even from the days of your fathers ye are gone away from mine ordinances, and have not kept them. Return unto me, and I will return unto you, saith the Lord of hosts. But ye said, Wherein shall we return? Malachi 3:6-7 (KJV)

Ah sinful nation, a people laden with iniquity, a seed of evildoers, children that are corrupters: they have forsaken the Lord, they have provoked the Holy One of Israel unto anger, they are gone away backward. Isaiah 1:4 (KJV)

Let them be blotted out of the book of the living, and not be written with the righteous. Psalm 69:28 (KJV)

Yet now, if thou wilt forgive their sin--; and if not, blot me, I pray thee, out of thy book which thou hast written. And the Lord said unto Moses, "Whosoever hath sinned against me, him will I blot out of my book." Exodus 32:32-33 (KJV)

And if any man shall take away from the words of the book of this prophecy, God shall take away his part out of the book of life, and out of the holy city, and from the things which are written in this book. Revelations 22:19 (KJV)

NEW TESTAMENT PEOPLE WHO FELL FROM GOD'S GRACE:

1. Jesus' Disciples
    a. Disciples for some time believed. (Luke 8:13). Drew back (Hebrews 10:26-39). Fell from grace. (John 1:12; 1 John 5:1)
    b. After these things the Lord appointed other seventy also, and sent them two and two before his face into every city and place, whither he himself would come. Luke 10:1 (KJV)
    c. Jesus spoke to His disciples of eating His flesh and drinking his blood. (John 6:53-59) Many therefore of his disciples, when they had heard this, said, This is a hard saying; who can hear it? From that time many of

his disciples went back, and walked no more with him. John 6:60,66 (KJV)

d. And Jesus said unto him, No man, having put his hand to the plough, and looking back, is fit for the kingdom of God. Luke 9:62 (KJV)

2. Judas

a. Jesus trusted Judas. My own familiar friend, in whom I trusted (Psalms 41:9). Judas' name was in the Book of Life. (Acts 1:20; Psalms 69:25-28)

b. Judas was a bishop of the church Christ was building. (Acts 1:20; Psalm 109:8) He had part of the Apostolic ministry. (Acts 1:17, 25) He had power to cast out spirits and heal all manner of sickness. (Matthew 10:19-20). Like the other apostles he was ordained by Christ. (Mark 10:19-20) Judas fell from the ministry. (Luke 22:3, John 13:2). Judas had eternal life. (John 17:2).

c. Jesus answered them, Have not I chosen you twelve, and one of you is a devil? He spake of Judas Iscariot the son of Simon: for he it was that should betray him, being one of the twelve. John 6:70-71 (KJV)

d. But go rather to the lost sheep of the house of Israel. And as ye go, preach, saying, "The kingdom of heaven is at hand. Heal the sick, cleanse the lepers, raise the dead, cast out devils: freely ye have received, freely give." Matthew 10:6-8 (KJV)

e. And they went out, and preached that men should repent. And they cast out many devils, and anointed with oil many that were sick, and healed them. Mark 6:12-13 (KJV)

f. And it came to pass in those days, that he went out into a mountain to pray, and continued all night in prayer to God. And when it was day, he called unto him his disciples: and of them he chose twelve, whom also he named apostles; And Judas the brother of James, and

Judas Iscariot, which also was the traitor. Luke 6:12, 13, 16 (KJV)

g. That he may take part of this ministry and apostleship, from which Judas by transgression fell, that he might go to his own place. Acts 1:25 (KJV)

h. (Jesus Speaking) "Yea, mine own familiar friend, in whom I trusted, which did eat of my bread, hath lifted up his heel against me." Psalm 41:9 (KJV)

3. Ananias and Sapphira were saved. (Acts 4:32, 5:1-9) Great grace was upon them. (Acts 5:1-11, Acts 4:33) Peter spoke to Ananias and Sapphira who lied. They both died and were buried.

4. The Galatians began in the Spirit (Galatians 3:2-4) were soon removed. (Galatians 1:6-5:4)

5. Demas left the church and went back to sin. (Colossians 4:14, 1 John 2:15-17)

a. For Demas hath forsaken me, having loved this present world, and is departed unto Thessalonica; Crescens to Galatia, Titus unto Dalmatia. 2 Timothy 4:10 (KJV)

b. Love not the world, neither the things that are in the world. If any man love the world, the love of the Father is not in him. For all that is in the world, the lust of the flesh, and the lust of the eyes, and the pride of life, is not of the Father, but is of the world. And the world passeth away, and the lust thereof: but he that doeth the will of God abideth forever. 1 John 2:15-17 (KJV)

6. Hymenaeus and Alexander went from faith to shipwreck;

a. Holding faith, and a good conscience; which some having put away concerning faith have made shipwreck: Of whom is Hymenaeus and Alexander; whom I have delivered unto Satan, that they may learn not to blaspheme. 1 Timothy 1:19-20 (KJV)

b. Alexander the coppersmith did me much evil: the Lord rewards him according to his works: Of whom be thou were also; for he hath greatly withstood our words. At my first answer no man stood with me, but all men forsook me: I pray God that it may not be laid to their charge. 2 Timothy 4:14-16 (KJV)

7. Many coveted money and left the faith. (1 Timothy 6:10,21)
8. Young widows cast off their first faith and were damned. (1 Timothy 6:11, 13)
9. Hymenaeus and Philetus left the faith and caused others to leave (2 Timothy 2:17-19)
10. Apostates were once saved, but fell and departed from the Faith. (Romans 1:21-32, Hebrews 6:4-8, 10:26-29, 2 Peter 2:20-22)
11. Many in the churches were once saved, but did not repent of later sin. (Revelations 2:5,10,16, 20-23; 3:3,11,16)

Along with the above individuals, and others that fell from grace, there are over 200 warnings in scripture against falling mentioned by Joshua, Samuel, Solomon, prophets, Paul, James, Peter, John, Jude, Christ and others.

SPEAKING IN TONGUES IS REAL:

For with stammering lips and another tongue will he speak to this people. To whom he said, This is the rest wherewith ye may cause the weary to rest; and this is the refreshing: yet they would not hear. Isaiah 28:11-12 (KJV)

And it shall come to pass afterward, that I will pour out my spirit upon all flesh; and your sons and your daughters shall prophesy, your old men shall dream dreams, your young men shall see visions: And also upon the servants and upon the handmaids in those days will I pour out my spirit. And I will shew wonders in the heavens and in the earth, blood, and fire, and pillars of smoke. The sun shall be turned into darkness, and the moon into blood, before the great and terrible day of the Lord come. And it shall come to pass, that whosoever shall call on the name of the Lord shall be delivered: for in mount Zion and in Jerusalem shall be deliverance, as the Lord hath said, and in the remnant whom the Lord shall call. Joel 2:28-32 (KJV)

In the law it is written: "With other tongues and through the lips of foreigners I will speak to this people, but even then they will not listen to me, says the Lord." 1 Corinthians 14:21 (NIV)

And they were all filled with the Holy Ghost, and began to speak with other tongues, as the Spirit gave them utterance. Acts 2:4 (KJV)

And these signs shall follow them that believe; In my name shall they cast out devils; they shall speak with new tongues; Mark 16:17 (KJV)

But when the Comforter is come, whom I will send unto you from the Father, even the Spirit of truth, which proceedeth from the Father, he shall testify of me: John 15:26 (KJV)

SPEAKING IN TONGUES IS FOR TODAY:

Matthew 7:7-11 Ask and receive.

Romans 8:26-27 The Spirit intercedes for us.

Ephesians 6:18 Praying always in the Spirit.

1 Corinthians 14 In this chapter speaking in tongues is mentioned seventeen times. Chapters 12 and 13 are also on the Holy Spirit's presence.

1 Corinthians 14:39 … and forbid not to speak in tongues.

1 Corinthians 13:1 Though I speak with the tongues of men and angels.

1 Corinthians 12:7, 8, and 10 But the manifestation of the Spirit is given to every man to profit withal. For to one is given by the Spirit . . . divers kinds of tongues; another interpretation of tongues.

Jude 20 (KJV) But ye, beloved, building up yourselves on your most holy faith, praying in the Holy Ghost,

Martin Luther claimed he spoke in tongues every day, the same as millions of people do today.

SPEAKING IN TONGUES WILL CEASE:

1 Corinthians 13:8, 10-11 Speaking in tongues, along with knowledge and prophesy will vanish away when that which is perfect comes. In Vines Complete Expository Dictionary the Greek word used for "perfect" is "teleios"; which is defined as "having reached its end", "finished", "complete", "perfect".

The only thing that was perfect that walked the face of the earth was Jesus Christ, so when He comes back in the second advent, we will no longer need tongues and prophecy as Jesus the King will rule and reign 1,000 years, and all mysteries will be revealed.

BLESSINGS OF A RIGHTEOUS MAN: PSALMS 32:1-11

1. Sins forgiven. Verses 1-5
2. Sins covered (atoned for). Verse 1
3. Not charged with sin. Verse 2
4. Freedom from sin.
5. Mercy from God Verse 6
6. Not overwhelmed with sorrow.
7. God is a hiding place. Verse 7
8. Preservation from trouble.
9. Encompassed with songs of deliverance.

10. Divine instruction. Verse 8
11. Guidance from God
12. Encompassed with Mercy. Verse 10

Psalms 32:11 (KJV) Be glad in the Lord, and rejoice, ye righteous: and shout for joy, all ye that are upright in heart.

CHAPTER 7

God's Curses on Sin cannot be Ignored

A CURSED SIN:

A lesson learned on the mission field is that the God cursed sins of unforgiveness, disobedience, idolatry, etc. cannot be ignored as they will cost you everything if you do not repent, and forgive where applicable.

When the Lord spoke to me in answer to my prayer concerning salvation (Romans 10:9) and unforgiveness (Matthew 6:15), He said, "Unforgiveness will give you a life of misery, lead to an early grave and put you in the Lake of Fire."

In other words, if you hold unforgiveness towards anyone, you are not saved; and you will end up in the Lake of Fire unless you repent and forgive.

"For if you forgive men their trespasses, your Heavenly Father will also forgive you. But if you forgive not men their trespasses, neither will your Father forgive your trespasses." (Matthew 6:14-15 KJV)

"And when you stand praying, forgive, if you have ought against any; that your Father also which is in heaven may forgive you your trespasses. But if you do not forgive, neither will your Father which is in heaven forgive your trespasses." (Mark 11:25-26 KJV)

An evangelist from South Africa told of a pastor friend who died and went to heaven. The Holy Spirit said the Lord was not finished with him on earth and he needed to return. He asked to see the Lake of Fire before he returned and it was granted. He saw people in terrible agony and he recognized the face of his mother-in-law. He said, "No she couldn't possibly be here as she was always in the church working, etc." The Holy Spirit responded, "But she refused to forgive her sister."

SAVED OR UNFORGIVING:

Since 1979 I have observed thousands of people who call themselves Christians and would state they are saved; however, many of them go to the altar in response to any salvation call. In 1981 I noted that about 1/3 of the people in American churches would not receive a healing or deliverance until after they had repented, or read out loud, a prayer for forgiveness of all unforgiveness in their heart. Unforgiveness was obviously a blockage to their healing, deliverance and salvation. After repentance, forgiveness, breaking curses and renouncing satanic influence; God's healing was fully received. These prayers are Appendix A and B in the book "A Challenge to Live"; and to this book which is a sequel, "Lessons Learned on the Mission Field."

SATAN LOVES UNFORGIVENESS:

Unforgivess is one of Satan's most destructive forces, both individually and collectively. His dirty work is found in all aspects of society. A society where individuals, marriages, families, friendships, business, ministries, government and international relations have been perverted and corrupted so as to prevent people from receiving God's intended blessings and His desired communion with His creation.

"The thief comes not but for to steal, kill and destroy. I am come that they might have life, and that they might have it more abundantly." (John 10:10 KJV) Through unforgiveness, satan is able to steal, kill and destroy.

As a boy I remembered the Second World War when German generals made an offer to kill Hitler and stop the war in Europe if Germany would retain its prewar boundaries. Stalin, Churchill and Roosevelt did not forgive and rejected the peace offer. As a result, the war continued in Europe with hundreds of thousands of people killed and millions suffered terribly. Paul speaking, "To whom you forgive, I forgive also—in the authority given me by Jesus, lest Satan should get an advantage of us, for we are not ignorant of his devices." Paraphrased (2 Corinthians 2:10-11)

As I write this book, I am observing the terrifying results of unforgiveness in the U.S. Forces of darkness that represent total corruption of society are attempting to impose themselves by force, or any other evil means, on all aspects of our life.

The guiding principles of our founding fathers are scoffed at: morality, honesty, integrity and righteousness, developed over hundreds of years of civilization are discarded. Free enterprise, property ownership and Christianity are declared obsolete. Responsibility is replaced by, "If it feels good, do it." Without the light of moral absolutes, the people, including children, flounder in the darkness where they are taught to hate (not love or forgive).

CHRISTIANS ADDRESSED IN THE BOOK OF REVELATION:

Speaking of End Times to Christians in the Book of Revelation; John quotes the Holy Spirit's comments to each of the seven churches in Asia. The comments are very specific and I recommend everyone should read them. They should activate the holiness, righteousness and fear of God in every Christian. Here are quotes of John's comments to three of the seven Christian churches:

EPHESUS, REVELATION 2:1-7 (KJV)

To the angel of the church of Ephesus write: He who holds the seven stars in His right hand, who walks in the midst of the seven golden candlesticks, says these things: I know your works, your labor and your patience, and that you cannot bear those who are evil. And you have tested those who say they are apostles, but are not, and have found them to be liars. You have endured, and have been patient, and for My name's sake have labored and have not grown weary. But I have something against you, that you have abandoned the love you had at first. Remember therefore from where you have fallen. Repent, and do the works you did at first, or else I will come to you quickly and remove your candlestick from its place, unless you repent. But this you have: You hate the works of the Nicolaitans, which I also hate. He who has an ear, let him hear what the Spirit says to the churches. To him who overcomes, I will give permission to eat of the tree of life, which is in the midst of the Paradise of God.

SARDIS, REVELATION 3:1-6 (KJV)

To the angel of the church in Sardis write:

He who has the seven Spirits of God and the seven stars says these things: I know your works, that you have a reputation of being alive, but you are dead. Be watchful, and strengthen the things which remain but are ready to die, for I have not found your works perfected before God. Remember therefore how you have received and heard; hold fast and repent. Therefore, if you will not watch, I will come upon you as a thief, and you will not know what hour I will come upon you.

"You have a few names even in Sardis who have not soiled their garments. They shall walk with Me in white, for they are worthy. He who overcomes shall be clothed in white garments. I will not blot his name out of the Book of Life, but I will confess his name before My Father and before His angels. He who has an ear, let him hear what the Spirit says to the churches."

LAODICEA, REVELATION 3:14-22

To the angel of the church of the Laodiceans write:

The Amen, the Faithful and True Witness, the Beginning of the creation of God, says these things: I know your works, that you are neither cold nor hot. I wish you were cold or hot. So then, because you are lukewarm, and neither cold nor hot, I will spit you out of My mouth. For you say, I am rich, and have stored up goods, and have need of nothing, yet do not realize that you are wretched, miserable, poor, blind, and naked. I counsel you to buy from Me gold refined by fire, that you may be rich, and white garments, that you may be dressed, that the shame of your nakedness may not appear, and anoint your eyes with eye salve, that you may see. Those whom I love, I rebuke and discipline. Therefore be zealous and repent. Listen! I stand at the door and knock. If anyone hears My voice and opens the door, I will come in and dine with him, and he with Me. To him who overcomes will I grant to sit with Me on My throne, as I also overcame and sat down with My Father on His throne. He who has an ear, let him hear what the Spirit says to the churches.

WHAT IS FORGIVENESS?

Forgiveness does not mean you condone what they did. They still have to face the consequences of their actions with God and perhaps the law of the land. Forgiveness is not forgetting. People who want to forget all that was done to them will find they cannot do it. Don't put off forgiving those who have hurt you, hoping the pain will one day go away. Once you choose to forgive someone, then Christ can come and begin to heal you of your hurts. But the healing cannot begin until you first forgive.

Forgiveness is a choice, a decision of your will. Since God requires you to forgive, it is something you can do. Sometimes it is very hard to forgive someone because we naturally want revenge for the things we have suffered. Forgiveness seems to go against our sense of what is right and fair. So we hold on to our anger, punishing people over and over again in our minds for the pain they've caused us. But we are told by God never to take our own revenge (see Romans 12:19). Let God deal with the person. Let him or her off your hook because as long as you refuse to forgive someone, you are still hooked to them. You are still chained to your past, bound up in your bitterness.

By forgiving, you let the other person off your hook, but they are not off God's hook. You must trust that God will deal with the person justly and fairly, something you simply cannot do. You might say, "But you don't know how much the person hurt me!" You're right. We don't, but Jesus does; and he tells you to forgive. Until you let go of your anger and hatred, the person is still hurting you. You can't turn back and change the past but you can be free from it. You can stop the pain, but there is only one way to do it - forgive.

You forgive others for your sake so you can be free. Forgiveness is mainly a matter of obedience to God. God wants you to be free, there is no other way.

Forgiveness is agreeing to live with the consequences of another person's sin, but you are going to live with those consequences anyway whether you like it or not. The only choice you have is whether you will do so in the bondage of bitterness or in the freedom of forgiveness. But no one truly forgives without accepting and suffering the pain of another person's sin. That can seem unfair and you may wonder where the justice is in it, but justice is found at the Cross, which makes forgiveness legally and morally right. Jesus took the eternal consequences of sin upon Himself. "God made Him who knew no sin to be sin on our behalf, that we might become the righteousness of God in Him" (2 Corinthians 5:21 NIV). We, however, often suffer the temporary consequences of the people's sins. That is simply a harsh reality of life all of us have to face.

Do not wait for the other person to ask for your forgiveness before forgiving him or her. They may never do so. Remember, Jesus did not wait for those who were crucifying Him to apologize before He forgave them. Even while they mocked and jeered at him, He prayed, "Father, forgive them, for they know not what they do." (Luke 23;34, KJV)

How do you forgive them from your heart? You allow God to bring to the surface the painful emotions you feel toward those who have hurt you. If your forgiveness doesn't touch the emotional core of your life, it will be incomplete. Too often, we're afraid of the pain so we bury our emotions deep down inside us. Let God bring them to the surface so He can begin to heal those damaged emotions.

Forgiveness is choosing not to hold someone's sin against him or her anymore. It is common for bitter people to bring up past issues with those who have hurt them. They want them to feel bad. But we must let go of the past and choose to reject any thought of revenge. This doesn't mean you must continue to put up with the future sins of others. God does not tolerate sin and neither should you. Don't allow yourself to be continually abused by others. Take a stand against sin while continuing to exercise grace and forgiveness toward those who hurt you. You may need help in setting wise limits and boundaries to protect yourself from future abuse.

Don't wait to forgive until you "feel like" forgiving. You will never get there. Make the hard choice to forgive even if you don't feel like it. Once you choose to forgive, satan will have lost his power over you in that area and God's healing touch will be free to move. Freedom is what you will gain right now, not necessarily an immediate change in feelings.

FORGIVENESS EXAMPLES:

One of my early cases was a 9 year old boy who came up for prayer after the service was over (in the service many were healed and 11 received the Holy Spirit.) The boy had a boil on the left side of his neck. I placed my hand over it and commanded it to be gone in Jesus name. Nothing happened. I said "Lord, what is going on?" The reply, "He has anger in his heart." I told the boy he had to repent for the healing to manifest. He said, "Yo no quiero." (I don't want to) - but he did. I placed my hand again over the boil and commanded it to go in Jesus name - it disappeared.

The need to get rid of unforgiveness before healing will manifest has been demonstrated thousands of times in the Lord's work through Eternal Love Ministries. I have found it best to lead everyone in a prayer to break unforgiveness before ministering healing.

In a church service in Texas, as each person came forward, they told me their need, (problem, sickness, etc.) The Holy Spirit then told me what caused the problem. In every case the person had caused their own problem by unforgiveness.

Over the years, I observed several cases where an individual had refused to forgive themselves. A Christian lady in Southern Mexico came for prayer about every six months over several years for a migraine headache. The headache would always leave; however over time it returned. I ministered in her son's church and talked to him as to why his mother suffered the headaches. He indicated she blamed herself for a family split fourteen years before. After ministry, she forgave herself and has continued to do so since with no more migraines.

A recent case in Temple, Texas was a lady who came for prayer who was obviously dying. The Holy Spirit said she is "blaming herself" (apparently in reference to some aspect of her family relationship). She agreed, repented of her sin and forgave herself. Over a few months we watched her return to her normal healthy self.

A Temple, Texas woman's second husband became a cocaine addict. Investigation revealed that the wife was extremely bitter at her first husband and she had never forgiven him. Her unforgiving attitude impacted the second husband who received the blunt of her continued animosity and he turned to drugs as an escape. With forgiveness prevailing, she and her second husband now live in peace.

In Rio Grande, Mexico a lady came for prayer who was bitter at her husband. She suffered back pain and had one leg shorter than the other. After a prayer of forgiveness the pain ceased and when told to do so, her leg grew out equal to the other. Two weeks later I saw her and her husband as they were acting like two love birds.

In Saltillo, Mexico a pastor and the entire congregation except his wife received the Baptism of the Holy Spirit. We spent several hours with her but she did not receive. Finally, I turned aside and asked the Holy Spirit what was going on. He said, "She hates her husband." I mentioned this to her and she looked at her husband and said, "I have hated you for fifteen years." Later that day she repented and did receive the Holy Spirit. She indicated that during the years of hatred, God seemed so far away she would never be able to reach Him.

The cases of unforgiveness are too numerous to be included here. Most people have a happy ending; however, sometimes the Lord would say, "Don't pray for him or her." I knew or suspected they had repeatedly rejected God and had been in unforgiveness, bitterness, hatred or other depravity for many years.

When someone is holding onto unforgiveness, they are telling God that He is not needed in their situation. They have placed themselves in God's shoes by judging someone else for what they have done. They say, "I will execute judgement here" and forget that vengeance belongs to God.

THE LORD'S COMMENTS ON UNFORGIVENESS:

In looking over prior notes of when the Holy Spirit instructed me, I found several comments pertaining to unforgiveness. His comments are in quotation marks.

"Ignore critics for they will surely come."

If you are doing damage to satan, he will have his critics, even among Christians.

"Bless those who criticize you."

Luke 6: 28 Bless them that curse you, and pray for them which despitefully use you.

Matthew 5:44 Love your enemies, bless them that curse you, do good to them that hate you and pray for them which despitefully use you and persecute you.

Romans 12:14 Bless them that persecute you, bless and not curse.

1 Corinthians 4:12 And labor, working with your hands: being reviled, we bless, being persecuted, we suffer it.

"Obedience is better than witchcraft which you practice on occasion when you speak evil of someone."

1 Samuel 15:23 "For rebellion is as the sin of witchcraft, and stubbornness is as iniquity and idolatry."

"Sit in judgment only when I say so!"

Luke 6:37 Jesus states. Judge not, and you shall not be judged: condemn not, and you shall not be condemned: forgive and you shall be forgiven.

John 5:30 Jesus speaking: I can of myself do nothing; as I hear, I judge: and my judgment is just because I seek the will of my Father who sent me."

Romans 12:19 Vengeance belongs to the Lord.

Matthew 7:1 Judge not, that ye be not judged.

Romans 14:10 Why do you judge your brother?

1 Corinthians 11:31 Judge self.

1 Corinthians 4:4 He that judgeth me is the Lord.

"Bless those who needle you. They are only trying to be friendly."

WE ARE COMMANDED IN SCRIPTURE TO FORGIVE:

Matthew 6:12, 14,15. Covered earlier.

Matthew 18:21-22 (KJV) "Then came Peter to him, and said, Lord, how oft shall my brother sin against me, and I forgive him? till seven times? Jesus saith unto him, I say not unto thee, Until seven times: but, Until seventy times seven."

Matthew 18:32-35. Jesus telling of the wicked servant who was turned over to the tormenters. Verse 35: "So likewise shall my heavenly Father do also unto you, if you from your hearts forgive not everyone their trespass."

Mark 11:25-26. "And when you stand praying, forgive, if you have aught against any: that your Father also, which is in heaven may forgive you your trespasses. But if you do not forgive, neither will your Father which is in heaven forgive your trespasses."

Ephesians 4:22-23. Paul in verse 32 states "be kind to one another, tenderhearted, forgiving one another, even as God for Christ's sake has forgiven you."

WE ARE TO FORGIVE AS JESUS FORGAVE:

I John 1:9. "If we confess our sins, He is faithful and just to forgive us our sins, and to cleanse us of all unrighteousness."

Colossians 3:13. "forbearing one another and forgiving one another, if any man have a quarrel against any; even as Christ forgave you, so also do ye."

Colossians 1:12-14. "Giving thanks unto the Father, which hath made us meet to be partakers of the inheritance of the saints in light. Who has delivered us from the power of darkness and hath translated us into the kingdom of his dear Son. In whom we have redemption through his blood, even the forgiveness of sins."

JESUS AND STEPHEN FORGAVE EVEN WHILE BEING KILLED:

Luke 23:32-34. Two criminals were led out to be executed with Jesus at a place called the skull. There all three were crucified - Jesus on the center cross. Jesus said, "Father forgive these people for they don't know what they are doing."

Acts 7:59-60. And as murderous stones came hurling at him, Stephen prayed, "Lord Jesus receive my spirit," and he fell to his knees shouting "Lord don't charge them with this sin," and with that he died.

UNFORGIVNESS CAN BE A CHALLENGE:

Staying free from unforgiveness has been the most difficult of all lessons learned on the mission field. Like idolatry, it also is a cursed sin. A sin that God has specifically stated must be repented of even if it is committed seventy times seven. Forgiveness is an absolutely necessary ingredient before your sins can be forgiven by our Heavenly Father. It is a great burden on anyone until they forgive everyone who has offended them. It demands action on your part to become free of sin's shackles which separate you from God's blessings and eternal life.

See also the comments on unforgiveness in the book, "A Challenge to Live."

CHAPTER 8

Patience

A hard lesson learned on the mission field was that a missionary must exercise extreme patience at all times. In my fifty years before I went on the mission field I had not experienced the need for patience to the degree I did on the mission field. I had been accustomed to a strict environment; including 26 years in the army, where everything was done as soon as possible and where delay was wasted time that accumulated into an intolerable backlog.

On the mission field everything had to be done as part of a vast number of actions, by many people, angels and the Holy Spirit, all orchestrated at the exact times for the desired results. Concurrently, the Lord was teaching each person to have faith, to trust in Him, to be patient, and do whatever else each person needed to become the man or woman God desired. God's time schedule, for something to be accomplished, was obviously subject to change to accommodate the complexity of the individual situations involved. This was evident to me every time we were to change facilities and or city, or country locations. It could be days, weeks, months or years before completion.

There were always good reasons for the delays such as becoming familiar with the roads, streets, public facilities, churches, etc.; understanding how to survive in the local culture and keeping up with the constantly changing political climate. In some cultures, time appears to be irrelevant. Much time is wasted because people arrive hours late for a function, service, etc. If your support (healing, deliverance, movies, etc.), is important to people, they will change their culture one service at a time to receive it.

(James 1:4 But let patience have her perfect work, that you may be perfect and entire wanting nothing. KJV)

A CHINA PATIENCE EXPERIENCE (HOW EASILY WE CAN BECOME IMPATIENT):

In the book "A Challenge to Live, I didn't say much about China; however, I believe I am to include it in "Lessons Learned on the Mission Field." The chapter on Patience seems like an appropriate place as it required extreme patience on my part. I am including it here under the possibility that the Lord will send me back to fulfill prophesies which I received about some future events in China.

POST OFFICE 51:

In a dream, I was working in a Post Office and over a loud speaker I was told that I had been transferred to Post Office 51. On another occasion, I had been told China, but didn't know where; China proper, Hong Kong, Taiwan or Macao. An internet search revealed a post office 51 in Hong Kong and another in the capital of Mongolia (not a part of China). Helen and I went to Hong Kong, where we found out that the post offices there were not numbered, they only had names. I thought maybe the British had a number 51 post office when Hong Kong was under their control. The British Consulate referred me to the Post Office headquarters in London, England. I telephoned them and they asked me to call back in fifteen minutes, which I did. I was greeted politely with the words, "Colonel Luepnitz." My mind thought, they know all about me. When in Hong Kong they only had one Post Office, it was number one and it was located on Hong Kong Island. They had a Post Office 51 in

Canada. As I made contacts, several people were checking on Post Offices in Taiwan, Macao and China main land. I didn't receive any positive answers; however, I had another dream which gave an outline of the China coast and a single dot inland.

OUR HONG KONG STAY:

During our three month stay in Hong Kong while attempting to locate Post Office 51, I ministered in two different denominational church groups and, a few independent churches. In one church, a young lady asked me to go with her to a hospital where the doctor had stated her mother was dying. The mother received her healing and the next morning went home. When the young lady told me of the mother's discharge from the hospital, she offered to go with me to Communist China to locate Post Office 51. We crossed the border the next morning and went to the closest Post Office. They couldn't tell us anything except that a large office of the Postal Service was in a nearby city. We went there and, starting on the first floor, we worked our way up the chain of command to the lady in charge on the ninth floor. She couldn't tell us anything either, but took me to another office where a man sat behind a huge desk. I felt sure he was the "Political Officer," from the Communist Party. His questions of me were the same as everyone else. Why did I want to know where Post Office 51 was? I told him of my dream and that I too wanted to find out why. He swiveled in his chair, took a brochure off a stand, opened it, pointed to a dot in the middle of Guangzhou and said. "There is Post Office 51."

For six weeks of our stay in Hong Kong, Helen and I lived in a facility occupied by only Christians from many different countries. I noted that each one was suffering from an unnatural affliction, (different than the people in Mexico experienced), and I sought the Lord for an answer. I had a vision of the insides of a Buddhist

Temple. In front, facing away from the altar, were girls pointing and speaking. When I informed the occupants of the vision, a man spoke up and said, "Yes, if you look out the windows at one a.m., you will see this building surrounded by Buddhist who are burning incense, pointing at this building and speaking curses over us, just as Carl saw in his vision. I gave them copies of scripture from the Bible which basically said, "No Word Spoken Against me shall Prosper" and told them to be speaking these scriptures and the blood of Jesus over themselves every day. The next morning at 4 A.M., I started to slip out of the top bunk to use the restroom and noted Helen was on the floor next to the lower bunk. Her right arm had slipped out of the shoulder joint and she was in pain. As I further exited my bunk, it felt like I was stabbed in the back. I hadn't prayed over Helen or myself like I told others to do and obviously we were under demonic attack. Helen's arm in a sling was a good distraction with customs officials.

We heard several reports of brutal treatment of Christians by communist officials to include:

- In some areas senior male pastors no longer existed because of continual disabling persecution and prison.
- I was told that a group in the U.S. published a photo of 20 to 30 Chinese people they were to see on a trip to China. On arrival they found all of them had been killed.

Another story was of two girls that were tortured to force them to say the pastor raped them. They refused to lie and were left nearly dead from the beatings. As a precaution I have not maintained communication with anyone in China.

Carl and Helen in Hong Kong

The day our three month visa expired, Helen and I left Hong Kong by airplane for the U.S.

After a brief U.S. stay for medical and other business, we obtained new visas for mainland China, flew into Hong Kong and prepared for the train trip to Guangzhou. Missionary friends went with us, but they had to return to Hong Kong after we registered in a Guangzhou hotel (where no one spoke English and there were no English signs or menus). I had to flap my arms and say cock-a-doodle-doo to indicate we wanted chicken eggs at breakfast.

I had a vision that showed a route into an area of the city, a home in the middle of the street, and the name of a woman. That Sunday, a man took us to an expatriate church, (for people with foreign passports), in the center of Guangzhou. After church, we sat down to eat in a restaurant with a couple from the church. I mentioned my dream to them and the husband exclaimed, "You just described the route to our apartment and the name is that of my wife." Each day we went with the wife to look at apartments in the area. It was a very frustrating time as the only usable apartments were $2,000 to $12,000 dollars a month. Cheaper apartments that we saw were not usable and would need a major expenditure to put them in serviceable condition. The wood floors had all been flooded with water and were totally warped and unusable. There were no homes in that area of the city like I saw in the vision. After some weeks, Helen and I were both becoming very frustrated and this is when I hollered "Lord, where are we supposed to live?" The answer was, "My son, don't you trust me?"

Instantly, many thoughts went through my mind as I pondered His response.

> I just came half way around the world to do the work the Lord has for me.

> God is supposed to know me better than I know myself.

> Is there something wrong in me that I am not aware of?

> Maybe my patience is being tested.

> Without a place to live, how long will it be before Helen states, "I am leaving."

> What can I say?

Then I immediately repented of these thoughts.

I remembered the several times, when I was in the Army that people prophesied I would fail God. These people left a lingering element of fear which I rebuked each time the thought came. In 1984, while living in Saltillo, Mexico, the Lord stated I would not fail Him as He ordained my success.

I didn't know what to say and I didn't say anything. As I was writing this book, the Lord said, "Every path I took, He had put me on it."

(Luke 21:19 In your patience possess ye your souls. KJV)

After some more days, a friend we knew from Hong Kong came and took us to an apartment about forty-five minutes further south in Guangzhou. A week or so later the wife who had been showing us apartments said she had their former apartment for sale. She no longer had the keys, but we were able to see the outside of the building. I sensed in my spirit that it was where the Lord had intended for us to live. It didn't look anything like what I saw in the vision, which apparently was symbolic. She offered the apartment a week late as we now had a rental commitment further south in Guangzhou, where we lived the rest of our time in China.

A NEAR DEATH AFFLICTION:

What I didn't know, at the time we were looking for the place we were to live, was that I had a massive infection of the skull which was affecting my ability to calculate anything. The last time I was in the United States I had mentioned the strange brain and skull feeling to my V.A. primary care doctor; however, he apparently had no influence over the Orthopedic Department and nothing was done.

I also talked to a doctor in China about the strange feeling in my skull. He indicated I needed to see a specialist in the United States as the problem could be very serious. At this time air pollution in China was very bad, and, when I returned to the U.S. I was suffering from chronic sinusitis and a terrible bronchial infection. I went to Kings Daughter's Hospital in Temple, Texas. The doctor was shocked that I could hardly remember anything such as a telephone number, street address, etc. He consulted with two other doctors and called my wife, Helen, to come drive the car. Some time later,

I developed a very painful tooth ache and went to see my dentist. He took one x-ray and said you need to see a higher level dentist immediately. He sent me to see Dr. Heggen. He took one x-ray and came to me with four pills in his hand. He said, "Take these; we do surgery in an hour". This is when I found out that I had a massive skull infection. A second surgery was performed a week later and I was put on three months of heavy antibiotics. Two and a half months later the strange feeling was leaving. This infection started from teeth roots split ten years or more before in a southern Mexican village when the pit of a plum I was eating, slipped in between the teeth causing the fracture.

ANOTHER NEAR DEATH AFFLICTION:

In southern Mexico, I spent twelve days trying to pass a kidney stone which was too large to pass into the bladder. I ended up in Austin, Texas where the stone was removed by being broken up with pincers inserted through the urethra and the bladder. In so doing, the urethra was damaged; ultimately causing restricted urine flow. Over several years the problem grew worse; resulting in my return from China with a massive bladder infection, causing grand mall seizures and the need for emergency surgery. The poison from the infection had been adversely affecting all of my body functions over several years to include loss of short-term memory, discernment and constructive thought. Amongst these problems, I was taking Mandarin language classes with little success. I would study a lesson in the evening thinking I have it covered. The next morning, I didn't remember it. I believe the Lord had me write the two books, in part, to help me get my memory back. I am still working on the memory.

Since the bladder infection, I had surgery to remove the middle lobe of my right lung which had a fast growing cancer. In the surgery a right rib was broken and removed. It left a part of my spine damaged severely affecting my ability to keep my shoulders straight. I am also currently on oxygen each night for COPD. I believe God will remove all physical and memory problems from my body.

"And so after he had patiently endured, he obtained the promise." (Hebrews 6:15 KJV)

CHINA'S GOVERNMENT

I love the wonderful, hardworking Chinese people, but they have a major problem. As with most socialist states or communist societies, they are a dictatorship. There the rulers control almost everything and the people who do not obey, suffer severe punishment, death or both. I cite a true case involving China's one child policy.

A young girl asked me to pray for her parents, which I did. A week later she asked again. I asked for details of the need: Her mother and father decided to have a second child. When the second child was born, they were fired from their jobs, all utilities were cut off, and greedy officials seized all of their furniture (cook stove, heater, refrigerator, table, couch, all chairs and the bed.) Even the clothes they didn't have on were taken. Neighbors didn't dare assist them for fear of the same treatment. All four family members lost all government benefits for education, medical support and any other function.

These were like the same horrible things that the communist Stalin did in the Soviet Union and that the socialist Hitler did in Germany. To my amazement, I hear of many people in the U.S., some calling themselves progressives, who are pushing violently for the same type government and fostering its teaching in our schools.

TRANSPORTATION:

In China, everyone forfeits their right to drive at age 65. For Helen or I to have a vehicle in China I needed to establish a business, have the business purchase a vehicle and hire a full time driver (someone under 65 years of age.)

Of course, after seeing the roads, traffic and traffic accidents, we didn't want a vehicle or a driver's license. We lived 45 minutes driving time from the center of the city and relied on buses (all without toilets), taxis, friends, or our legs for transport. We had to get off the buses at stops other than those we wanted in order to find places that had an available toilet. This was especially bad for me during the last years in China when I had a terrible bladder infection.

MEETINGS:

In China, to have a meeting with six or more people, including Helen and myself, I needed a government permit and would probably have a government official present at the meeting. I estimate that this legally precluded 90% of desired meetings and 95% of the people who would attend. The places in the open where students wanted to meet without permits, left me standing a foot taller than the students who numbered about 20 on each occasion. Adults would see us and always come over to find out what we were doing.

I had to discontinue those outdoor meetings as the parents would not allow the meetings in their homes and these students could not find a sheltered place to go.

I had an English language copy of the Communist Party Directive that addressed teenagers. It was a felony to teach them about Jesus if they were 18 and under. Of course when they enforced it, the age was irrelevant as it also stated the books of Romans and Revelation would not be taught to anyone.

Invitations to speak at business meetings and colleges were frequent, especially businesses that automatically had everyone assembled once a week. Specialty schools such as bankers and other elites, left doors partially open to us. We were also in charge of an English Corner in a large fine restaurant. Everyone who spoke English and wanted to practice it, etc. could talk with us. It was an excellent position from which we met people from all aspects of Chinese life, including high level communists, business people of all types, professionals, students, etc. I would be patient while they talked and asked questions knowing that soon they would ask what I thought about China. I would state China has the capacity to be the greatest country in the world, but there are variables that can change that. They would ask what they were and I would tell how many empires have come and gone, destroyed by corruption and immorality; but China does not support Christianity, which tries to fight corruption and immorality.

This resulted in my words returning to me from a top meeting of the Chinese Communist Party in Beijing. In fact, at that time, the Communists worked hand in glove with the Buddhist to harass and speak curses over Christians. A war continues every day in Hong Kong and against missionaries scattered throughout China's provinces. My three pages of scripture on, "No word spoken against me shall prosper" was greatly appreciated by missionaries. I have noted in many parts of the world that Muslims and Hindus also corporately speak curses on Christians.

WILL ALL PEOPLE HAVE THE OPPORTUNITY TO RECEIVE JESUS AS THER SAVIOR BEFORE JUDGEMENT

This perplexing question is frequently asked of missionaries who may answer yes or no without a scripture base for their answer.

- Jesus suffered and died for our sins, (our salvation).

"For God so loved the world that he gave his one and only Son, that whoever believes in him shall not perish but have eternal life." (John 3:16 NIV)

"Salvation is found in no one else, for there is no other name under heaven given to mankind by which we must be saved." (Acts 4:12)

- Everyone has a desire to know God.
  In the early 1980's, while at a village site, the Lord spoke these words to me, "I have put a desire in every human to know me."

I have observed this desire in operation many times. A scientific publication, "Mapping the mind" by Rita Carter, indicates that there is a spot in the human brain that when touched during mapping caused each person studied to reply with a God oriented response.

- Several scriptures reference a God given ability to know Him.
  ... "to every one of you: Do not think of yourself more highly than you ought, but rather think of yourself with sober judgment, in accordance with the faith God has distributed to each of you." (Romans 12:3 NIV)

... "The righteous will live by faith." (Romans 1:17 NIV)

"since what may be known about God is plain to them, because God has made it plain to them." (Romans 1:19 NIV)

"For since the creation of the world God's invisible qualities - his eternal power and divine nature - have been clearly seen, being understood from what has been made, so that people are without excuse." (Romans 1:20)

- God reveals himself to everyone through what their five senses tell them. (See, hear, touch, smell and taste)
- Our conscience will convict us of sin.
- The Tremendous complexity of God's creation speaks to us.
- The Holy Spirit will pray for us and guide us. (Romans 8:26, 27, 34)

    ... "the Spirit helps us in our weakness. We do not know what we ought to pray for, but the Spirit himself intercedes for us through wordless groans." (Romans 8:26 NIV)

    ... "he who searches our hearts knows the mind of the Spirit, because the Spirit intercedes for God's people in accordance with the will of God." (Romans 8:27 NIV)

    "Christ Jesus ..... is also interceding for us." (Romans 8:34 NIV)

- For three and a half years the angels of God warn men not to believe in the antichrist or take his mark.

    "Then I saw another angel flying in midair, and he had the eternal gospel to proclaim to those who live on the earth—to every nation, tribe, language and people." (Revelations 14:6 NIV)

    ... "for the earth will be filled with the knowledge of the LORD as the waters cover the sea." (Isaiah 11:9 NIV)

    "He said in a loud voice, "Fear God and give him glory, ... Worship him who made the heavens, the earth, the sea and the springs of water."" (Revelations 14:7 NIV)

    "A third angel followed them and said in a loud voice: "If anyone worships the beast and its image and receives its mark on their forehead or on their hand, they, too, will drink the wine of God's fury ..... They will be tormented with burning sulfur in the presence of the holy angels and of the Lamb." (Revelations 14:9-10 NIV)

"Then I heard another voice from heaven say: "'Come out of her, my people,' so that you will not share in her sins, so that you will not receive any of her plagues; for her sins are piled up to heaven, and God has remembered her crimes." (Revelations 18:4-5 NIV)

"I tell you, no! But unless you repent, you too will all perish." (Luke 13:5 NIV)

"Not everyone who says to me, 'Lord, Lord,' will enter the kingdom of heaven, but only the one who does the will of my Father who is in heaven. Many will say to me on that day, 'Lord, Lord, did we not prophesy in your name and in your name drive out demons and in your name perform many miracles?' Then I will tell them plainly, 'I never knew you. Away from me, you evildoers!" (Matthew 7:21-23 NIV)

"As surely as I live,'says the Lord,'every knee will bow before me; every tongue will acknowledge God.'" So then, each of us will give an account of ourselves to God. (Romans 14:11-12 NIV)

"that at the name of Jesus every knee should bow, in heaven and on earth and under the earth, and every tongue acknowledge that Jesus Christ is Lord, to the glory of God the Father. (Philippians 2:10-11 NIV)

The First Resurrection:

> I saw thrones on which were seated those who had been given authority to judge. And I saw the souls of those who had been beheaded because of their testimony about Jesus and because of the word of God. They had not worshiped the beast or its image and had not received its mark on their foreheads or their hands. They came to life and reigned with Christ a thousand years. (The rest of the dead did not come to life until the thousand years were ended.) This is the first resurrection. Blessed and holy are those who share in the first resurrection. The second death has no power over them, but they will be priests of God and of Christ and will reign with him for a thousand years. (Revelations 20:4-6 NIV)

Satan's Doom:

> "When the thousand years are over, Satan will be released from his prison and will go out to deceive the nations in the four corners of the earth—Gog and Magog—and to gather them for battle. In number they are like the sand on the seashore. They marched across the breadth of the earth and surrounded the camp of God's people, the city he loves. But fire came down from heaven and devoured them. And the devil, who deceived them, was thrown into the lake of burning sulfur, where the beast and the false prophet had been thrown. They will be tormented day and night for ever and ever." (Revelations 20: 7-10 NIV)

The Second Resurrection. The Dead are Judged

> "Then I saw a great white throne and him who was seated on it. The earth and the heavens fled from his presence, and there was no place for them. And I saw the dead, great

and small, standing before the throne, and books were opened. Another book was opened, which is the book of life. The dead were judged according to what they had done as recorded in the books. The sea gave up the dead that were in it, and death and Hades gave up the dead that were in them, and each person was judged according to what they had done. Then death and Hades were thrown into the lake of fire. The lake of fire is the second death. Anyone whose name was not found written in the book of life was thrown into the lake of fire." (Revelations 20:11-15 NIV)

The New Jerusalem:

"Then I saw "a new heaven and a new earth, "for the first heaven and the first earth had passed away, and there was no longer any sea. I saw the Holy City, the new Jerusalem, coming down out of heaven from God, prepared as a bride beautifully dressed for her husband. And I heard a loud voice from the throne saying, "Look! God's dwelling place is now among the people, and he will dwell with them. They will be his people, and God himself will be with them and be their God. 'He will wipe every tear from their eyes. There will be no more death' or mourning or crying or pain, for the old order of things has passed away." He who was seated on the throne said, "I am making everything new! "Then he said, "Write this down, for these words are trustworthy and true." He said to me: "It is done. I am the Alpha and the Omega, the Beginning and the End. To the thirsty I will give water without cost from the spring of the water of life. Those who are victorious will inherit all this, and I will be their God and they will be my children. But the cowardly, the unbelieving, the vile, the murderers, the sexually immoral, those who practice magic arts, the idolaters and all liars—they will be consigned to the fiery lake of burning sulfur. This is the second death." (Revelations 21:1-8)

My answer based on these scriptures would be a clear yes. God is not confined to our methods and understanding and will allow every person the opportunity to accept or reject Jesus Christ before the judgement.

Appendix A

Prayer Renouncing Witchcraft, Occult, Etc. (Breaking Curses)

Lord, I repent and ask your forgiveness if I now or have ever dominated or controlled anyone contrary to the perfect will of God.

In the Name of Jesus Christ, I now renounce, break and loose myself from domination and subjection of my mother, father, grandparents and any other human beings, living or dead, that have ever in the past or are now dominating or controlling me in any way contrary to the perfect will of God.

In the Name of Jesus, I now renounce, break and loose myself and all my children from all psychic heredity, demonic bondage, occult bondage, physic bondage, bonds of physical or mental illness and disease, and all curses upon me and my family lineage as a result of sins, transgressions, iniquities, occult or physic involvements of myself, my parents, my ancestors, my spouse, parents of my spouse, their ancestors, and all ex-spouses, their parents and their ancestors. Thank you, Lord for setting me free.

In the Name of Jesus, I rebuke, break and loose myself and all my children from all the evil curses, charms, vexes, hexes, spells, jinxes, occult powers, physic powers, witchcraft, sorcery and hypnotic influence that have been put on me or my family lineage by any person, occult source or psychic source. I command all connected and related spirits to leave me now in Jesus Name.

I come to you, Lord, as my deliverer. You know all my problems, everything that binds, defiles and harasses me. I now refuse to accept anything from satan. I now loose myself from every dark spirit, from satanic bondage, from every evil influence, from every spirit in me that is not the Spirit of God. I command all such spirits to leave me now in Jesus Name. I confess that my body is the temple of the Holy Ghost: redeemed, sanctified, cleansed, justified by the blood of Jesus Christ. Therefore, satan has no place in me and no power over me. In the name of Jesus Christ, I now break all curses set against me according to Galatians 3:13, "Christ hath redeemed me from the curse of the law, being made a curse for me," and in Colossians 2:13-15, "Jesus quickened us together with him, having forgiven me all trespasses: blotting out the ordinances written against me which were contrary to me and took them out of the way, nailing them to his cross, triumphing over them in it."

Thank you, Lord for setting me free. In Jesus Name, Amen

Deuteronomy 7:25-26, 18:9-14, 24:1. 28:1, 2, 15, I Corinthians 6:9-11, 10:20-21, Exodus 34:7, Numbers 14:18, 33, Colossians 3:13-14, Lamentations 5:7, Jeremiah 31:29-34,32:18-19, Ezekiel 18:all, Ephesians 5:11, Galatians 3:13-14, 5:19-21, I Peter 2:24

Appendix B

Prayer to Close Door of Torment Because of Unforgiveness

ALMIGHTY FATHER, IN JESUS NAME, BY THE POWER OF YOUR HOLY SPIRIT AND BY AN ACT OF MY FREE WILL, I CONFESS TO YOU ALL UNFORGIVENESS IN MY LIFE, CONSCIOUS AND SUBCONSCIOUS, I ACKNOWLEDGE THAT IT IS SIN AND I ASK YOUR FORGIVENESS. I KNOW THAT IF I CONFESS MY SIN, YOU ARE FAITHFUL AND JUST TO FORGIVE ME AND CLEANSE ME OF ALL UNRIGHTEOUSNESS. I BELIEVE IN YOU WORD AND RECEIVE YOUR FORGIVENESS NOW. I THANK YOU FOR IT IN JESUS NAME.

I RELEASE ALL OF THOSE IN MY LIFE WHO HAVE WRONGED OR HURT ME AND I FORGIVE THEM ALL DEBTS REAL OR IMAGINED THAT THEY OWE ME. I SAY, "IT'S OK IF YOU NEVER PAY ME BACK." I RELEASE MYSELF AND FORGIVE MYSELF OF ALL SHORTCOMINGS AND WEAKNESSES AND FOR ALL I HAVE DONE TO HURT OR DISAPPOINT MYSELF AND OTHERS. AND FATHER, I FORGIVE YOU FOR ANY TIMES THAT I HAVE FELT THAT YOU LET ME DOWN. I KNOW AND DECLARE THAT YOU ARE GOOD, AND YOU ARE JUST IN ALL YOUR WAYS, I TRUST YOU WITH MY LIFE.

NOW, I WILL TO LET GO OF ALL BITTERNESS, RESENTMENT, ANGER, HATE, RAGE, WRATH, RETALIATION, REVENGE, ENVY, STRIFE AND ALL UNKINDNESS IN ANY FORM.

NOW, BECAUSE OF MY CONFESSION, BECAUSE I HAVE FORGIVEN, I AM FREE FROM TORMENT, IN JESUS NAME.

Matthew 6:12, 14, 15, 18:21-35; Mark 11:24-26; John 20:23; I John 1:9, 5:16; Philemon 2:13; Ephesians 4:32; Colossians 3:13

Appendix C

Healing Scriptures Work Sheet

1 PURPOSE – JESUS AND DEVIL

JOHN 10:10 THE THIEF COMES TO KILL, STEAL, DESTROY. JESUS COMES TO BRING LIFE

1 JOHN 3:8 JESUS IS HERE TO UNDO THE WORKS OF THE DEVIL

2 JESUS ALREADY BORE OUR SICKNESS

ISAIAH 53:4-5 PROPHESIED JESUS TOOK ALL SICKNESS

MATTHEW 8:16-17 DROVE OUT SPIRITS WITH A WORD - ISAIAH PROPHECY FULFILLED

I PETER 2:24 JESUS BORE OUR SINS ON THE CROSS, BY HIS WOUNDS YOU ARE HEALED

LUKE 10: 17-22 (19) SATAN IS DEFEATED - HE FELL, SERPENTS AND SCORPIANS UNDERFOOT

GALATIANS 3:13 JESUS TOOK OUR CURSES UPON HIMSELF ON THE CROSS

3 JESUS HEALED ALL SICKNESS

MATTHEW 4:23 JESUS WENT ABOUT HEALING ALL DISEASES

MATTHEW 9:35 JESUS HEALED EVERYONE

MATTHEW 12:15 MANY FOLLOWED JESUS AND HE HEALED THEM ALL

MARK 6:55-56 JESUS HEALS AS HE WALKS BY THE SICK, THEY TOUCHED HIM

LUKE 13: 11-13, 16 WOMAN HUNCHBACK HEALED

4 JESUS HEALED BY ANOINTING OF HOLY SPIRIT
ACTS 10:38 JESUS HEALED WITH POWER OF THE HOLY
SPIRIT
MARK 11: 13,14, 20 CURSE AT ROOTS (FIG TREE)
LUKE 4:40-41 JESUS LAID HANDS ON SICK AND HEALED
ALL—DEMONS FLED

5 JESUS IS THE SAME YESTERDAY, TODAY AND FOREVER
HEBREWS 13:8 JESUS IS THE SAME YESTERDAY, TODAY
AND FOREVER

**6 SAME HOLY SPIRIT IS IN THOSE BAPTIZED IN THE
HOLY SPIRIT AS WAS IN JESUS**
ROMANS 8:11 SAME HOLY SPIRIT IN JESUS IS IN YOU
JOHN 14:20 THE FATHER IS IN JESUS, AND JESUS IN US
I JOHN 4:4 GREATER IS HE IN YOU THAN HE THAT IS
IN THE WORLD

7 BELIEVERS HEAL BY POWER OF THE HOLY SPIRIT
MATTHEW 10:8 JESUS SAID HEAL THE SICK
MATTHEW 15:30-31 JESUS HEALED THE MULTITUDE OF
ALL SICKNESS
MARK 16:17-18 GREAT COMMISSION - BELIEVERS WILL
LAY HANDS ON THE SICK AND THEY WILL GET WELL
LUKE 10:1,9 JESUS SENT OUT TO HEAL
MATTHEW 16: 19 WHATEVER YOU BIND OR LOOSE ON
EARTH IS BOUND OR LOOSED IN HEAVEN
ACTS 3:6-8 PETER SPOKE TO CRIPPLE AT GATE AND HE
IS HEALED
ACTS 5:15 PETER'S SHADOW AS HE PASSED BY HEALED
THEM
ACTS 19:11-12 GOD USED PAUL'S HANDS TO DO MIRACLES
AND HEAL MANY

ROMANS 8:26-39 GOD IS FOR YOU, WHO CAN BE AGAINST YOU

8 JESUS SAID BELIEVERS WERE TO DO MORE THAN HE
JOHN 14:12 BELIEVE IN JESUS, THE WORKS THAT I DO SHALL BELIEVERS D0 ALSO, AND GREATER WORKS THAN THESE SHALL THEY DO; BECAUSE I GO TO THE FATHER
MATTHEW 10:1 JESUS CALLED THE DISCIPLES TO CAST OUT UNCLEAN SPIRITS AND HEAL ALL
ACTS 19:11-12 GOD USED PAUL'S HANDS TO DO MIRACLES AND HEAL MANY

9 FAITH IS IMPORTANT TO RECEIVE A HEALING
MATTHEW 8;5-13 CENTURION
MATTHEW 21:21-22 JESUS SAID, HAVE FAITH (AS TO KILL FIG TREE AND MOVE A MOUNTAIN) ASK AND RECEIVE
MARK 5:25-30,34 JESUS HEALS WOMAN WITH ISSUE OF BLOOD-FAITH
MARK 9:23 ALL THINGS ARE POSSIBLE TO THEM THAT BELIEVE
MATTHEW 17:20 IF YOU HAVE FAITH, YOU CAN MOVE MOUNTAINS
LUKE 17:6 IF FAITH AS BIG AS A MUSTARD SEED, CAN SAY TO A TREE, BE REMOVED
HEBREWS 10:23 JESUS IS FAITHFUL TO GIVE WHAT HE PROMISED
HEBREWS 11:11 GOD IS FAITHFUL TO HIS WORD (SARAH AND CHILD)

10 ASK AND RECEIVE

MARK 11:23-26 WITH FAITH SPEAK TO THE MOUNTAIN, DON'T DOUBT, BELIEVE, HE SHALL HAVE

MATTHEW 7:7-8 ASK AND YOU SHALL RECEIVE-EVERYONE WHO ASKS RECEIVES
JOHN 16:23-24 ASK ANYTHING IN JESUS NAME-YOU SHALL HAVE IT
ACTS 3:6-8 PETER SPOKE TO CRIPPLE AT GATE AND HE IS HEALED
JAMES 5:14-15 SICK, CALL ON ELDERS, ANOINT WITH OIL, PRAYER OF FAITH, LORD RESTORES
I JOHN 3:22 WE RECEIVE WHAT WE ASK BECAUSE WE OBEY HIM
I JOHN 5:14-15 ASK ANYTHING IN HIS WILL AND IT IS DONE
II TIMOTHY 1:7 GOD GAVE US A SPIRIT OF POWER, LOVE, WELL BALANCED MIND, DISCIPLINE AND SELF CONTROL

11 HOW TO KEEP YOUR HEALING

REVELATION 12:11 BLOOD OF JESUS AND WORD OF YOUR TESTIMONY
PROVERBS 4:20-24 WORDS OF GOD ARE LIFE HEALING HEALTH, GUARD SPEECH
PROVERBS 18:20-21 DEATH AND LIFE ARE IN THE TONGUE
PROVERBS 15:4 A WHOLESOME TONGUE IS A TREE OF LIFE
PROVERBS 16:24 PLEASANT WORDS ARE AS HONEY; SWEET TO THE SOUL
ISAIAH 55:11 MY WORD WILL NOT RETURN VOID, IT WILL ACCOMPLISH WHAT SENT FOR
JEREMIAH 1:12 I WILL HASTEN MY WORD TO PERFORM IT

12 GOD WANTS EVERYONE HEALED

EXODUS 15:26 I AM THE LORD WHO HEALETH THEE

EXODUS 23:25 GOD WILL TAKE SICKNESS FROM YOUR MIDST

DEUTERONOMY 7:13-15 DO GOD'S WILL AND HE WILL TAKE AWAY SICKNESSES

DEUTERONOMY 28: 1-14 OBEY GOD AND SICKNESSES WILL NOT COME ON YOU

DEUTERONOMY 30: 19 GOD SETS BEFORE US LIFE, DEATH. BLESSINGS 0R CURSES-WE CHOOSE

II KINGS 20:5 GOD HEARS OUR PRAYERS AND HEALS US

II CHRONICLES 7: 14 IF MY PEOPLE HUMBLE THEMSELVES, PRAY, SEEK MY FACE AND TURN FROM WICKED WAYS I WILL HEAR, FORGIVE AND HEAL

PSALM 30:2 I CRIED AND YOU HEALED ME

PSALM 33:18-19 THE LORD'S EYE IS UPON YOU TO DELIVER YOU

PSALM 34:20 THE RIGHTEOUS KEEPS ALL HIS BONES AND NONE ARE BROKEN

PSALM 91: ALL

PSALM 103:1-5 GOD HEALS ALL YOUR DISEASES

PSALM 107: 17-20 ILL BECAUSE OF TRANSGRESSIONS, GOD HEALS WITH HIS WORD

PSALM 146:8 THE LORD OPENS THE EYES OF THE BLIND AND HEALS THOSE BOWED

PROVERBS 3:7-8 FEAR AND WORSHIP THE LORD, NO EVIL, HEALTH TO YOUR BODY

PROVERBS 20:12 THE LORD MAKES THE SEEING EYE AND HEARING EAR

ISAIAH 35:10 THOSE IN THE LORD RECEIVE JOY AND GLADNESS-SORROW FLEES

ISAIAH 40:31 THOSE WHO WAIT ON THE LORD RENEW THEIR STRENGTH

ISAIAH 57:18-19 THE LORD WATCHES YOUR WAYS AND HEALS THE RIGHTEOUS

ISAIAH 58:6-12 SOME THINGS GOD REWARDS WITH GOOD HEALTH

ISAIAH 61:1-3 THE SPIRIT OF GOD HEALS THE BROKENHEARTED AND GIVES JOY

JEREMIAH 30: 17 GOD WILL RESTORE YOUR HEALTH, HEAL WOUNDS

JEREMIAH 33:6 GOD WILL RESTORE HEALTH, HEALING, CURE, G IVE PEACE, ETC

EZEKIEL 16:6 WHEN GOD SEES YOU BLEEDING, HE SAYS LIVE

MALACHI 4:2 THOSE WHO REVERE AND WORSHIP THE LORD ARE HEALED AND FREE

MATTHEW 8:14-15 PETER'S MOTHER-IN-LAW HEALED (LUKE 4:38-39)

MATTHEW 14:14 JESUS HEALED THE SICK

I CORINTHIANS 12:9 JESUS GIVES TO SOME GIFTS OF HEALINGS BY HOLY SPIRIT

PHILIPPIANS 2:13-16 GOD WILL WORK IN YOU, DON'T COMPLAIN, HOLD OUT TO THE END

HEBREWS 10:35 CAST NOT AWAY YOUR CONFIDENCE WHICH HAS GREAT REWARD

III JOHN 2 PRAY YOU ARE WELL EVEN AS YOUR SOUL PROSPERS

THE MISSION FIELD PICTURES

Students in the Trade School, Puerto Escondido, Oaxaca, Mexico
Taught Carpentry, Welding, Electricity,
Plumbing, Automotive and Construction

Kitchen cabinets under construction for
the Puerto Escondido apartments.
Puerto Escondido, Oaxaca

Church under construction on mountain over Monterrey, Mexico.

Classrooms and girls dormitory building under
construction. Puerto Escondido, Oaxaca

Near the guest house, visiting Americans rehearse
their program for the evening service.

Church ready for Roof Beams.

Carl ministering in the Auditorium in Saltillo, Coahuila, Mexico

The ministry in Mexico continues under son Carl, his wife
Marina and their three children Carl, Alegría and Roy

ABOUT THE AUTHOR

DRAMATIC AND TERRIFYING experiences at the tender, innocent age of kindergarten and first grade implanted anger and bitterness in Carl Luepnitz's brain. They kept the door open for ugly, demonic influence many years later, which would have destroyed him; his wife, Helen; their marriage; and the ministry, except for God's solution. In 1974, Carl attended a Kathryn Kuhlman meeting in which he received healing and encountered the truth of Christ in a profound and life-changing way. The Holy Spirit began to transform his heart and mind, and, soon, began to transform his family. Together, Helen and Carl made a commitment to God that would change the course of their lives forever. To dislodge demonic forces that had been entrenched many years required dedication by Carl and Helen to bring every thought under control. That is, no more negative or toxic thoughts; only positive thoughts reflecting biblical admonitions, thus causing the 'toxic brain material to fade away and the non-toxic to replace it. Throughout this process God was laying in Carl and Helen the groundwork for a ministry of deliverance and Holy Spirit power on the mission field.

After retiring from the army, God called Carl and Helen into the mission field, where they have continued for forty years to experience the supernatural. Between his military service and missions work, Carl has spent time in thirty countries.

The blessings and the happiness in this life were worth every bit of his effort. Helen and Carl will have been married sixty-six years on January 19, 2018.

After forty years, the mission continues through Eternal Love Ministries, fulfilling the Great Commission out of its bases in Saltillo and Puerto Escondido, Mexico. Join with us in this journey to reach the unreached and edify the church.

Contact the Author

FOR MORE INFORMATION about this book please visit our website, www.AChallengetoLive.com or contact us at achallengetolive@gmail.com.

Today, Eternal Love Ministries continues ministering out of the two bases in Saltillo and Puerto Escondido, Mexico, both providing rewarding opportunities for short-term mission teams. For information please visit our website at www.EternalLove.net or e-mail us at Eternal.Love.Min@gmail.com. Donations to Eternal Love Ministries are tax-deductible and are always applied prayerfully and efficiently to accomplish the work of the gospel in Mexico. Donations can be received online or by mail at the following address:

Donations
Eternal Love Ministries
PO Box 3
Buckholts, TX 76518

Correspondence
Eternal Love Ministries
PO Box 833
Temple, TX 76503

M000198239

urban & suburban Meadows

Bringing Meadowscaping to Big and Small Spaces

Catherine B. Zimmerman

maTrix media **press**

Published by Matrix Media Press
Silver Spring, MD 20901

For ordering information or special discounts for bulk purchases, please visit
www.themeadowproject.com.

Copyright ©2010 Catherine Zimmerman

All rights reserved.

No part of this book may be reproduced, stored in a retrieval system, or transmitted
by any means, electronic, mechanical, photocopying, recording, or otherwise, without
written permission from the publisher.

Distributed by Greenleaf Book Group LLC

Greenleaf Book Group LLC at PO Box 91869, Austin, TX 78709, 512.891.6100

Design and composition by Diane Buric Design and Illustration
Cover design by Diane Buric Design and Illustration
Editor Catherine Cummins
Unless otherwise noted all photos are by the author.

Library of Congress Control Number: 2010901686
ISBN: 978-0-9844560-0-0

TreeNeutral

Part of the Tree Neutral™ program, which offsets the number of trees
consumed in the production and printing of this book by taking proactive
steps, such as planting trees in direct proportion to the number of trees
used: www.treeneutral.com

Printed in Canada on acid-free paper
The pages within this book were printed on paper containing 10% Post-Consumer Fiber.

10 11 12 13 14 10 9 8 7 6 5 4 3 2 1

First Edition

Dedicated to my Mom and Dad

What beauty does the meadow hold
Whispering breezes caress sunflowers of gold
Finches, bees and butterflies flutter and dine
On seeds and sweet nectar so divine
Bird melodies all day trill
'til twilight falls and makes them still
Sunrise sparkles on dew clad grasses
As I stroll the path with buoyant gladness

creating a meadow

Helenium autumnale (Sneezeweed).

reflections

The great thing about practicing organic land care is you don't have to kill something with toxic chemicals to grow something.

I grew up on a small farm in the 50's and 60's. My Dad, a third generation vegetable farmer, who had an appreciation for balance in land use, formed my approach to the landscape. He didn't plant corn right up to the front steps nor did he squander too much of the six acres of land in lawn. There was enough grassy space for my three brothers and two sisters and me to play softball, badminton and to construct forts. The task fell on us to mow and many summer days were spent taking shifts on the push mower. The smell of that freshly mown lawn, sweet and fragrant with clover scent, is etched into my brain. The blitzkrieg of herbicides, which threatens to wipe out all but monocotyledonous blades of grass, had not yet arrived. We were blissfully unaware of the dangers to come.

Our land was productive and we spent most of our time planting, weeding and picking vegetables and berries. We sat around the kitchen table for hours snapping beans and hulling peas. When the bushel baskets were empty and every container in the house was filled, my oldest brother sliced up cool watermelon as a treat.

Mom and Dad were masters at canning all this produce. Jars and jars of pickles, rhubarb, raspberries and beans filled shelves in the cellar. We produced much of what we ate throughout the year. Fresh picked tomatoes and corn have never tasted as good.

Elmer Zimmerman checks bean crop.

Dad was a very hands-on, learn-by-doing, father. He gave us each a little patch of garden to plant whatever we wanted. I chose to plant flowers and made up a tune I would sing to them.

"O' flower, O' flower
O' grow for me
I'll water you night
I'll water you day
I'll water you all
The time away!"

I'm surprised the plants didn't just rot in the ground under such excessive watering. At the age of five, I was afraid that my flowers would wither away without my intervention.

Dad shared my love of flowers, or I should say that I inherited his passion for them. He found time to tend the roses, trim the lilacs, weigela and the Rose of Sharons. He planted large beds of zinnias for cut flowers and moss rose down by the barn bank. Oh, he claimed all this effort was for Mom's benefit, but I knew better. He even let a rather large patch of his favorite blue, wild flower, chicory grow behind the chicken house. He told me all those flowers would attract a lot of great bees and that would be good for the garden. I just liked smelling and looking at the flowers. I still ran away at the sight of a bee. I later discovered the wild patch behind the chicken house was considered an invasive species, not native and not too highly prized by the landscaping world. Now, every June, when I see those bright blue flower heads with their wiry stems poking out of some impossibly small crack in the pavement, I am reminded of my dad.

Dad offered a wealth of information about the organic practices he used growing up. He always rotated crops, never planted the same family of plants on the same ground two years in a row. He used cover crops such as annual rye to prevent erosion of the soil. Cover crops get tilled under to provide what is now referred to as "green manure" or nitrogen rich organic matter. This rich organic matter makes use of manure from the farm animals as the main source of fertilizer for the garden. Never use raw manure. It burns the plants roots.

Many farmers of Dad's era had little, or no, formal education. They chose organic practices more out of necessity rather than an understanding of their benefits over chemical practices. Manure was cheap and readily available for crop fertilization when Dad was a young boy. Horses were a major source of manure. A combination of factors changed organic farming practices. When automobiles replaced horse drawn transportation the source of manure became scarce. After World War II, farm workers migrated to factory jobs in the city. This loss of farm labor necessitated a shift toward "modern" agriculture and gardening that was more mechanized and

more dependent on synthetic fertilizers and pesticides. Farmers were seduced by the promise of larger crop yields, with less labor. Dad joined the movement. These practices seemed just fine.

By the late 70's I was out of college, employed and a first-time homeowner in the suburbs of Washington, DC. I owned a patch of land and I could plant whatever I wanted. I wanted what everyone in the neighborhood had—a great, green lawn. Fertilizer and pesticide use was in full swing. I didn't see any reason not to sign on. My parents were masters of canning. I became a master of the popular four-step fertilizer program. Everyone admired my yard. I told them how simple it was. I had converts. I thought I knew something about the soil.

The Ohio Farmer was the trade journal Dad had read for decades. After he retired, he also subscribed to *Mother Earth News*, an organically oriented publication, and he tuned in daily to NPR, National Public Radio. Dad was a very open-minded guy. He was exploring, starting to doubt his farming practices and reconnecting with his organic roots. He opened my eyes to the dangers of pesticides.

What are pesticides? Pesticides include herbicides and insecticides. I took a look at the word. I got the pest part, bad insects. "Cide" is Latin for "to kill". I was killing bugs, all bugs? Was I killing ladybugs? The kids and I released ladybugs every year to eat aphids on the roses. I was killing ladybugs and a lot of other good bugs. This stuff doesn't care what bug; it just wipes out bugs. By most accounts, the world was a better place.

As Dad and I talked, I began to question my own gardening practices. When did my "patch of earth" become a status symbol? When did I start treating it like a personal accessory? I began to really pay attention.

I read. I had no idea that agriculture and suburban lawn runoff creates the biggest source of water contamination. One hundred million pounds of synthetic pesticides and fertilizers are dumped on lawns each year. This is ten times more per acre than is used on farms![1] Algae blooms, caused by all these chemicals, were killing life in the Chesapeake Bay. Ecosystems were being destroyed. And the fuel-powered mowers, string cutters and leaf blowers used to maintain lawns were creating air pollution, as well as a cacophony of sound pollution. We were doing all this harm to the environment just so we could look out over green, grassy vistas.

I started to see all this was connected. Those beneficial insects I poisoned along with the pest insects were very important. They were actually keeping the bad guys in check, pollinating plants and providing a needed meal for the bird, amphibian and small mammal populations. Every landscaping choice I was making directly impacted my fellow critters. I was responsible.

Author and Dad, 1992.

I stopped using synthetic fertilizers and pesticides. I examined my grassy, monoculture "patch of earth". I decided to reduce my lawn, maybe get rid of it altogether! I set out to look for alternatives. *Urban and Suburban Meadows* is the result of that journey that began with my father.

[1]*Beyond Pesticides: Lawn Pesticide Facts and Figures,* see pg. 259.

"I think the meadow really evokes a connection to the earth and a sense of peace and calm... but then when you walk into a meadow it's so full of life; it's just teeming. It's noisy with the buzz of the pollinators, the chirping of the crickets, the flutter of the birds and the butterflies. It's really alive. It's much more than a field that needs to be mowed. It's full of life."

Peggy Bowers, Horticulturist

why a meadow?

WHY PLANT A MEADOW INSTEAD OF A LAWN? 10 REASONS

1 **No chemical pesticides/herbicides or fertilizers.** Eliminating toxic chemicals protects beneficial soil organisms that support the ecosystem, the plants and animals that live there, and the people and pets who visit there.

2 **Meadows** require minimal disturbance to the native landscape.

3 **Diversity.** Meadows are more than lawns that need to be mowed, they are habitats teeming with life. Meadows are home to many more different native plant, insect and animal species than monocultures (lawns).

4 **Only mow or burn** once between November and April. Meadows conserve fuel and labor.

5 **Sustainable.** Meadows thrive on a cradle-to-cradle cycle, using their waste to build soil organic matter that nourishes life.

6 **Year-round habitat.** Meadows provide year-round cover and food for insects and wildlife.

7 **Erosion control.** Unlike lawns that act as green concrete, the complexity and varying heights of meadow plants will soften rainfall and prevent water from rushing over the surface of the soil. In addition, the deep root systems hold and stabilize the soil.

8 **Bio remediation.** Meadows provide a matrix of microorganisms, fungi, green plants or their enzymes that can restore the natural environment altered by contaminants to its original condition. This is particularly important around bodies of water where meadow plants can block pollutant runoff from causing algae blooms.

9 **Low maintenance.** Once established, meadows require no watering, minimal mowing, no fertilizing, and no raking.

10 **Enjoyable.** The ever-changing beauty of a meadow evokes a sense of peace and calm, while the activity of its inhabitants provides endless enjoyment.

Aster novae-angliae 'Purple Dome' (New England aster) and *Panicum virgatum* 'Shenandoah' (Red switchgrass).

Connecticut meadow as a front lawn alternative. Native *Buchloe dactyloides* (Buffalograss) edges the meadow. Michael Nadeau, Plantscapes, Inc.

introduction

I set out to understand exactly how to create meadows as lawn alternatives. My journey led me to a fascinating group of expert plant people and meadow designers scattered throughout the United States. They generously shared their time and knowledge. This guide is the result of those travels, interviews and research. I hope to take the mystery out of meadowscaping by showing readers how to successfully establish a beautiful, diverse meadow or prairie habitat.

MEADOWS

What is a meadow? A meadow is a field of natural grasses and native wildflowers typically occurring in the eastern part of North America. Eastern meadows have a high proportion of cool season grasses. Meadows are found where the forest canopy has been opened by fire, flood or agricultural activities. Meadow plants are some of the first plants to vegetate an area, such as abandoned farmland or "old field meadows", where the soil has been disturbed. But meadows are a temporary ecological community. Without some type of natural or man made intervention, woody plants and trees will take over and shade out the grasses and flowers and the meadow will eventually turn into forest. This process is referred to as plant succession.

People often confuse the terms prairie and meadow. Prairie is the French word for meadow. Prairies are similar plant communities found in Midwestern North America,

Bruce Jones

Old field meadow, Rappahannock County, Virginia.

dominated primarily by warm season grasses, also with a variety of wild flowers. "The Midwestern prairies and eastern meadows share many of the same species of flowers and grasses. In many cases prairies and meadows possess close relatives of different species in the same genus, such as Asters, Goldenrods and False indigos. Even though some species might be slightly different from an eastern meadow to a midwestern prairie, the appearance is often similar between the two plant communities."[1]

There are different types of prairies due to the amount of rainfall. Drier prairies, in the west, have shorter grasses than wetter prairies found to the east. Prairies do not transition to forests because low rainfall, grazing, and burning prevent woody growth. Prairie plants have extremely deep root systems that help them withstand drought and gives them

an advantage over more shallowly rooted non-prairie species. The prairie is sustained because prairie plants can withstand these extreme conditions, including severe hot and cold temperatures.

Fire is a very important element in a sustainable prairie. Burning a prairie suppresses non-prairie plants, returns the dead vegetation to the soil as carbon and balances the nutrients in the soil. The ground is left open to the sun's warming rays and heat-loving prairie plants vigorously sprout again.

The same techniques and considerations for organic site preparation, design, planting and maintenance are applicable to both meadows and prairies. For these purposes, I use the terms meadow and prairie interchangeably in this guide.

Larry Engel

Storm brews over vast, short grass Montana prairie.

ECOSYSTEMS

Ecosystems are natural groups formed by the interaction of a community of microorganisms, plants and animals, with their physical environment. With the advance of human activity such as farming, industry, housing and commercial development, ecosystems have been fragmented and lost. When ecosystems are destroyed, many animal species also disappear.

Meadows are very diverse ecosystems containing many types of grasses and flowers at varying heights, attracting scores of insects and wildlife. Meadows function as soil stabilizers, pollutant filters, homes and food sources for its inhabitants. And, meadows are self-sustaining requiring no human inputs to thrive.

Lawns are the exact opposite. Unlike the biodiverse meadows, lawns are virtual monocultures. Lawns are purposefully planted with grass, and sometimes clover, and maintained at a low, even height for cosmetic reasons. They offer little potential for diversity of animal species. Typically, maintaining luxuriant, green, weed-free lawns requires constant watering and the use of fertilizers and pesticides. The extravagant use of precious water resources alone is very problematic. As human populations grow, more and more demand is placed on water and water is not an unlimited resource.

Turf monocultures, such as lawn areas in this housing development, deprive wildlife of habitat and food.

SYNTHETIC PESTICIDES AND FERTILIZERS

When we use pesticides on our lawns and landscapes, we eliminate the target pests, but other pests actually proliferate once their natural enemies are killed. We also end up destroying beneficial organisms. Our interference creates an imbalance in the ecosystem.

Likewise, use of synthetic fertilizers and even excessive use of organic fertilizers can overload the soil with nutrients and disrupt both biological and chemical interactions in the soil. Based on the soil PH, the degree of soil acidity of alkalinity, added nutrients such as nitrogen, phosphorous and potassium, may not be absorbed by plants. Instead they escape into the groundwater either through runoff or leaching. These nutrients end up in streams, ponds, lakes and bays where they disrupt the balance in aquatic ecosystems. The overload of nutrients, particularly phosphorous, causes the rapid growth of algae, which robs the water of dissolved oxygen critical to the lives of aquatic organisms. Some algae generate bio-toxins that are deadly to birds, fish and other mammals.

This is the real danger. *Pesticides and fertilizers are out of our control once applied*: Not

Algae bloom from pollutant runoff.

only can they end up doing considerable damage to ecosystems, but there are also human costs. Of the "30 commonly used lawn pesticides 13 are probable or possible carcinogens, 13 are linked with birth defects, 21 with reproductive effects, 15 with neurotoxicity, 26 with liver or kidney damage, 27 are sensitizers and/or irritants, and 11 have the potential to disrupt the endocrine (hormonal) system. Pregnant women, infants and children, the aged and the chronically ill are at greatest risk from pesticide exposure and chemically induced immune-suppression, which can increase susceptibility to cancer."[2]

Planting a meadow habitat, using organic methods and a diversity of native plants that are adapted to the soil conditions, eliminates the need to use any pesticides or fertilizers. It is one way to begin reversing the damage we have carelessly caused the environment. In doing so we begin to work with nature, creating habitat for insects and wildlife, providing filters for pollutant runoff, and bring healthy, sustainable ecosystems to our own backyards.

[1]Neil Diboll, Prairie Ecologist ,Prairie Nursery, Inc.
[2]Beyond Pesticides Lawn Pesticides Facts and Figures (see lawn fact sheets pg. 259)

Prairie plants filter pollutant runoff. Jack Pizzo & Associates, Ltd.

Jack Pizzo

COST FACTORS: LAWNS VERSUS MEADOWS

Beyond the growing loss of diversity, damage to our ecosystems and depletion of water resources, lawns cost money. There is no getting around the fact that if we choose to plant our lawns in non-native grass species like Kentucky Blue Grass, we will wage a constant battle maintaining that lush, green carpet. It is no mystery why Kentucky Blue Grass, for instance, must be closely tended and meticulously watered following even a mild dry spell. First, it is a cool season species, which goes dormant in heat and drought. Second, it has barely any root system! (See left side of diagram). Take a look at the neighboring native prairie plants in the diagram. It is easy to see how these tough plants survive erosion, fire, and drought. In many cases, most of the plants biomass is underground, out of harm's way. The prairie plants massive root system delivers nutrients and water to the shoots, leaves, and flowers above ground.

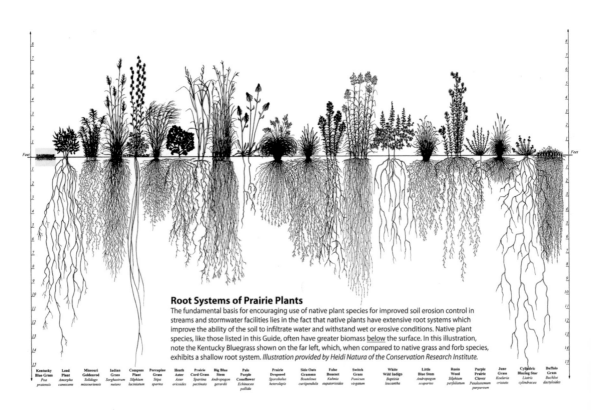

Root Systems of Prairie Plants
The fundamental basis for encouraging use of native plant species for improved soil erosion control in streams and stormwater facilities lies in the fact that native plants have extensive root systems which improve the ability of the soil to infiltrate water and withstand wet or erosive conditions. Native plant species, like those listed in this Guide, often have greater biomass below the surface. In this illustration, note the Kentucky Bluegrass shown on the far left, which, when compared to native grass and forb species, exhibits a shallow root system. *Illustration provided by Heidi Natura of the Conservation Research Institute.*

Reprinted from the Natural Resources Conservation Service (NRCS) Illinois Native Plant Guide, *Illinois Native Plant Guide: Root Systems of Prairie Plants.*

LOW COST, LOW MAINTENANCE, NATIVE LAWN ALTERNATIVES

In areas where you would like to retain lawn, consider planting a native grass like *Buchloe dactyloides* (Buffalo grass), a good drought tolerant, low mow turf grass. Buffalo grass has roots that can extend seven feet into the soil to reach a water source.

Native seed nurseries around the country are developing warm and cool season, low-mow native grass seed mixes adapted to specific regions. Because they are adapted to the region, watering becomes an infrequent necessity. No fertilizer inputs are required and mowing is minimal, needed only once or twice a year. If you want a natural look, mow only once in the spring. For a more manicured look, mow once a month, to a height of three to four inches.

Saxon Holt

above: *Festuca rubra* (Creeping red fescue) as a lawn substitute in Southern California meadow garden. Cool season fescues are best planted in northern climates but selections from California do well in drier conditions. Creeping red fescue is not native to all ecoregions. If not native to your area, it is considered a weed and not appropriate to plant in a meadow or prairie. Chuck Stopherd design.

Charles Mann

left: A large lawn of mown *Buchloe dactyloides* (Buffalo grass) accents a classic craftsman-style house at the Antique Rose Emporium in Brenham, Texas.

To work with a non-native existing lawn, go organic! There are several good resource books that walk you through establishing and sustaining healthy soil and grass, naturally. Healthy turf is highly beneficial. It requires less water, resists insect pests and diseases, and out-competes weeds. The NOFA Organic Lawn and Turf Handbook is one of the most detailed and practical guides available. It covers site analysis, soil health, amendments, cultural practices, weeds, insects, and diseases. The handbook is based upon Northeast Organic Farmers Association (NOFA) & National Organic Program (NOP) organic agriculture practices that are modified for land care. It was produced by the NOFA Land Care Committee combining information from agricultural extension programs and the technical knowledge of organic land care professionals who successfully and economically maintain hundreds of acres of organic lawns and athletic turf. Visit www.organiclandcare.net for more information and to obtain the *NOFA Organic Lawn and Turf Handbook.*

Connecticut meadow in June. The lawn and meadow are 100% organically managed. Michael Nadeau, Plantscapes, Inc.

COST COMPARISON CHARTS

Just *how* cost effective is a meadow or prairie? The following charts compare lawn and meadow installation and maintenance costs for a one-third acre seeded site. The rates are based on typical water, material, and contractor rates in the Northeast and Mid-Atlantic regions. Rates will vary around the country. The charts reflect two scenarios: 1) work that is contracted, and 2) work executed by the homeowner.

Meadows and prairies can be maintained either by spring burning or mowing or a combination of the two methods. Burning in a two-to-three year cycle is the most effective maintenance tool for a healthy meadow or prairie. Burning is not permitted in all jurisdictions; included in the charts are costs for both burning and mowing management.

Mowing achieves much the same effects as burning. However, the burn process helps seeds that require fire to germinate, hastens nutrient recycling, and releases nitrogen into the atmosphere, making it less available for plant growth. Meadow and prairie species thrive under low nitrogen levels, giving them a huge advantage over nitrogen needy undesirable species.

Whether a meadow or prairie is maintained by burning or mowing, the costs over a ten-year period are considerably less than maintaining a non-native lawn on the same site.

NON-NATIVE LAWN VERSUS NATIVE MEADOW/PRAIRIE INSTALLATION BASIC COST COMPARISON FOR A ¹/₃ ACRE SITE

Procedures & Materials	Seeded Turf Contractor	Seeded Turf Homeowner	Seeded Meadow/ Prairie Contractor	Seeded Meadow/ Prairie Homeowner
Synthetic Herbicide (cost based on 2 applications)	$80	$80		
Organic Herbicide (cost based on 6 applications)			$450	$450
Starter fertilizer	$65	$65		
Grass Seed	$150	$150		
Meadow/Prairie seed mix			$450	$450
Straw	$160	$160	$160	$160
Backpack sprayer		$85		$85
Spray Equipment & Labor (2 workers @ $160/hr.)	$640		$1,920	
Equipment & Labor-tilling/grading/seeding/straw	$960	$125		
Lightly rake soil/mix seed/seeding/roll seed/straw			$960	$60
Total	**$1,905**	**$665**	**$3,940**	**$1,205**

Assumptions:
- Costs for synthetic and organic herbicide application can vary depending on type of vegetation being killed and the number of times a site has to be treated to kill that vegetation.
- Organic herbicide used to kill off vegetation on meadow site.
- Contractor bills man hour and equipment at $80/hour per worker (rate incorporates overhead such as: equipment, travel, insurance, special clothing & wages.)
- Homeowner rents tiller & buys back pack sprayer. (Lawn)
- Homeowner rents metal roller and & buys back pack sprayer. (Meadow)
- No costs for lawn irrigation system.
- No costs for design and contractor/client meetings.

NON-NATIVE LAWN VERSUS NATIVE MEADOW/PRAIRIE MAINTENANCE 10 YEAR COST COMPARISON FOR $^1/_3$ ACRE

	Contractor	Contractor	Contractor	Contractor	Contractor	Contractor	Contra
	Year 1	Year 2	Year 3	Year 5	Year 6	Year 7	Year
Maintenance Lawn							
Install	$1,905						
4 step fertilization program	$480	$494	$509	$540	$556	$573	$608
Aerating and overseeding		$300			$338		
Mowing	$1,440	$1,483	$1,528	$1,621	$1,669	$1,719	$1,824
Municipal Water	$1,342	$1,382	$1,424	$1,510	$1,556	$1,602	$1,700
Annual expense	$5,167	$3,660	$3,461	$3,671	$4,119	$3,895	$4,132
Cumulative expense	$5,167	$8,827	$12,288	$19,842	$23,961	$27,856	$36,358
Maintenance Meadow/Prairie using Burn & Mowing Management							
Install using organic practices	$3,940						
Invasive management/ maintenance	$600	$618	$637	258	265	273	290
Mowing	$180	$124			$140		
Burn (mowing costs in years 4 and 8 not shown)			$1,400	$1,485		$1,576	$1,672
Municipal Water	$447						
Annual expense	$5,167	$742	$2,037	$1,743	$405	$1,849	$1,961
Cumulative expense	$5,167	$5,909	$7,946	$10,070	$10,475	$12,324	$14,71
Savings	$0	$2,918	$4,342	$9,772	$13,486	$15,532	$21,64
Percentage savings	0%	33%	35%	49%	56%	56%	60%

Nearly $26,000 saved over 10 years

	Contractor	Contractor	Contractor	Contractor	Contractor	Contractor	Contra
Maintenance Meadow/Prairie Using Mowing Management							
Install using organic practices	$3,940						
Invasive management/ maintenance	$600	$618	$637	258	265	273	290
Mowing	$180	$124	$128	$135	$140	$144	$153
Municipal Water	$447						
Annual expense	$5,167	$742	$764	$393	$405	$417	$442
Cumulative expense	$5,167	$5,909	$6,673	$7,448	$7,853	$8,270	$9,141
Savings	$0	$2,918	$5,614	$12,394	$16,108	$19,586	$27,21
Percentage savings	0%	33%	46%	62%	67%	70%	75%

$31,000 saved over 10 years

All years calculated. Due to space limitations years 4 and 8 are not displayed.

Assumptions:
(Costs will vary around the country due to contractor availability, rates, materials and travel time to site)
• Mowing lawn weekly for 24 weeks.
• Mowing rate for contractor based on $60 per mow.
• Mowing cost for home owner based on $100 per year mower cost & maintenance and $4 per week for gasoline.
• Mowing management for meadow/prairie: three times 1st year, twice in 2nd year and once a year thereafter.
• Homeowner rents aerator.

...ractor r 10	Homeowner Year 1	Homeowner Year 2	Homeowner Year 3	Homeowner Year 5	Homeowner Year 6	Homeowner Year 7	Homeowner Year 9	Homeowner Year 10
	$665							
	$338	$348	$359	$380	$392	$404	$428	$441
		$200			$225			$253
9	$196	$202	$208	$221	$227	$234	$248	$256
1	$1,342	$1,382	$1,424	$1,510	$1,556	$1,602	$1,700	$1,751
6	$2,541	$2,132	$1,990	$2,111	$2,400	$2,240	$2,376	$2,701
94	$2,541	$4,673	$6,664	$11,037	$13,437	$15,677	$20,600	$23,301
	$1,205							
	$112	$111			$121			$136
			$1,400	$1,485		$1,576	$1,672	
	$447							
	$1,764	$111	$1,400	$1,485	$121	$1,576	$1,672	$136
70	$1,764	$1,875	$3,275	$4,874	$4,994	$6,570	$8,370	$8,505
24	$777	$2,798	$3,389	$6,163	$8,443	$9,107	$12,230	$14,795
	31%	60%	51%	56%	63%	58%	59%	63%

Nearly $15,000 saved over 10 years

	Homeowner Year 1	Homeowner Year 2	Homeowner Year 3	Homeowner Year 5	Homeowner Year 6	Homeowner Year 7	Homeowner Year 9	Homeowner Year 10
	$1,205							
	$112	$111	$114	$121	$125	$129	$137	$141
	$447							
	$1,764	$111	$114	$121	$125	$129	$137	$141
7	$1,764	$1,875	$1,989	$2,228	$2,353	$2,482	$2,751	$2,892
97	$777	$2,798	$4,674	$8,809	$11,084	$13,195	$17,849	$20,409
	31%	60%	70%	80%	82%	84%	87%	88%

$20,000 saved over 10 years

- Lawn water usage based on watering 18 times over the growing season at 1 inch per, using water rate of $6.21/ccf (1 ccf=100 cubic feet).
- Meadow/prairie water usage based on $1/3$ that of lawn in the 1st year. Watering may not even be necessary the 1st year. After meadow/prairie is established, no watering required.
- Burning management for meadow/prairie in areas where permitted. Assumes homeowner hires professionals. Site burned every other year starting in year three. Mowing on off years.
- Cost of living increase 3% annually, rounded to the nearest dollar.

site preparation

I became intrigued with urban meadows when I met Michael Nadeau. He was teaching a section on lawn alternatives for the NOFA (Northeast Organic Farmers Association) Land Care Course. He showed a series of slides of one of his meadow installations. The meadow went right up to the patio! It was breathtaking! I was hooked!

This chapter is inspired from video interviews and many conversations with Michael Nadeau, Plantscapes Inc.

HOW TO CHOOSE A MEADOW SITE

Whenever and wherever possible, return areas planted in lawn to more ecological habitat using native meadow plants. Native plants are plants that have been known to naturally occur in an area without human intervention from pre-European development.

Meadow plants are typically drought tolerant sun lovers. The most important consideration in site choice is an area with at least a half day of direct sunlight. However, there are native meadow plants that grow well along the woodland edge and can be used in a site with partial sun, for example: *Lobelia cardinalis* (Cardinal flower), *Physostegia virginiana* (Obedient plant), *Carex muskingumensis*, (Palm sedge), *Carex grayi* (Morning star sedge), and *Chasmanthium latifolium* (River oats) to name a few.

Here are some meadow site possibilities:

- New construction sites where the soil is poor, often compacted and rocky. This

left: Urban hillside meadow, Washington, DC; *Baptisia australis* (Blue false indigo). Lauren Wheeler, Natural Resources Design, Inc.

Turn the loss of a tree into a sunny meadow habitat.

This constructed wetland and rain garden or "wet meadow" replaces an area of lawn at Sidwell Friends School in Washington, DC. The rain garden manages storm water runoff and the constructed wetlands aid in treating the school's wastewater. Andropogon Associates, Ltd.

Deep root system of prairie plants controls erosion on slope in Missouri housing development. Jon Wingo, DJM Ecological Services

is an ideal site for a wildflower meadow because meadow plants like these conditions. Attempting to plant a lawn on such degraded, infertile soil requires a great deal of resources to establish and maintain.

- An area where a tree needed to be removed creates a great sunny meadow location.

- Lawns, where childhood sports and games are no loner played, are perfect for a meadow.

- Areas where woods and lawn meet are lovely settings for a meadow. Allow the meadow to encroach into the lawn. Mow a path through the meadow to connect to the woods.

- Slopes where erosion is a problem and mowing grass is difficult. The matrix of diverse meadow plants will soften rainfall and moderate erosion and runoff.

- Areas where heavy rains cause flooding can be remediated with a wet meadow planting or "rain garden".

> **TIP**
>
> **The key to choosing a site is sunlight and matching the plants with the site.**

Community school meadow project. Fairfax County, Virginia.

The sidewalk and street form borders for a Wisconsin suburban prairie garden.

CREATING THE SHAPE

Sidewalks, fences or natural borders such as, a stream or woodland edge may already form some of the meadow boundaries. The key is to delineate the edges to look very natural. Simple tools that can be used:

- Flexible garden hose. Just lay the hose down and move it around until the desired shape is achieved.
- Mower with the blade set low.
- Flags.
- Water soluble marker paint.

START WITH A CLEAN SLATE

Meadow creation is a departure from the typical urban and suburban landscape. By creating meadows, we are rebuilding ecosystems that existed before the land was developed and lawn became the prevalent landscape.

Preparing the site for planting requires removing or killing unwanted, existing vegetation. Conditions will vary from bare, disturbed ground to lawns to overgrown weedy patches filled with invasive and woody plants. Weed seeds, which can lay dormant for years, also present a problem and should be left undisturbed. For example, tilling will bring dormant seeds to the soil surface where exposure to sun will allow them to germinate. A bumper crop of weeds will ensue making it more difficult to grow a meadow.

This chapter outlines five organic techniques for site preparation. Sites may require a combination of methods or hand removal if there are "thug" plants present. Our goals are to work with nature by taking a "Do No Harm" approach, disturbing the site as little as possible, retaining soil organic matter and protecting soil organisms.

When it comes to site preparation for meadows, there are two camps, the organic proponents and the synthetic chemical proponents.

The argument for using synthetic herbicides (the most common one is Roundup™) is that they are very effective in killing plants and cost less than natural, organic herbicides. That's a good argument until one reads scientific studies on glyphosate (the active ingredient) and the interaction with the inert ingredients in the product. The accumulating scientific evidence shows links to human health hazards, death, or mutations in non-target species such as beneficial insects, fish, birds and small mammals.[1]

The proponents of an organic approach contend that these synthetic herbicides poison the environment. When trying to create a more environmentally friendly landscape (meadow), they say there is no right way to do the wrong thing.

Using an organic herbicide may require more applications and a higher initial cost than does clearing the site with potentially toxic chemicals. However, organic herbicides do not add to ground water pollution or result in any of the other serious problems that are caused by glyphosate-based products and other synthetic pesticides. With proper timing of organic herbicide treatments, effective results are achieved. [2]

The length of time it takes to clear the site can vary depending on the type of vegetation being killed and the method used. Don't rush into seeding or planting. Time spent on site preparation, making sure the site is completely clear of vegetation, means less time spent controlling weeds in your meadow later.

[1]Beyond Pesticides Fact Sheet: Glyphosate [with citations] pg. 263.
[2]See pg. 38 "Spray".

Smother

Use organic materials to smother and kill vegetation.

Tools
Wheelbarrow
Mower
Shovel
Rake

Materials
Newspaper
Cardboard
Organic products that decompose
Mulch

Benefits
- Minimizes site disturbance.
- Plant and smother material decomposes and adds organic matter to the soil.
- Controls erosion.
- Weed seeds remain undisturbed or die.
- Inexpensive.
- Does not require herbicide use.
- Re-uses materials (old wool rugs, natural fiber underlayment, old plywood, etc.) that would become landfill items.

Considerations
- Waiting period to plant or seed meadow.
- Will kill desirable vegetation, too.
- May not kill weed seeds.

Best results
- Plan ahead.
- Prepare the site in summer or fall for spring planting.
- Use material that will decompose to smother vegetation. Do not use clear or black plastic.
  - Plastics do not decompose creating environmental concerns at disposal time.
  - Black and clear plastic blocks air and water from the soil and the heat generated can "cook" soil organisms.
  - Clear plastic acts like a green house and will accelerate weed growth.

TIP

Laying out sheets of newsprint is undoubtedly a tedious task if you have a large area. A trip to your local daily newspaper facility may be the answer.

Newspapers are printed from huge rolls of newsprint, then cut into sheets and assembled for delivery. The press machine is calibrated to automatically sense when the roll is nearly finished and mechanically switches to a new full roll of newsprint. The end of the old roll is sent to recycling. End rolls can also be purchased, usually priced by the pound. The facility may even donate the material. An average end roll has about 20 to 30 yards of usable newsprint. It is very handy and less time consuming to simply roll the newsprint over the area you want to smother.

What about newspaper inks? Are they toxic? Today newspaper ink is soy-based and non-toxic, even the color pages. You might want to avoid the glossy, shiny pages. The coating delays the breakdown of the paper in the soil.

TIP

A garden hose, spray paint or flags can also be used to define edge of the meadow.

Step 1 Mow the edge or perimeter of the space being prepared for planting the meadow habitat to create the shape of the meadow.

Step 2 Cover vegetation with newspaper 4-5 layers thick, overlapping for full coverage. Only one layer is necessary if using cardboard.

Step 3 Spread two to four inches of weed free mulch over newspaper. Level mulch evenly with rake.

Step 4 Wait 3 months and possibly up to a year for vegetation to die off depending on the weeds you are trying to control.

> **TIP**
>
> **Wet newspaper to keep it in place before spreading mulch.**

Step 5 When the underlying vegetation is dead, plant your meadow plants or plugs. Some smother material may not be decomposed. Simply cut a slit in the cardboard or newsprint, fold back corners, put the plant through the slit, fold the corners back and put the mulch back around the plants.

Step 6 When seeding, remove smother material and plant seed in bare soil.

Step 7 Water until plants are established.

Step 8 If a nurse crop is used, mow to maintain a 6" height for the first season to allow sunlight to penetrate to the meadow seed for germination.

> **TIP**
>
> **Before layering newspaper, spray area with non-synthetic natural herbicide to accelerate vegetation kill off.**

Strip

Remove existing vegetation and roots with sod cutter or hand tools.

Tools
Sod cutter
Mattock
Hand or power edger
Wheelbarrow
Shovel
Rake
Gloves
Garden hose, paint or flags

Materials
Smother material
Natural herbicide
Wood chips or mulch

> ### TIP
> It's important that when you are composting weeds, that you make sure the roots sides are up and not down because they *will* start to grow in the compost pile.

Benefits

- Quickly removes vegetation.
- Covers large areas.
- Stripped plant material can be composted.
- Green material is full of nitrogen.
- Brown material, roots and soil, great carbon source.
- Composted sod quickly becomes very rich soil.
- Shape of meadow can easily be sculpted to desired shape.

Considerations

- Equipment rental cost.
- Transporting sod cutter to meadow site and requires a person experienced in operating a sod cutter.
- Some subsequent plant growth from missed plant rootlets.

Step 1 Define edge or perimeter of the meadow with garden hose, paint or flags.

Step 2 Strip vegetation using a sod cutter or mattock.

Step 3 Remove plant material to compost pile.

Step 4 Spray any subsequent vegetation growth with natural herbicide until site is clear of vegetation.

TIP

For small meadow areas, try using a smother material such as newspaper to prevent plant re-growth after stripping. Plugs or container plants can be planted through smother material. Make sure smother material is as close to the plant as possible without covering the crown of the plant. Mulch or wood chips will need to be applied to keep newsprint in place. Do not use this smother technique when seeding.

Spray

Use non-synthetic natural herbicides to topically kill vegetation.

Tools
Backpack or tank sprayer
Safety glasses
Gloves
Spreader
Dust mask
Chemical resistant measuring cup

Materials
Colorant
Blood meal or Alfalfa meal
Water
Non-synthetic natural herbicides

Benefits

- Covers large areas.
- Best method when preparing slopes. Plant root matrix remains intact and diminishes erosion.
- Prevents the use of toxic synthetic herbicides.

Considerations

- May have to spray up to six times to kill off all vegetation.
- Expensive. Buy in concentrated form to reduce cost.
- Does not control all plants, including woody plants.

How Does it Work? Natural herbicides burn off the waxy cuticle that protects the cells in the plants leaves, dehydrating the plant and destroying its ability to photosynthesize. The herbicide affects only the coated plant foliage and does not go into the plant's root system or the soil as in the case of synthetic herbicides. Any subsequent regrowth needs to be sprayed until the plant is dead.

Caution: It is very important to carefully follow label directions when mixing. Although these are naturally derived products, breathing vapors and contact with skin and eyes is extremely irritating and can be dangerous. Proper safety precautions and equipment must be used. Proper storage is essential.

> ### TIP
> These herbicides work best on lush vegetation. To encourage flush of growth, treat meadow site with an organic source of nitrogen, such as blood meal or alfalfa meal, a week to ten days before spraying. Wear a dust mask when applying for nuisance dust.

Step 1 Define meadow shape.

Step 2 Measure area to be treated. Mix natural herbicide concentrate with water. Mix only the amount of herbicide necessary to cover the meadow site.

Step 3 Spray natural herbicide evenly over area.

Step 4 Spray any subsequent plant growth, repeat until all vegetation is killed off.

Step 5 Plant or seed the meadow.

> **TIP**
> Mix colorant with herbicide so even coverage can be seen, areas will not be skipped over. Do not use regular dyes. There are specific dyes for use with herbicides.

Natural herbicides

Burnout—Highly concentrated vinegar, lemon juice and clove oil-best on hot humid days on herbaceous plants like grasses.

Matran—50% clove oil & 50% other ingredients including wintergreen—controls actively growing green vegetation, both annual and perennial broadleaf and grassy weeds.

Scythe—Pelargonic acid, derived from geraniums- best on cooler days, works better on tough to kill plants.

Nature's Avenger—contains D-limonene-oil from citrus skin-which strips the weed of its waxy skin.

Singe

Use a propane torch to burn tops of plants and some of the root system to kill vegetation.

Benefits
- Minimal site disturbance.
- Effective vegetation kill off.
- Easily portable propane torch.
- No residue to rake or remove.

Considerations
- Cost of purchasing propane torch and filling tank-rental option readily available.
- Working with fire-follow safety precautions.
- Petroleum-based.
- Non-selective.

Step 1 Work in a team. One member operates the torch, the other team member is ready with water to douse any live embers and watches out for the operator.

Step 2 Define meadow edge or perimeter.

Step 3 Wet down surrounding areas not being burned.

Step 4 Pass flame over vegetation being careful not to burn the soil.

Tools
Propane torch
Garden hose
Safety glasses
Gloves
Flame resistant clothing and stout boots

Materials
Propane
Water

TIP

Torch has a low roar when in operation. This is normal.

Step 5 Thoroughly wet singed area to kill any live embers.

Step 6 Repeat steps 3-5 for subsequent growth until site is clear of vegetation.

Step 7 Plant or seed meadow.

Speed

Just stop mowing! Then you can add meadow plants in the lawn and allow them to establish together in the emerging meadow.

Tools
Mower
Wheelbarrow
Shovel

Materials
Meadow plants-container
Mulch-shredded leaf mulch is best
Poor soil for backfilling plants

Benefits

- Minimal site disturbance.
- No site preparation cost for labor or materials.
- Quickly establishes into a meadow.
- Can add or "edit" plants as meadow grows.
- Reduces mowing, watering, pesticide use, labor, noise & air pollution, etc.
- Looks so much more beautiful than a lawn.

Considerations

- Reduced lawn area for recreational use.
- May require removal of invasive or "thug" plants that establish.

Step 1 Create meadow shape with mower.

Step 2 Select meadow plants and place in meadow.

Step 3 Using a shovel, remove existing sod in a diameter twice the size of plant container. Shake lose dirt back in planting hole. Compost removed sod. The green portion of the sod has a lot of nitrogen; the brown portion of the sod has a lot of carbon. It also has all the microbes necessary to break down the sod and it will become excellent soil in less than a year.

Step 4 Dig planting hole, place plant in center. Plant crown should be just above ground level.

Step 5 Fill planting hole with poor soil. Meadow plants can grow in poor soil without any problem. Plus, the nursery has given the plant plenty of fertilizer to be able to grow for the first year. Using poor soil also slows the root system from the surrounding sod from growing into the planting hole. The plant can then become established and competes with surrounding sod.

Step 6 Mulch deeply, about four inches to keep weed seeds from blowing onto bare soil of the planting hole. Shredded leaves make the best mulch. Keep mulch at least one inch from plant stem. Mulching too closely could rot the plant crown.

Step 7 Water plants until established.

Step 8 As your lawn turns into a meadow and grows in together with the meadow plants, edit what you like and don't like.

Step 9 Mow once in early Spring.

Michael Nadeau demonstrates a "Speed" meadow.

why native plants?

Why Native Plants?

Finding a native plant can be something of a chore. Nurseries are inclined to sell ornamental, non-native plants because they are "pest free". Rarely will you find tags on plants indicating where they originated. You might have a clue if Chinese or Japanese are included in the plant name. Until I heard Doug Tallamy relate his research on the native plant-insect connection, I wasn't sure planting native plants was all that necessary.

This is a passage from my video interview with Douglas Tallamy, Professor and Chair of the Department of Entomology and Wildlife Ecology, University of Delaware.

Absolutely every animal on this planet obtains it's food directly from plants by eating a plant or indirectly by eating something that ate a plant. Plants are the only organisms that can capture the sun's energy and turn it into food.

The most important group of animals, in that they take energy from plants and pass it to other animals, are insects that eat plants. We'll call them insect herbivores. Most insect herbivores are only able to eat a particular group of plants and we call that specialization. They can only eat the plants that they have co-evolved with because plants defend themselves with nasty chemicals and it takes long periods of time for insects to develop the physiological ability to digest those chemicals.

left, Inside a Virginia meadow with *Libellula luctuosa*, a female Widow skimmer dragonfly.

right, *Papilio polyxenes* (Black swallowtail) caterpillar.

When we create a meadow we are in effect restoring an ancient food web. This works best if we use the native plants that were originally part of that food web. We favor native plants because the insect herbivores that have evolved in your meadow's location evolved in concert with those native plants. They have specialized on those native plants over many, many thousands of years, which have enabled those insects to eat them. Those same insects have no evolutionary exposure to plants that evolved in China and Europe. They won't be able to eat these plants. They won't be able to digest them.

They won't even recognize them as food plants. So if you are creating a meadow, choose meadow plants that are native to your area of the country.

A good example of an insect that specializes on one group of plants, because of that plant's chemistry, is the monarch butterfly. It eats milkweeds and nothing else because it's able to breakdown the nasty chemicals that are in milkweeds. But it is unable to digest any other type of plant. If we cut milkweeds down, then monarch larvae can't crawl off and eat some other type of plant. Ninety

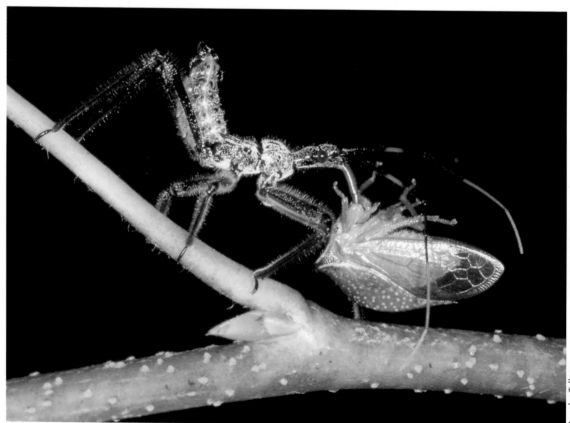

Douglas Tallamy

Natural enemies keep insect population in balance. Assassin bug takes on a leaf hopper.

percent of our insects are specialists just like the monarch. So, if we destroy the plants that these insect herbivores have specialized on, they will have nothing to eat and will be doomed to extinction.

Stop and think about it. So many animals depend on insects for their food. All amphibians eat insects. So do many of the reptiles and rodents. Ninety six percent of our terrestrial birds rear their young on insects. If we replace our native plants with non-native plants then all of those animals won't have enough to eat.

That will greatly effect biodiversity. That is exactly what we have done by creating lawns and landscaping with non-native plants that evolved outside our local ecosystems.

Remember what a meadow is all about. It's not just a beautiful place but also a place where things can live. Living things have two requirements. They need food and they need a place to live. Your meadow provides both. It provides food because of the plants that you have put in your meadow. If you put many different types of plants in your meadow, there will be a diversity of food for a diversity of insects. There will also be a diversity of natural enemies that will eat those insects.

The meadow provides habitat, hiding places, those little niches where the birds and other meadow creatures can nest and rear their young.

Red-winged blackbird chicks in a meadow nest.

Planting a native wild flower meadow is so much more beautiful and dynamic, both structurally and in terms of the species, than planting a monoculture, such as a lawn.

Somebody once said that gardening is a way of showing you believe in tomorrow. I think that has never been more true than today, because the way we garden, the way we create places like meadows is going to determine what life looks like tomorrow.

meadow design

My mission to learn about meadowscaping, led me to Larry Weaner, a remarkable naturalistic landscape designer. During my interviews with Larry while strolling through his meadow creations, I began to realize that there is a little more to creating beautiful meadows than picking my favorite pink, yellow or blue flower.

The following concepts comprise the basis for sustainable meadow design. Larry Weaner, Larry Weaner Landscape Design Associates

NATURE'S DESIGN

The successful establishment of a sustainable meadow requires the understanding of how a meadow develops in nature. We need to understand the underlying ecology and the relationship the plants have to the soil, sun and other meadow plants. You cannot approach a meadow like you would a garden, where plants are chosen based on what you like. We have more latitude when planting a garden—if you are a little off on plant materials, it's easy to fertilize, weed and water to maintain plant viability.

One of the reasons we want to trade in our lawn for a meadow is the sustainability factor. The plants must do the majority of the work. Even if our meadow planting is small and within spitting distance of the nearest hose bib, we want to be much more attuned to whether the plant is adapted to the specific conditions and native to the meadow site so we can bi-pass inputs usually required for a traditional garden or lawn.

The three key ecological concepts to understand when creating a meadow are:

- **Site Analysis:** pick the plants that are adapted to a situation.
- **Plant Communities:** right plant, right place-group together the plant species that naturally grow with one another.
- **Process of Change:** understand the process of change that takes place in a meadow over time.

Once you have a sound ecological foundation, you have the tools to go ahead and make plant selections. The key is first picking the plants that are adapted to the site. Then, and only then, will you be able to make the more aesthetic decisions such as plant color, texture and sequence of bloom.

Meadows at Milton Hershey School in Hershey, PA. Design, Timothy Hoover.

Site analysis

The first step after identifying where you want to plant your meadow is careful site analysis. What is the soil type? How much direct sunlight is available? How much moisture is retained in this particular soil? Is the site sloped or level? A north-facing slope might be treated differently than would be a south-facing slope.

The basic criterion for selecting plants is choosing native plants that are adapted to the specific area. Plants like Little bluestem, a beautiful blue tinged grass that turns red in winter, and butterfly weed, that has a vibrant orange flower and attracts monarch butterflies, are found in dry meadow situations. If you have poor, gravely or sandy soil, you may think it a difficult place to grow a meadow, however, if you select plants that are adapted to those particular conditions, they will perform well.

This site analysis checklist will help you evaluate your meadow location. A site may contain more than one condition or soil type.

HOW TO DETERMINE SOIL TYPE

There are three basic soil types: sandy, loamy and clay.

Sandy soils are lighter and have particles big enough to see with the naked eye. These are poor soils, low in organic matter, and thus low in fertility. Water moves quickly through the soil taking with it nutrients and leaving persistently dry conditions. Sandy soils feel grainy and course to the touch.

Loamy soils are of medium texture, easy to work with, and with good organic matter (average garden soil). The organic matter helps retain moisture and provides good drainage. The soil particles vary in size between sand and clay soils and are slightly rough.

Clay soils have very fine particles packed tightly together. This limits drainage and causes the soil to be heavy and difficult to work with. If in doubt, take damp soil and roll between the palms of your hands. Clay soils will form a smooth rope.

Many meadow and prairie flowers are adapted to clay conditions and have deep tap roots that break up the clay, aerating the soil so water can slowly permeate. *Silphium laciniatum* (Compass plant), *Dalea purpurea*

Dalea purpurea (Purple prairie clover) vigorously blooming in late July. The plants long tap root delivers moisture in this clay soil prairie condition.

Site analysis checklist

✓ Draw a diagram of the meadow area, note where north is to help determine the path of the sun over the area. As you examine the site make sure to mark areas that differ in soil, light or water conditions.

✓ Take a soil sample. If you have noted different soil types and conditions, make sure to do a separate sample of that area. The soil test evaluates soil pH (how acid or alkaline is the soil), buffer pH (value used to determine how much lime or sulfur should be added to bring soil to desired pH), soil nutrients and minerals and the organic matter content.

✓ Determine soil type, texture and structure—clay, sandy or gravely, silt, loam.

✓ Moisture level:
• low spot where water drains
• high water table
• poorly drained soil

✓ Make note of sun and shade conditions. Is there at least a half-day of sunlight?

✓ Topography—Flat? Hills or slopes? And which direction do they face?

✓ Is the site in its native state or has mulching, or removal or addition of topsoil altered it?

✓ Does the site have periods of water inundation or natural standing water areas/wetlands?

(Purple prairie clover) and *Baptisia australis* (Blue false indigo) are just a few that possess these remarkable, deep tap roots. Grasses like *Andropogon gerardii* (Big bluestem), *Sorghastrum nutans* (Indiangrass), and *Elymus canadensis* (Canada wild rye) are also great clay busters!

SOIL TESTING

To achieve a healthy, green lawn the soil must have the proper balance of minerals, nutrients, organic matter and soil organisms. Soil testing is particularly important so unnecessary nutrients are not used. Unfortunately, relatively few lawns are ever tested and excessive nutrients are indiscriminately applied, directly affecting soil health and ground water.

Meadows are the exact opposite. They do not rely on inputs to thrive. Meadow plants flourish because they are adapted to the soil conditions in which they are growing. A soil test is useful in determining the percentage of organic matte, soil pH and buffer pH. If the site has rich soil (soil high in organic matter, high fertility) you can expect an increase in pressure from weeds. Therefore, you should choose more competitive meadow plants such as *Monarda fistulosa* (Wild bergamot), *Pycnanthemum virginianum (*Virginia mountain mint), *Heliopsis helianthoides* (Ox eye false sunflower) and *Sorghastrum nutans* (Indian grass). An alternative tactic would be to lower the pH by adding the recommended amount of sulfur to the soil. Nutrients are less available in soils with low pH. Meadow plants grow just fine in those soil conditions and will out-compete the weeds.

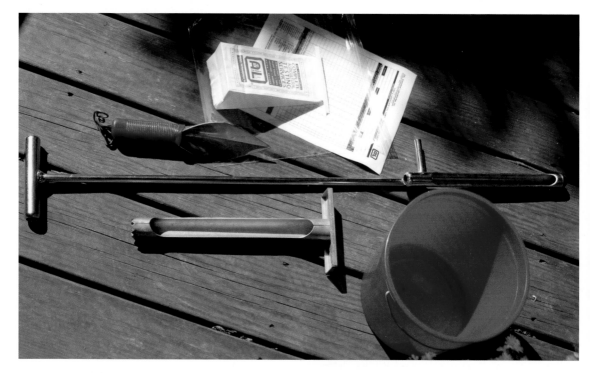

Tools:

- Soil auger, spade or shovel, soil sampling tube. Augers or tubes should be stainless steel.
- Clean sampling equipment and containers.
- Clear plastic zip top bag or sample bag provided by lab.
- Screwdriver to help push soil out of auger.

Step 1 Use appropriate tool for soil condition.

Step 2 Scrape away any plant material before taking sample.

Step 3 Take from 10-20 sub-samples. Dig each to a 6" depth.

If you have noted different soil types and conditions be sure to do a separate sampling of that area.

Step 4 Mix together the sub-samples to form sample for lab. The sample size should be 1 to 1½ cups of soil. Bigger soil samples may be needed if determining soil type. Check with the lab on amount of soil needed.

Do not mix sub-samples from different soil conditions. For example wet/dry or sun/shade.

Step 5 Indicate on sample form type of "crop" to be grown. For example: meadow plants/warm season grasses. You may have to write this in under other crop. If in doubt, just call the lab.

Step 6 Send to a government or professional lab for analysis. Based on the crop indicated, the lab will give recommendations for amendments or pH adjustments. (See resource section for list of soil testing labs).

TIP
When sampling compacted or frozen soils, a soil auger works best.

Plant communities—right plant, right place

Plants do not grow individually in nature. Generally, they grow in association with other specific species based on habitat. This is known as a plant guild or plant community. These plants have evolved for thousands of years together. There are plant interactions taking place that even the most brilliant ecologists don't understand.

Take a walk in a naturally occurring meadow. There are specific plants growing under different circumstances. You can see *Solidago speciosa* (Showy goldenrod), likes to grow with *Aster laevis* (Smooth aster) and *Schizachyrium scoparium* (Little bluestem) in dry meadow conditions. In wet conditions, you'll find certain species like *Asclepias incarnata* (Swamp milkweed), *Liatris spicata* (Gayfeather) and *Carex vulpinoidea* (Fox sedge). Not only do they thrive because they are in a site that they like, but also, over the millennium, they have learned to compliment each other and share resources. One plant might have a very deep root system, another a shallow root system and yet another companion likes their roots shaded. When all these plants are together and are interacting in a positive manner, the meadow tends to

Dry soil, low fertility *Solidago speciosa* (Showy goldenrod) *Aster novae-angliae* (New England aster) and *Schizachyrium scoparium* (Little bluestem).

work better on it's own. It is not a coincidence when you look out over a natural meadow that there are very few weeds. The native plant communities, growing in the meadow, are so well adapted to the site that they grow quickly, dominating the site and preventing the weeds from growing.

We can take our cues from natural meadow plant guilds and, based on our site conditions, replicate those plant communities in our own meadow designs.

Wet soils retain moisture. *Liatris spicata* (Dense blazingstar), *Lobelia cardinalis* (Cardinal flower), *Iris virginica* var. *shrevei* (Wild iris).

Mesic/Medium, average garden soil, *Heliopsis helianthoides* (False sunflower), *Eryngium yuccifolium* (Rattlesnake master), *Parthenium integrifolium* (Wild quinine).

Process of change

A meadow is an unfolding scenario that changes not only over the season but also over time.

In the early stages of a naturally occurring meadow, you see plants that germinate and flower quickly, dominating. If you come back in the third year those plants will be gone and instead you will see a completely different composition of plants. When you come back in the fifth year, the composition will have changed once again.

If the meadow is composed of only early stage plants—short-term species, mostly annuals, biennials and short-lived perennials—it will fade out in a year or two. If the meadow has only the long-term species, there will be nothing of significance to provide competition and weeds will invade. Once you understand this process, you realize

the importance of including short and long-term plant seed in your seed mix. By doing so, your meadow planting will unfold similar to a meadow unfolding in nature.

In analyzing the success of your meadow in its early stages, look beyond simply the big plants you see flowering. Take a look underneath them at the new growth that will follow the early stage plants. You should find the emerging, long-term species, and their presence tells you if the meadow is on the way to becoming a dense meadow composition

Not only do the plants themselves change over time in a meadow, but the general aesthetic feel of it evolves as well. What you'll find

Misty, morning view at Neil Dibolls' Wisconsin home. Neil Diboll, Prairie Nursery, Inc.

First year meadow, Maryland. Kara Bowne-Crissey, Good Earth Gardeners.

flowering in an early stage meadow will be plants like: Partridge pea, Black-eyed Susan and Dotted mint. There may be a lot of nice flowers, but the meadow will have a bit of a rough and tumble appearance.

By the fourth or fifth year, the longer-lived plants will have settled into a very graceful equilibrium. You may see five different plants in one square foot, yet it doesn't look overgrown. It doesn't look unkempt because these plants have evolved together to a point where they have complimentary growth habits, making the whole composition very elegant.

Parthenium integrifolium (Wild quinine), *Echinacea purpurea* (Purple coneflower), *Heliopsis helianthoides* (False sunflower), *Rudbeckia subtomentosa* (Black-eyed Susan), *Ratibida pinnata* (Yellow coneflower) naturally intermingle in ten year old Connecticut meadow. Larry Weaner, Larry Weaner Landscape Design Associates.

Ian Caton

Not only is the meadow changing over a period of years, but it's different in every season. One of the really interesting things about meadows is they tend to be very strong late in the season, when most gardens have finished blooming. The Asters, the Goldenrods, Pink turtlehead, are all plants that begin blooming in September and continue to bloom well into October. Grasses are some of the most beautiful and graceful

The André Bluemel Meadow over the seasons at River Farm, the American Horticultural Society headquarters. Design Kurt Bluemel, Kurt Bluemel, Inc.

aspects of any meadow. Not only do they bloom in summer, but during fall, the seed heads become prominent and the leaves often turn a bronze-red color that lasts, along with the dry seed heads, throughout the entire winter. Meadows are vibrant habitats, evolving over the course of several years and changing throughout the calendar year, providing a beautiful, four-season spectacle.

Design aesthetics

Armed with your site analysis and new understanding of the inner workings of meadows, you're ready to choose plants and consider design aesthetics. Consult a plant list appropriate to the soil, moisture and light conditions of the site.

PLANT FORM

When designing a meadow habitat, it's not only important to select which plants you are going to use, but in what form you are going to plant them. By form I mean seed, plugs or potted plants. Plugs are actually very small plants that you can buy in trays. You can also buy plants similar to what you would buy in a garden center and plant them in the meadow.

You might want to plant plugs and mature plants in a meadow habitat because doing so will decrease the time it takes for that meadow to develop when compared to planting seed. You also have the ability to design it more. When you plant a seed mix over an area, you are not in control of which plants will germinate where. However, by planting drifts of plugs, you are able to add a personal design element. You can arrange plants in a manner that makes it look more like an intentional garden and less like something that happened on it's own.

David Hughes

Planting foreman Chris May uses a gas-powered auger/drill to install front entrance meadow plants. This site has two distinct light conditions, sunny and dry to the left of the walk and dry shade to the right. Fringetree Design Studios, LLC.

Ian Caton

Larry Weaner hand broadcasts seed in small Connecticut meadow. Larry Weaner, Larry Weaner Landscape Design Associates.

Designed meadow garden from live transplants includes 20 species of forbs, grasses and sedges all native to North Carolina. In the foreground *Liatris spicata* (Dense blazingstar), *Coreopsis major* (Greater tickseed) *Parthenium integrifolium* (Wild quinine). Snow Creek Landscaping, LLC.

Drifts of *Heliopsis helianthoides* (Ox eye sunflower), *Schizachyrium scoparium* (Little bluestem) and *Pycnanthemum virginianum*, (Virginia mountain mint) planted from seed. Larry Weaner, Larry Weaner Landscape Design Associates.

SENSE OF PLACE

Meadows have gotten a bad reputation. They are often considered messy and unsuitable, particularly in a small urban settings. If you plan to put your meadow in the front yard, consider smaller stature meadow plants and mow a border to make it look more appropriate in connection to the other landscapes nearby. You may want Joe Pye weed, an eight-foot tall plant with huge pink flowers that attracts butterflies. You might just plant a few of these taller plants strategically located from a design standpoint. It gives you the tall plant with beautiful flowers, but doesn't give you a meadow dominated by 8' plants.

The mowed border allows tall plants like *Eupatorium maculatum* (Joe Pye weed), *Vernonia noveboracensis* (Ironweed) and *Heliopsis helianthoides* (Ox eye sunflower) to gracefully flank, without overwhelming, the driveway entrance of this New England home. Michael Nadeau, Plantscapes, Inc.

Michael Nadeau

Bart Johnson

Low profile front yard prairie. All species are native to the Oregon's Willamette Valley upland prairie ecosystem. Design, Bart Johnson and Aryana Ferguson.

North Carolina planting forms a meadow habitat border between properties. Snow Creek Landscaping, LLC.

COLOR

Begin working with colors you like and color combinations. Think about bloom sequence; make sure there is always something blooming throughout the season. Again, grasses are particularly beautiful, changing color as the season progresses.

Penstemon digitalis 'Husker Red' (Beard tongue). Consider foliage color as part of the color palette. Gardens of the Three Graces.

left: Blue inflorescences of *Baptisia australis* (False indigo) provide a complimentary backdrop for blush red and yellow *Aquilegia canadensis* (Wild red columbine).

below: June Virginia meadow awash in fuchsia, lilac and gold color. Jeff Wolinski, Ecologist.

Larry Weaner

Schizachyrium scoparium (Little bluestem) bends with the wind in Connecticut meadow. Larry Weaner, Larry Weaner Landscape Design Associates.

Spiky seed head of *Bidens frondosa* (Devils beggarticks) in foggy December meadow.

Horizontally layered flowering spikes of *Solidago rugosa* "Fireworks" (Fireworks goldenrod).

GROWTH FORMS

Some plants have very interesting architecture in their growth forms. It's important not to forget the non-flowering aesthetic aspects of a meadow such as swaying grasses in the breeze.

above: Afternoon breeze ruffles inflorescences of *Elymus canadensis* (Canada wild rye) and *Ratibida pinnata* (Yellow cone flower).

top right: Unique flower heads of *Eryngium yuccifolium* (Rattlesnake master) take center stage in twilit Illinois prairie.

bottom right: *Silphium laciniatum* (Compass plants) tower like watchful sentries over prairie landscape.

PATHS

Consider having paths mown or constructed through your meadow so that you may stand inside of it and better appreciate the intricacies of the foliage combinations, flowers and all of the insects and birds feeding and inhabiting the meadow's interior.

Matching these different aesthetic elements with the meadow or prairie ecology is what makes a successful, thriving meadow or prairie habitat.

opposite page top: Graceful, curving path beckons exploration of Wisconsin prairie. Michael Healy, BioLogic Environmental Consulting.

below: Mulched path divides tall meadow from short stature meadow plants. Snow Creek Landscaping, LLC.

Gravel path encircles prairie wetland. Fitchberg Center, Wisconsin.

Upright, bright, bluish-purple flowers of *Agastache foeniculum* (Anise hyssop), airy *Heliopsis helianthoides* (Ox eye sunflower) and billowing *Panicum virgatum* (Switchgrass) provide visual texture and movement along meadow path in Yellow Springs, Ohio.

Meadow grasses

Grasses are a vital component to the whole meadow community. In addition to their esthetic characters of color, texture and movement, grasses offer quite a few other functions.

- Deep root systems of some grasses help prevent erosion.
- Grasses allow for drought survival because their roots systems can be as much as ten feet deep.

- Grasses act as support for taller meadow flowers.
- Grasses act as a very important food source and provide nesting material and habitat for wildlife.

Grasses are very competitive plants and keep the weeds out. Grasses should make up at least 40% of the mix in order to get the weed inhibitive function successfully established.

Lavendar, greens, golden browns and reds of *Schizachyrium scoparium* (Little bluestem) and *Andropogon gerardii* (Big bluestem) in a September meadow. Neil Diboll, Prairie Nursery, Inc.

above: During winter months, grasses provide habitat, food and cover for small mammals, birds and insects. Fringetree Design Studios, LLC.

left: *Chasmanthium latifolium* (River oats) grows by pond in suburban New York state meadow. Larry Weaner, Larry Weaner Design Associates.

TIP

Beware *Panicum virgatum* (Switch grass). It is very aggressive and may push out other meadow plants, forming a monoculture. Use a less competitive cultivar.

The height of grasses and flowers are an important consideration in your design. Low profile grasses such as meadow and prairie mainstays, *Schizachyrium scoparium* (Little bluestem), *Sporobolus heterolepsis* (Prairie dropseed), and *Bouteloua curtipendula* (Sideoats grama) are good choices when designing around your home or an entryway. These clump forming, shorter grasses do not obscure the flower blossoms or corner the market on resources below ground as taller, more aggressively-spreading grasses will.

This is not to say that you should eliminate tall grasses from your meadow plan. Well placed tall grasses can be useful as focal points. This Judith Phillips meadow design layers shorter grasses and wild flowers throughout the front with the taller *Andropogon gerardii* (Big bluestem) located toward the back.

In an urban setting, taller grasses may be best planted with taller meadow flowers in side or back yards. In this backyard meadow design (right photo), seven-foot tall *Panicum virgatum*, 'Cloud Nine' (Switchgrass) has room to spread its feathery, panicle umbrella over *Solidago speciosa* (Showy goldenrod).

Grasses extend the prairie meadow beauty and appeal well beyond the flower-blooming period. Their graceful foliage brings texture and movement to a meadow or prairie while buff, amber, and red hues brighten the winter landscape.

New Mexico front yard meadow. Judith Phillips' Design Oasis.

Ohio backyard prairie in September. Gardens of the Three Graces.

Ian Caton

Dried inflorescences of *Andropogon virginicus* (Broom sedge) and *Tridens flavus* (Purple top) sparkle in morning sunlight of a snowy winter meadow. Larry Weaner, Larry Weaner Design Associates.

LIVE PLANTS

Use live plants in smaller areas in a garden setting that is 50 to 1000 square feet. Plant plugs or larger container plants.

Benefits

- Control design—can locate plants exactly where you want them.
- Faster results—many plants bloom in 1st season but not all. Some slower growing species may require two or three years to mature.
- Plants establish quickly.
- Will require less maintenance than a traditional garden because an established prairie meadow garden does not require watering, fertilizing or pesticide applications.
- Can tell which plants are weeds in the garden and control any problems right away. In a seeded meadow, problem weeds can become established before you can identify them and will require more effort to eradicate.

Considerations

- More expensive than seeding a meadow.
- More labor-must plant each plant individually.
- Must mulch to control weeds until plants fill in.

TIP

As with seeded meadows and prairies, planting times are subject to adjustment for different climates, ecoregions and the ability to water. Make sure plants get proper watering in the first year.

LIVE PLANT PLANTING GUIDELINES

Plugs

- Optimum plug planting in spring: April 1st through May 30th.
- Plant plugs in early fall September 1st through September 20th. Later planting may not give plants enough time to establish root before winter and they may heave out of the ground during freeze-thaw cycles.

Container plants

Container plants have a more established root system and there is more latitude in planting timing. Plant April through early July and again in late August through September.

opposite page: Using container plants brings immediate results but at a considerably higher cost than a seeded meadow or prairie.

right: *Lupinus texensis* (Texas bluebonnet) and *Castilleja indivisa* (Texas paintbrush) bloom in March while many meadows in the north slumber under a blanket of snow. Lady Bird Johnson Wild Flower Center, Austin, Texas.

below: Urban meadow awaits spring thaw in Hastings-on-Hudson, NY. Larry Weaner, Larry Weaner Landscape Design Associates.

Saxon Holt

Clark Montgomery

Hand seeding

Best for small areas or sites where it would be difficult to use a tractor.
General Seeding Rate: ¼ lb *Pure Live Seed* (PLS) per 1,000 square feet. Most seed mixes come with a suggested seeding rate.

Tools
Large tub or bushel basket
2 Five gallon buckets
Rake
Big metal roller filled with water

Materials
Native flower and grass seed mix
    (¼ lb/1,000 sq. ft)
Inert material (For every ¼ lb of meadow/
    prairie seed mix use 2 bushels of inert
    material. A bushel is equal to 8 gallons.)
    • Saw dust
    • Peat moss
    • Vermiculite
    • Perlite
    • Kitty litter
    • Other similar material
Straw mulch

Step 1 Start with clear site—make sure all vegetation is killed off.

Step 2 Lightly rake soil, or till lightly and rake level if soil is not loose.

Step 3 Choose seed mix based on site analysis and design considerations. Make sure your meadow/prairie seed mix is regionally adapted to your climate, soil and light conditions.

Step 4 In a large tub, mix seed with an inert, slightly damp material. Mix thoroughly.

Step 5 Divide mixture into two equal parts, and then use a five gallon pail to carry it onto the area to be seeded.

TIP
Beware seed mixes sold in garden centers. Many contain non-native plants often with a high portion of annuals and biennials and few grasses. There are a number of mail order nurseries that specialize in this area. You can find a list in the resource section of this book.

Neil Diboll demonstrates hand seeding.

Step 6 Take ½ the mixture and broadcast over planting area.

Step 7 Take the rest of the mixture and broadcast over entire area going in the opposite direction you went the 1st time.

Step 8 Rake lightly. Native wildflower seeds are very small and will not germinate if placed too deeply in the soil. Seeds should be planted an average 2-3 times as deep as their diameter.

TIP

Sun Requirements: Meadows and prairies require at least one half day of sun. This is difficult to translate into hours per day, because it varies by the season, and from latitude to latitude.

Step 9 Take a heavy metal roller filled with water and roll to firm the seeds into the soil.

Step 10 Cover with straw mulch 1 to 1½ inch thick. This will hold the moisture in the soil and encourage germination. This is especially important if the site cannot be watered.

Step 11 Watering—Water every morning for 10-15 minutes or until the soil is damp. If water begins to run off, stop watering. If the soil is moist in the morning, no need to water that day.

TIP

Do not use large bark chips as mulch. Bark chips are heavy and do not allow the emergence of small seedlings. Some bark chips also seem to have compounds in them that inhibit the growth of prairie plants, and can also deplete the soil of nitrogen.

BRILLION

Broadcast seeder spreads seeds on worked up soil surface, packing wheels then firm seed into the soil.

Benefits

- Heavy cast iron packing wheels provide superior seed to soil contact on loose soils.
- One of the more precise of the broadcast type seeders for metering seed.
- Good seed placement in the soil.
- Can be used as a "no-till" seeder is when planting in the fall onto loose, open sandy soil. The Brillion will push the seed into the loose soil and during the winter freeze cycle, seed will work further down into the soil.

Considerations

- Typically requires soil tillage.
- Tilling process brings up weeds from the lower soil causing higher weed densities.
- Grass box seeding rate setting mechanism is more primitive and more subject to error than the Truax. Both the Brillion and Truax forb (flower) metering is precise.

Step 1 Start with clear site- make sure all vegetation is killed off.

Step 2 Choose seed mix based on site analysis and design considerations.

Step 3 Load the seed boxes. Truax no till drills can be purchased with either two or three seed boxes. One is for fluffy grasses, one is for small forbs and small round grass seeds, and the third is for a nurse crop such as annual oats or annual rye. The Brillion seeder is available with either one or two boxes. The single box models seed only grass, so the seed needs to be mixed with a dilutant to ensure that the small seeds do not settle out into the bottom of the box and fall through during the first few passes across the field. With the double box Brillion, the fluffy grass seeds are placed in the larger grass box, along with large forb seeds such as members of the genus *Silphium*. Small, round grass seeds, such as Switchgrass and Prairie dropseed are placed in the small forb box with the other forb seeds.

Step 4 Calibrate seeding rate on seeder.

Step 5 Seed the meadow, constantly monitoring the rate of seed flow to ensure that the seeder is not set too high so that the seed runs out before the field is covered.

Step 6 If possible, water until established.

> ### TIP
>
> When seeding a meadow or prairie, use a nurse crop such as annual oats (*Avena sativa*) for spring seeding or winter wheat (*Triticum aestivum*) when seeding in the fall. A nurse crop is an annual crop used to assist in the establishment of the meadow. Nurse crops hold the seeds in place, protect the soil from weather, prevent erosion and shelter tender meadow seedlings.

Planting a meadow or prairie with plugs

Tools

Trowel
- Works in all soil types including, rocky soil.
- If planting more than 50 plants may become tiresome.

Dibble
- Good for planting small plugs.
- Use in loose soils like sandy, sandy loam and loamy soils.
- Do not use in heavy clay. Dibble will compact planting hole sides *and prevent root growth.*

Soil auger
- Attach to electric drill.
- Plant many plugs: quick, easy, fast.

- Use appropriate sized auger to leave enough space around plug for packing with soil. For example, for a 1½" plug use 2½" auger.
- Rocky soil may pose problem. Rocks lodge in auger. Auger can get bent and may hurt the drill.
- Difficult to use in clay soil that is very dry or wet and gummy. Make sure soil is drained but not dried out.

Bulb planter
- Use if you don't have access to a drill and auger.
- Use appropriate size, slightly larger than plug.

Materials

Native meadow plugs—buy in flats

Mulch—helps weeds from germinating and holds moisture in soil

Winter wheat straw

Leaf mulch

Shredded bark

TIP

Plugs and small container plants have shallow root systems and need to be watered more often than quart or gallon containers.

Step 1 Start with clear site—make sure all vegetation is killed off.

Step 2 Choose plug plant based on site analysis and design considerations.

Step 3 Choose appropriate planting tool based on number of plugs to be established, soil type and soil conditions.

Step 4 Dig planting hole to plug depth (2-4") and slightly larger than plug in width.

Step 5 Place plug in hole, pack soil around roots firmly, making sure there are no air pockets around the plant. Cover the top of the plant soil media with ½ inch of native soil to prevent wicking of moisture out from artificial soil materials in the soil media the plug came in. Do not cover crown of plant. The crown is the part of a plant just above and below the ground from which the roots and shoots branch out.

Step 6 Cover with a couple of inches of mulch up to where the plug just comes out of the ground.

Step 7 Water thoroughly so water saturates down into soil.

Step 8 Watering—Water plugs thoroughly once every few days after planting. Occasional deep watering is better than daily shallow watering. Be careful not to overwater, especially on clay soils that retain lots of moisture. If plant shows signs of wilting, water immediately.

Prairie planting on infertile construction soil one year after planting plugs.

Planting a meadow or prairie with container plants

Tools
Shovel for large container plants, quart, gallon, etc.
Small spade or trowel for small container plants
Knife or pruning clippers
Wheelbarrow

Materials
Winter wheat straw
Shredded bark mulch
Leaf mulch

TIP

Often larger container plants may become root bound. The roots begin to grow around the inside walls of the container. This happens when the plant has been in the container for a long time. Take a knife or pruning clippers and score or cut the roots about a ½ inch into the root mass all around the pot. This helps to break up the mass and allow the plant to grow properly in the ground. This will not hurt the plant.

Step 1 Start with clear site—make sure all vegetation is killed off.

Step 2 Choose plant based on site analysis and design considerations.

Step 3 Using a shovel or for a small container plant, a trowel, dig the planting hole to just below the depth of the plant crown and twice the diameter of the plant container. The crown is the part of a plant just above and below the ground from which the roots and shoots branch out.

Step 4 Remove plant from container and place in planting hole.

Step 5 Firmly pack the soil around the plant to get rid of air holes that will dry out the plant roots.

Step 6 Mulch around the plant. Keep mulch at least an inch from plant crown.

Step 7 Water plant thoroughly until soil is saturated.

Step 8 Water larger (1 gallon) container plants thoroughly, about once a week. If weather is hot, dry and windy, more frequent watering may be necessary. Smaller container plants will require watering every two to three days if it does not rain, more frequently under drought conditions. Water regularly, for the first month or so, until the plants are well established.

Physostegia virginiana (Obedient plant).

Storm water is successfully captured and filtered this by prairie swale at the commercial retail and residential development, Fitchberg Center, Inc. in Fitchberg, Wisconsin. Controlled burns maintain the site. Prairie swale concept, Landscape Architect John Harrington. Prairie plant installation, Prairie Nursery, Westfield, Wisconsin.

maintaining a meadow or prairie

One of the most valuable benefits of planting a meadow or prairie instead of a lawn is maintenance.

In nature, meadows are maintained, born and/or rejuvenated by naturally occurring disasters, such as lightning strikes. Natural meadows are merely a transition in the landscape from bare earth to old growth forests. Left alone, woody growth and trees take over and a meadow becomes a forest. Planted meadows share this progression. They are low maintenance landscapes, but not no-maintenance landscapes. Timely meadow management is required. But how do we know when to time that management?

Plants are generally divided in temperate regions into cool season and warm season plants. Most prairie flowers and grasses are warm season plants, meaning they grow well with warmer temperatures between 75 and 90 degrees, and sometimes over 100 degrees. Most cool season plants grow better when temperatures are around 50 to 60 degrees or in the low 70's.

Some of our biggest problem weeds in meadows are cool season, non-native plants, such as quack grass, Kentucky Blue grass, smooth broom grass and in some cases, the fescues. They emerge earlier in the spring than do meadow and prairie flowers and grasses because they germinate and thrive in the cooler temperatures. This gives us a great opportunity to manage against them and manage for, or in favor of the warm season prairie plants. By using well-timed

annual mowing or biennial burning, we will do maximum harm to the unwanted, cool season plants and provide maximum advantage to the desirable, warm season, native meadow and prairie plants. Generally speaking, when the buds of the sugar maple are opening, which can vary up to four weeks in any given year, this is the best time to mow or burn a meadow or prairie to achieve optimal results.

One exception is if the meadow has a high proportion of early, spring-blooming flowers or a lot of desirable, cool season grasses. In this case, the best time to burn or mow is either in the fall after everything has gone dormant, usually sometime in November or in relatively early spring before the flowers appear from the ground. Otherwise, early blooming flowers will be damaged and the effect of your meadow will be lost for that year.

When established, meadow management for a seeded meadow or a meadow planted with live plants is the same—annual mowing every spring right down to the ground. Leave the shredded cuttings to provide soil organic matter or rake off the cuttings to further expose the soil and warm it up even faster. Or burn every other year. Burning biennially is sufficient to prevent woody plants and invasive plants from getting a toehold in the meadow. Biennial burning also maintains the optimal balance between the flowers and the grasses within the meadow. Management of your meadow is by far cheaper and less time consuming than lawn management. Weekly mowing, trimming and watering are replaced with meadow or prairie watching.

Maintenance for a seeded meadow or prairie

A seeded meadow requires more mowing maintenance to control weeds in the first two years than a meadow planted with live plants. After the seeded meadow is established the maintenance is the same, once a year mowing or if possible, biennial burning.

Tools

- String trimmers (weed-whackers, either gas or electric) for areas of ½ acre or less. Will take 2 hours for ¼ acre.

- Walk behind mower—will have to spend more time chopping up tall meadow plants.

- Tractor mounted mowers for areas of ½ acre or more.

- The best mower to use is a flail type mower, as it shreds the cut material and deposits it gently on top of the vegetation where it can dry out.

- Rotary mowers, including bush hogs, tend to accumulate the cut material on the housing, often dropping large clumps on the ground where they can bury the seedlings.

- Most people have rotary type mowers, and these will usually work fine when cutting only modest amounts of weeds. When the weeds are dense and tall, that's when you get clumping of large quantities of cut material.

- Hand scythe on small areas of a few thousand square feet. It's a lot of work to use on large areas. Expect to spend over 2 hours for ¼ acre.

TIP

Wait until the 2nd season when seedlings have established root systems to hand remove or dig out weeds. Otherwise, delicate seedlings may be pulled out, damaged or killed.

Fresh meadow emerging.

annual weeds

6" meadow seedlings

6" maintenance mowing

1st growing season

- Perennial meadow plants grow slowly and only get 2"-6" tall.
- Annual weeds predominate, grow more quickly.
- Prevent weeds from getting higher than 12-16" tall.
- Mow 3-4 times. Keep mowed to 6".

TIP

It's not a good idea to install live plants at the same time you put in your meadow seed because the management program for the 1st year is to keep it mowed back to 6". Transplants will grow higher than 6" and either be cut off during that management process or you'll have to mow around all of your individual transplants or live plants. If you want to add plants that are perhaps not available by seed or more difficult to establish from seed, you can wait until the spring of the 2nd growing season when you are going to be mowing at closer to 12" or you can wait until the spring of the 3rd season and install them because at that point the mowing management will be completed.

annual weeds

12" meadow seedlings

15" maintenance mowing

2nd growing season

- Perennial meadow plants getting taller.
- Now have biennial weeds and annual weeds.
- Keep weeds to 12". Start mowing in late May, early June. Mow 2-3 times over the season.
- Very important to prevent formation of weed seeds by biennials which can reseed into the meadow and become a long-term problem.

3rd growing season

- Most annual and biennial weeds under control.
- Change management practices to spring mowing or burning.
- No mid season mowing.

Maintenance for a container planted meadow or prairie

Maintenance on a meadow or prairie garden installed with live plants is a little bit different than a seeded planting because it's a more controlled environment.

School meadow designed by Peggy Bowers, Horticulturist.

Tools

String trimmers (weed-whackers, either gas or electric)

Small hand tools—can be used in small meadow gardens but tends to be labor intensive, especially cutting back well, established grasses.

Wheelbarrow

Rake

Shovel

Trowel (for hand weeding)

Materials

Mulch

> **TIP**
>
> **String trimmers are good because it's easy to control the height of your mowing. They can be used on uneven ground, slopes and wet areas.**

Installation

- Mulch around transplants to prevent weeds from developing.

1st and 2nd Season

- In early spring, before new growth appears, cut previous seasons plants to the ground.
- Mulch around new growth to prevent weeds.
- Throughout the season gently pull or dig problem weeds. Make sure to firm any soil disturbed around meadow plants.

3rd Season

- Cut old growth to the ground.
- Perennials should be completely filled in and their roots and above ground shoots and leaves will prevent most weeds from invading.
- Continue to watch out for any stray weeds and remove before seed heads develop.

Guidelines for burning a meadow or prairie

Prairies evolved over time under the influence of regular fires caused either by lightning strikes or intentionally set by Native Americans as a land management tool to maintain high quality hunting grounds. Controlled burning is the best method for maintaining a healthy meadow or prairie.

Don Sweeney

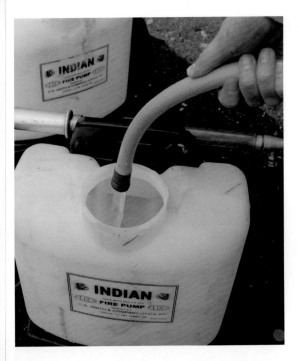

Tools

Mower (to mow fire breaks around and within meadow).

Matches, lighter or propane torch (small areas under an acre).

Drip torch (large areas over half an acre).

Flapper (rubber treated webbing, attached to 5' handle). If you do not have access to a flapper use a large, flat bottom scoop shovel. Both tools are used to smother flames in small blaze situations.

Firm tine garden rakes used to distribute fire along fire line when doing small burns.

TIP

Very Important: Never wear clothing made of nylon, polyesters, plastics or other synthetic fibers. These materials melt at low temperatures and can fuse to the skin when exposed to fire.

Water: For small burns, use garden hoses and or back pack style fire pump for areas where hoses will not reach. For large burns, use 250 gallon water tank with small engine powered pump to provide pressure to water hoses. The tank and pump can be mounted on a truck bed or three point hitch of a tractor.

Backpack style fire pump (used when pressurized water is unavailable).

Two way radios (allow for communication with crew members on larger burns).

Protective Gear

Fire resistant Nomex fabric or non-flammable heavy cotton clothing with loose fitting long sleeve shirts and long pants. Pants should cover shoe tops to prevent embers from getting into boots.

Heavy duty, high top, leather boots-no steel toes. Steel toes can get really hot.

Heavy leather gloves that cover wrists and forearms.

Cotton undergarments and either cotton or wool socks.

Face protection, goggles or visor.

Fire resistant hat or hard-hat if working under trees.

Step 1 Determine optimum time to burn depending on management goals.

- Most cool season weeds and grasses can be effectively controlled with a mid spring burn. Burning when the buds of the sugar maple (Acer saccharum) are just breaking open will do minimal damage to warm season meadow flowers and grasses, while significantly setting back undesirable cool season plants.

- Early spring blooming meadow plants are often damaged in mid-late spring burning. These meadows are best burned in fall after vegetation has gone dormant.

- To achieve maximum control of invasive woody plants burn as late in spring as possible after woody plants have leafed out. Mowing the standing dead plant material just prior to the burn places fire fuel closer to the ground. The fire will burn hotter and longer under these circumstances and do proportionately more damage to woody vegetation. The later you wait in spring to burn the less flammable the meadow will become. This is due to the increased ratio of green plant growth to flammable dead vegetation from the previous year. Beware of late spring burns; they tend to produce heavier smoke due to the higher percentage of new green plant growth.

Step 2 Develop a burn plan. Consider: area to be burned, number of burn crew members needed, weather, wind direction, tools, firebreaks, water sources, and fuel load. The fuel load is the quantity, and structure (plant height) of dead plant material. The higher the fuel load the hotter the fire will burn. The taller the plant height the higher the flames will reach.

Fairfax County Park Authority burn team reviews burn plan prior to large controlled burn.

Step 3 Get a burning permit from the appropriate agency.

Step 4 Establish firebreaks. A firebreak can be a pond, river, road, plowed field, closely mowed grass, burned area or anything else that stops a fire and contains it within a burn area. Good firebreaks are essential when burning next to areas with high fuel loads that may ignite due to errant embers or creeping fire. Firebreaks should be designed into the meadow planting during the landscape planning process to simplify burn preparation. If firebreaks will need to be mowed along the meadow edges or bordering grassy areas, mow them the previous fall for an upcoming spring burn. The mowed material will rot over the winter and become less flammable. If fall mowing is not possible, rake mowed material and

Path designed into meadow doubles as firebreak during controlled spring burn.

Retention pond and mowed firebreaks contain fire within prescribed burn area.

Mowing firebreak in Milton Hershey School Meadow.

duff from spring mowing well into area to be burned. This will remove any large quantities of flammable material from the firebreak and adjacent grassy edges.

Mow firebreaks down to ground level to remove flammable plant stubble that might allow the fire to carry across the firebreak. Mow the appropriate width firebreak to match meadow or prairie size and fuel load to be burned.

- For small burns of a half acre or less with a short grass prairie meadow and moderate fuel load, ten to fifteen feet firebreaks are usually sufficient.
- For larger, multi-acre burns especially in a tall grass meadow with high fuel loads, firebreaks thirty to forty feet may be necessary.

Safe Burning Tips

Burn when winds are 5 MPH or less. Burn in the evening when temperature is lower and humidity is higher. If burning in late spring with high levels of fresh, green plant growth the fire may not carry during the evening. It may be necessary to conduct the burn in mid to late afternoon to insure successful ignition.

Fires move more quickly uphill because flames preheat fuel making it burn more rapidly. Always burn down hill at least twenty to thirty feet to create a good backfire blackline. If the wind is blowing down hill, do not attempt to burn because this produces a headfire. Wait to burn until wind is blowing uphill against the fire.

Step 5 Notify local fire department and neighbors of proposed burn date and time. Some agencies require that you call again when the burn is complete so they know any fire calls afterward are valid.

Step 6 Weather is the most important factor in a controlled burn. The fire direction, speed, intensity, and smoke drift depend on wind direction and velocity, relative humidity and air temperature. Check weather conditions the day of the burn. If changes in wind direction or an increase of winds over five miles an hour are predicted, wait to proceed with burn until after wind shift has occurred and wind speed has dropped. Wind shifts during a burn can result in a dangerous situation that will require rapid tactical adjustments to the fire plan and may lead to a breach of firebreaks. The best decision you can make under unsettled weather conditions is to cancel the burn.

Step 7 Position water hoses so any out of control fire can be easily sprayed. In order to halt a fire with water, direct the stream of water in a sweeping motion at the base or point of advance of the fire. Use a backpack type pump sprayer if a water source is not available. The crew should have the

Don Sweeney

appropriate fire control equipment and be situated so the entire area can be monitored. When working in larger areas, use 2 way radios to stay in communications with other members of the team.

Step 8 Set a small test fire and observe smoke and wind direction. This gives the crew a chance to observe and correct potential problems before the actual burn.

Step 9 If sufficient water is available, soak down firebreaks thoroughly immediately before starting the burn. The backfire firebreak is the most critical because the wind is blowing against the fire creating the highest chance of embers and fire creeping into the firebreak.

Soaking firebreak before small controlled burn at Milton Hershey School.

Don Sweeney

Igniting backfire on large scale prescribed burn carried out by Fairfax County, Virginia Park Authority.

Step 10 Start by igniting the fire into the wind. This is known as a backfire. For example, if the wind is coming out of the south, start your backfire line along the north side firebreak in the NE corner. The fire will creep slowly at ground level against the wind. Extend the backfire line westward gradually, maintaining control at all times. Any smoldering embers at the edge of your firebreak can reignite and spread across the firebreak if left untended. Position a crewmember at the NE corner to monitor the fireline that will inevitably creep southward along the east side firebreak. If the east firebreak is nonflammable such as a pond, river, road, plowed field or closely mowed grass, the corner monitor is not necessary.

Don Sweeney

Monitoring fireline.

Black line established by backfire.

Complete the backfire line across the entire north side. Once the backfire has burned 20-40 feet southward into the meadow, this creates a black line (burned area). Since the fuel in the black line area has been consumed this extends your original firebreak. Flank fires on the east and/or west sides can now be started.

Flank fires burn parallel to the wind direction. Flank fires will burn more rapidly than a backfire. So extend them gradually making sure that the fire has burned well into the meadow and that your flank firebreaks are completely extinguished as you go. If you have only one burn team, start only one flank fire at a time. Retaining one team member as a monitor on the eastern firebreak, the fire crew can now extend the fireline southward

along the west firebreak. Once the west firebreak has been completely burned in, retain a monitor in the southwest corner. The fire starter crew member can proceed to the eastern firebreak to extend the eastern flank fireline southward to the SE corner. Once the back and flank fires have burned well into the meadow on three sides, the fire has little chance of "jumping" across the newly burned areas.

A headfire, burning with the wind, can now be gradually started on the south perimeter in either the SW or SE corner. Headfires move rapidly with the wind, have high flames and radiate a great deal of heat. If the headfire begins to spread into the south side firebreak, do not put yourself at risk by trying to extinguish the flames immediately. Allow the

Headfire burning intensely with the wind.

headfire and heat to travel away from the firebreak line before attacking the fire. It is critical to monitor wind speed and direction closely. Winds over five miles an hour may result in hard to control fires and may carry or blow embers across the firebreaks. Have water sources at the ready and immediately douse embers that land outside the prescribed burn area.

Step 11 The fire will burn itself out as it moves toward the center, consuming all the fuel. Do not leave the fire unattended. When all the vegetation has been burned down, wait for all live embers to burn out completely. Any burning logs, stumps, hollow trees and branches must be extinguished completely before leaving the site.

Sources:

Neil Diboll, Prairie Nursery, Inc. Westfield, Wisconsin

Minnesota Department of Natural Resources

Northern Prairie Wildlife Research Center

Fairfax County, Virginia Park Authority

1. Start backfire line in NE corner.
2. Gradually move backfire line along north side toward NW corner.
3. When backfire line is complete go back to NE corner and start 1st flank fire moving along the east side to SE corner.
4. Start 2nd flank fire in NW corner moving along west side to SW corner.
5. Start headfire in SE corner gradually moving west along south perimeter.

WIND DIRECTION COMING OUT OF SOUTHWEST

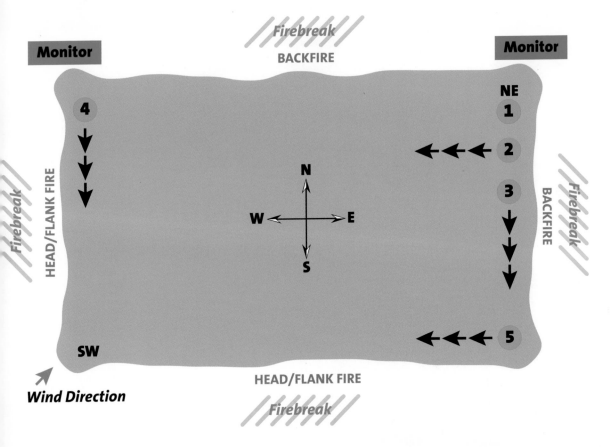

1. Start backfire line in NE corner.

2. Gradually move backfire line along north side toward NW corner.

3. When backfire line is complete go to NE corner and start another backfire moving along the east side to SE corner (it becomes a 2nd backfire because the wind is blowing out of the SW toward both N and E sides).

4. Start flank/headfire fire in NW corner moving along west side to SW corner.

5. Start flank/headfire in SE corner gradually moving west along south perimeter to complete the burn.

meadow and prairie plant lists

RIGHT PLANT, RIGHT PLACE

The site analysis gives us the ability to choose plants that are adapted to the meadow or prairie site and combine them with other plants that prefer the same condition and work well together. The native plant lists are organized according to three basic kinds of sites:

- Dry-good drainage, sand, gravel and rocky soils.
- Mesic/Medium (average garden soil)-well drained, loam, silt loam, sandy loam soils.
- Wet-poorly drained soils that retain subsoil moisture all summer long, clay soils.

The map is divided into nine geographic regions to help simplify the process of finding plants native to your area. However, there are numerous ecological communities in any given region or state that cross these man-made boundaries. Not surprisingly, there are many plants that do not fit these limitations. In some cases a plant may be found in one county yet is absent in the neighboring county. The lists are intended as a starting point. My primary sources for native status are the USDA Natural Resources Conservation Services Plants Database and the Ladybird Johnson Wildflower Center Native Plant Information Network. To compile the plant lists I used numerous books and web based native plant sources. An excellent native plant guide is *Armitage's Native Plants for North American Gardens*. Dr. Allan Armitage

provides in-depth descriptions of native perennials, biennials, and annuals including information on habitat, hardiness and appropriate site conditions. A comprehensive guide, which details native grasses and their cultural requirements, can be found in *The Encyclopedia of Grasses for Livable Landscapes* by Rick Darke. Refer to the regional resource section in this book to refine plant lists in your area. The regional resources provide local experts to help narrow your native plant selection and outlets for finding seed mixes and live plants that are native to your part of the country.

The plant lists contain only native species of wildflowers and grasses. Non-native species (aliens) and cultivars are not included in the lists. And why is that? We want to avoid using "alien" species, plants that have originated outside North America. Some wildflower seed mixes contain these non-native species. Aliens are often aggressive, crowding out native plants, which results in a decrease of biodiversity and habitat in the affected ecosystem. Also, our native insects rely on native plants as host plants and food sources.

Two examples that demonstrate how serious a problem alien species can become are Crown vetch (*Coronilla varia*) and Purple loosestrife (*Lythrum salicaria*). Crown vetch was introduced as an erosion control ground cover planted mostly along highways. This species forms dense mats of vegetation, which excludes all other plants, including

Vibrant meadow plants. Snow Creek Landscaping, LLC.

Spring blooming native plant *Baptisia australis* (Blue false indigo).

native species. It is difficult to control or eradicate Crown vetch and thus it has blanketed many natural areas across North America.

Purple loosestrife is a wetland perennial, native to Europe, introduced in the early 1800's. It is a beautiful plant but a prolific seeder that has escaped into waterways spreading from New England to the west coast. It threatens and destroys native wetland plants and endangers fish and other wildlife. The damage to wetlands is so severe that there is a national effort by state natural resource and environment agencies, universities and nursery trades associations to raise awareness of the threat posed by this invasive plant. Preventing further spread is a top priority and many states have prohibited or banned the sale and planting of Purple loosestrife.

One reason these plants run amuck in our ecosystems is a lack of natural enemies. Natural enemies would likely hold these same plants growing in their own native ecosystem in check. So consider the possible environmental hazards and steer clear of non-natives. Besides, there is a plethora of beautiful native plants to select from for your meadow or prairie planting!

Whether to choose cultivars should also be given thoughtful consideration. Cultivars are plants created or selected for specific characteristics such as early blooming or flower color. They are propagated by vegetative means or by cross breeding two plants to attain those traits. There are

TIP

The long-lived species, such as *Baptisia australis* (Blue false indigo) may take years to get to the flowering stage but could also live for one hundred years in the prairie.

numerous new cultivars of native plants being introduced into the nursery trade every year. So many, in fact, that finding a native plant at the local nursery can be a daunting task. Fortunately, the demand for native plants is on the rise and an increasing number of garden centers and mail order nurseries specialize in selling native plants and meadow seed mixes. If you decide to use a cultivar, inquire about the origin of the parent plant to determine if the species is native to your area.

Other important considerations when choosing cultivars of native plants:

- Insects respond to chemicals that are in plant leaves. If the cultivar leaf chemistry has changed from the native parent plant, that will affect whether insects feed on the plant.
- Pollinators respond to flower bloom time, color and shape. If the cultivar changed these traits or reduced the nectar load, it will matter to the pollinators.
- Is the cultivar sterile? A sterile plant provides no benefit to seed or nectar feeders. Double flower plants are always sterile.
- Cultivars are bred and raised under garden conditions and are not necessarily adapted to the local conditions as are their native parents. They may require more inputs to thrive. Remember, one goal in planting a meadow is to reduce inputs such as water and fertilizer.
- Cultivars may contaminate the native gene pool by cross-pollinating with the native species.

Resources:

Purple Loosestrife: What you should know, what you can do Minnesota Sea Grant, www.seagrant.umn.edu

Defining Native Plant for Purposes of Restoration, Revegetation & Landscaping Colorado Native Plant Society

Native Plants: An Overview Jeffrey G. Norcini, Associate Professor of Environmental Horticulture, Native Plant Specialist, North Florida Research & Education Center, Quincy, FL 32351

Douglas Tallamy, Professor and Chair of the Department of Entomology and Wildlife Ecology, University of Delaware

Neil Diboll, Prairie Ecologist, Prairie Nursery, Westfield, Wisconsin

Landscape Restoration Handbook, Second Edition Donald Harker, Gary Libby, Kay Harker, Sherri Evans, Mark Evans

- Many cultivars do not have the genetic variation of the parent native. Generally, greater genetic diversity increases long-term sustainability.

Much more research needs to be done comparing cultivars with their parent natives and determining the impact cultivars have on the wildlife that rely on native plant species for survival.

regional and zone maps

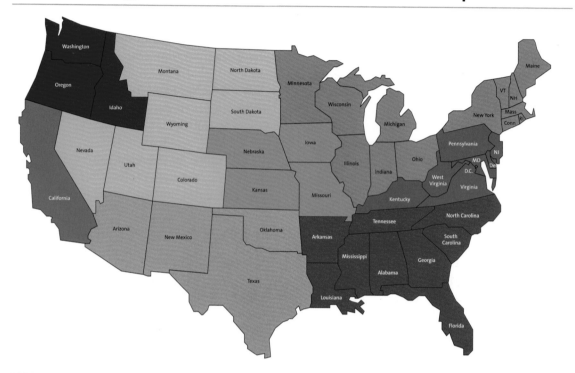

USDA PLANT HARDINESS ZONE MAP

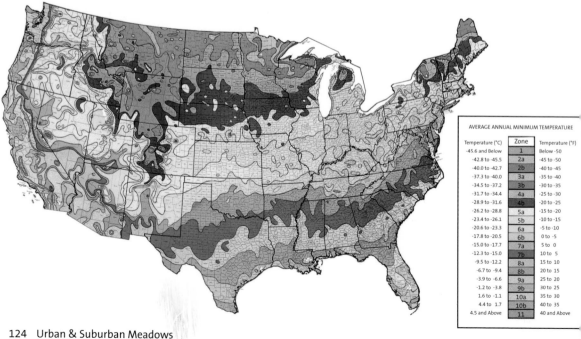

AVERAGE ANNUAL MINIMUM TEMPERATURE		
Temperature (°C)	Zone	Temperature (°F)
-45.6 and Below	1	Below -50
-42.8 to -45.5	2a	-45 to -50
-40.0 to -42.7	2b	-40 to -45
-37.3 to -40.0	3a	-35 to -40
-34.5 to -37.2	3b	-30 to -35
-31.7 to -34.4	4a	-25 to -30
-28.9 to -31.6	4b	-20 to -25
-26.2 to -28.8	5a	-15 to -20
-23.4 to -26.1	5b	-10 to -15
-20.6 to -23.3	6a	-5 to -10
-17.8 to -20.5	6b	0 to -5
-15.0 to -17.7	7a	5 to 0
-12.3 to -15.0	7b	10 to 5
-9.5 to -12.2	8a	15 to 10
-6.7 to -9.4	8b	20 to 15
-3.9 to -6.6	9a	25 to 20
-1.2 to -3.8	9b	30 to 25
1.6 to -1.1	10a	35 to 30
4.4 to 1.7	10b	40 to 35
4.5 and Above	11	40 and Above

plant key

NATIVE TO THESE REGIONS

■ Northeast   ■ Midwest Great Lakes
■ Mid-Atlantic   ■ Rocky Mountain
■ Southeast   ■ Pacific
■ Southwest   ■ Northwest
■ Central Plains

*States are noted as "plus or minus" where
exceptions occur.*

NAME

The first name is the genus (broad group
of plants or animals that share a range of
characteristics) and the second name is
the specific epithet (descriptive word) for
example, *Solidago rugosa. Rugosa* is Latin
for rough. Together these names form the
unique name for the species.

COMMON NAME

One of many imprecise names given a plant
often leading to confusion when identifying
the plant. For example: Priest's crown, Irish
daisy, Monk's head, Telltime, Faceclock,
Blowball, Lion's tooth, Butter flower, Black
endive, Dog's lettuce, Child's chain grass,
Worm rose, Sow milk, also known as
Dandelion.

LIGHT

Amount of sunlight a plant needs to thrive
during the growing season.

S = Sun—6 hours of direct sunlight.

PS = Part—Sun 3-6 hours of direct sunlight.

SH = Shade—less than 3 hours of direct or
filtered light.

HEIGHT

Mature size of plant including flowers rising
from foliage.

COLOR

Normally refers to flower color
(except grasses).

BLOOM

Months plant is in bloom. This may vary
in from region to region.

FEATURE

Notable aspect of plant for example
outstanding fall color.

WILDLIFE

Plant benefits to insects and animals.

Butterflies—Food source or host plant
for butterflies.

Beneficial Insects—Attracts pollinators
and pest control insects.

Hummingbirds—Plants that attract
hummingbirds.

Small mammals—Offers food or cover
for small mammals.

Deer resistant—Plant less prone to deer
browsing.

Birds—Used for food, nesting and cover.

MEADOW AND PRAIRIE FLOWERS

Native to these regions	Zone	Scientific Name	Common Name	Sun	Height	Color
(plus NV, MT, WY)	5–10	*Eriophyllum lanatum*	Oregon sunshine	S	1-2'	Bright Yellow
CA, OR	4–9	*Eschscholzia californica*	California poppy	S	1-2'	Orange, Yellow
(plus SD, OK, TX)	4–7	*Euphorbia corollata*	Flowering spurge	S	1-3'	White
(minus NV; plus MN, NM, AZ)	3-8	*Gaillardia aristata*	Great blanket flower	S	2-3'	Red-Yellow
(minus OH, IN; plus NY, IA)	1–5	*Geum triflorum*	Prairie smoke	S, PS, S	6-8"	Pink
(minus TN, AR; plus TX)	8–11	*Helianthus debilis*	Dune sunflower	S	2-4'	Bright yellow
(minus VT, NH, FL, MN)	4–9	*Helianthus mollis*	Downy sunflower	S, PS	4-6'	Yellow
(plus CO, WA)	4–9	*Heliopsis helianthoides*	False sunflower	S, PS	4-6'	Gold
MA, AZ, UT, CA	4–9	*Layia platyglossa*	Tidy tips	S	>1'	Yellow
(plus NY, WV, ND, SD)	4–9	*Liatris aspera*	Rough blazingstar	S, PS	3-5'	Purple/P
(minus IN, AR, UT, NV; plus TN, AR, LA)	3–7	*Liatris punctata*	Dotted blazing star	S	1-3'	Purple/P
(minus VT, FL, MS, KY, MN; plus MO, AR)	5–9	*Liatris scariosa*	Northern blazing star	S, PS	2-4'	Reddish-
(plus AL, LA, MI, MN, WV)	3-9	*Linum lewisii*	Prairie blue flax	S	1-2'	Blue-Pur
(minus TN, OK, AR)	4–9	*Lupinus perennis*	Wild lupine	S, PS	1-2'	Blue
FL, LA, OK, TX	8–9	*Lupinus texensis*	Texas bluebonnet	S	1-3'	Blue Wh
(plus NM, CO, UT, ID, WY)	4–9	*Penstemon eatonii*	Firecracker penestemon	S, PS	1-3'	Scarlet
	3–9	*Penstemon gradiflorus*	Large flowered beardtongue	S, PS	2-4'	Lavende
AZ, CA, CO, NM, UT, WY	3-8	*Penstemon strictus*	Rocky Mountain beardtongue	PS	1-3'	Blue-Pur
(plus NY, ND, SD)	4–9	*Phlox pilosa*	Downy phlox	S, PS	1-2'	Pink
(plus NH, MI, WI, MN, NM, AR)	5–8	*Potentilla gracilis*	Slender cinquefoil	S	1-2'	Bright Yellow

Bloom	Feature	Wildlife
e-Sept	Grows in well branched clumps	Host *Colias eurytheme* (Orange sulfur), *Vanessa atalanta* (Red admiral), *Polygonia progne* (Gray comma), *Pyrgus communis* (Skipper), birds, butterflies, bees
-Oct	Annual, easily grown, reseeds, found throughout most of the US	Butterflies
e-Oct	Small, white, fragrant flowers in flat topped clusters, long lasting	Waterfowl, shorebirds
-Sept	Daisy-like flowerheads, red with yellow rims, very drought tolerant.	Butterflies
il-June	Cup shaped flowers	Butterflies
r round	Blooms repeatedly, winter interest, may be aggressive	Butterflies, bees
g-Sept	Erect, deeply veined ray florets	Butterflies, birds
e-Sept	Adaptable, very long bloom time	Hummingbirds, butterflies, birds
y-Sept	Annual, profuse bloomer	Butterflies, birds
g-Sept	Dense spikes	Hummingbirds, butterflies
g-Oct	Deep rooted, very drought tolerant, native to short grass prairies.	Butterflies, birds
g-Sept	Less dense spikes, interrupted clusters	Butterflies
rch-Sept	Pale blue flowers veined in darker blue, flowers from bottom up, grows at an angle.	Birds, butterflies
y-June	Pea-like flowers	Host *Plebejus melissa* (Karner blue), *Callophrys irus* (Frosted elfin), hummingbirds, butterflies
rch-May	Fragrant, showy blooms, reseeds	Host *Strymon melinus* (Hairstreak), *Microtia elva* (Elfin) butterflies, bees, insects
y-Aug	5 to 10 long narrow tubular blossoms top stems.	Hummingbirds, honeybees, songbirds
y-June	Tubular flowers	Hummingbirds
y-June	Evergreen, sub-alpine, profuse, long lasting, large spires of royal-blue-purple flowers.	Butterflies
y-June	Saucer shaped flowers	Hummingbirds, butterflies
e-July	Good in low profile meadow	Larvel host to butterflies

MEADOW AND PRAIRIE FLOWERS

Native to these regions	Zone	Scientific Name	Common Name	Sun	Height	Color
	3–7	Rudbeckia hirta	Black-eyed Susan	S, PS	1-3'	Yellow
(minus NV, NM)	3–9	Ruellia humilis	Haity wild petunia	S, PS	1'	Lavender
AL, AR, FL, GA, IL, IN, KS, KY, MO, OH, OK, TN	5–8	Silene regia	Royal catchfly	S, PS	2-4'	Red
CA, OR	3–9	Sisyrinchium bellum	Western blue-eyed grass	S, PS	1'	Blue
(minus ME, FL, AL, MT, VT)	3–8	Solidago speciosa	Showy goldenrod	S, PS	1-4'	Yellow
(minus ND, SD)	4–9	Sphaeralcea munroana	White-stem globe-mallow	S	2-3'	Apricot-Orange
(minus VT)	5–8	Tradescantia ohiensis	Ohio spiderwort	S, PS	2-3'	Blue
(minus VT, FL)	4–8	Viola pedata	Birdsfoot violet	S, PS	4"	Blue

MEADOW AND PRAIRIE GRASSES

Native to these regions	Zone	Scientific Name	Common Name	Sun	Height	Color
(minus IA, MO; plus MN, AR)	5–9	Achnatherum hymenoide	Indian ricegrass, Sand grass	S	1-3'	Yellow, Green
(plus AZ)	4–9	Andropogon gerardii	Big bluestem	S, PS	5-8'	Purplish-
(minus VT, RI, ME, MN, NE; plus TX, OK)	3–8	Andropogon virginicus	Broom-sedge	S, PS	2-3'	Yellow
(minus VT, NH, MA, RI, NC, NV)	4–8	Bouteloua curtipendula	Side oats grama	S, PS	1-3'	Straw
(minus VT, NH, IL; plus SC, FL, ID)	3–9	Bouteloua gracilis	Blue grama, mosquito grass	S	8-36"	Red turn straw
(minus GA, FL, AL, MS, LA)	3–8	Elymus canadensis	Canada wild rye	S, PS	5'	Yellow, Green, Brown
(minus MT, VT)	5–8	Eragrostis spectabilis	Purple lovegrass	S, PS	1-2'	Pink/Pur
(minus ID; plus MT)	7–11	Festuca califonica	California fescue	S, PS	3-6'	Yellow
(minus ND)	4–9	Fescue idahoensis	Bunchgrass fescue	S, PS	1-3'	Yellow

Bloom	Feature	Wildlife
e-Sept	Daisy-like flowerheads	Host *Chlosyne gorgone* (Gorgone checkerspot), *Chlosyne lacinia* (Bordered patch), deer resistant, birds, butterflies
e-Aug	Low profile meadow	Hummingbirds
y-Aug	Needs excellent drainage	Hummingbirds
-May	Flowers last one day, dies back in summer heat	Hummingbirds, butterflies, bees, beneficial insects
g-Sept	Showy flowers-threatened	Numerous pollinators
e-Sept	Silver green foliage, spreads by under ground runners	Butterflies, bees, birds
e-Sept	Showy clusters of blue, three-petaled flowers	Unknown
y-June	Large pansy-like flowers	Host *Speyeria idalia* (Regal Fritillary), birds, butterflies, small mammals
e-Sept	Cool season, clump forming, airy appearance, seed heads ivory colored	Host *Hesperiidae* (Skipper butterflies), birds, butterflies, small mammals
g-Sept	Warm season, clump forming, very tolerant of conditions	Host *Anatrytone logan* (Delaware skipper), *Atrytonopsis hianna* (Dusted skipper), deer resistant, birds, small mammals
t-Nov	Warm season, clump forming, very adaptable to conditions, fall seed heads radiant in sunlight	Host *Poanes zabulon* (Zabulon skipper), butterflies, birds, cover, nesting, food
g-Sept	Warm season, clump forming, flowers purple turning to straw	Host *Hesperia viridis* (Green skipper), *Hesperia attalus* (Dotted skipper), deer resistant, birds, butterflies
e-Sept	Warm season, clump forming, one of the shortest native grasses	Host *Oarisma garita* (Garita skipperling), *Hesperia uncas* (Uncas skipper), *Hesperia pahaska* (Pahaska skipper), *Hesperia viridis* (Green skipper), *Polites rhesus* (Rhesus skipper), *Amblyscirtes simius* (Simius roadside-skipper), birds, butterflies
rch-June	Cool season, clump forming, self sows, fast growing, nurse crop	Host *Poanes zabulon* (Zabulon skipper), deer resistant, butterflies, birds, small mammals
y-Sept	Warm season, clump forming low profile meadow, colorful	Deer resistant
ril-July	Cool season, clump forming, elegant, blue green foliage	Deer resistant
ril-July	Cool season, clump forming, blue to gray-green foliage, rocky slopes	Host *Polites sonora* (Sonora skipper), deer resistant

DRY SOILS (WELL-DRAINED SAND, GRAVEL, AND ROCKY SOILS)

MEADOW AND PRAIRIE GRASSES

Native to these regions	Zone	Scientific Name	Common Name	Sun	Height	Color
■■■■■■ (plus NY, VT, ME, PA, MD, DE, KY, AL, MS, LA, AR)	4–9	*Koeleria macrantha*	Prairie junegrass	S, PS	1-2'	Lt Green to Buff
■■■■ (minus VT, NH, ME, NM, AZ, IA, NE; plus OH, IN, IL)	6–9	*Muhlenbergia capillaris*	Hairawn muhly	S	1-3'	Pink purp
■■■■■■ (plus ID)	3–9	*Panicum virgatum*	Switchgrass	S, PS	3-8'	Straw
■■■■■■■■ (minus OR, NV)	3–8	*Schizachyrium scoparium*	Little bluestem	S, PS	2-3'	Bluish
■■■■■■■	3–9	*Sorghastrum nutans*	Indian grass	S, PS	2-7'	Copper G
■■■■■■	3–8	*Sporobolus heterolepsis*	Prairie dropseed	S, PS	2-4'	Gold
■■■■■■■ (minus AR)	5–10	*Tridens flavens*	Purpletop	S, PS	2-5'	Purple

Aster oblongifolius

Bouteloua gracilis

Saxon Holt

Bloom	Feature	Wildlife
ny-June	Cool season, clump forming, goes dormant in summer in hot, humid conditions	Birds
t y	Warm season, clump forming, grows in a variety of habitats & soils	Deer resistant
eg-Nov	Warm season, clump forming and rhizomatous, aggressive, airy, purple seed heads	Host *Anatrytone logan* (Delaware skipper), birds, butterflies
g-Sept	Warm season, clump forming, turns red in fall	Host *Hesperia ottoe* (Ottoe skipper), *Hesperia sassacus* (Indian skipper), *Polites origenes* (Crossline skipper), *Atrytonopsis hianna* (Dusted skipper), *Hesperia meskei* (Dixie skipper), *Hesperia metea* (Cobweb butterfly), deer resistant,
y y-Sept	Warm season, clump forming and some rhizamatous spread, very adaptable	Host *Amblyscirtes hegon* (Pepper & salt skipper), deer resistant, birds, butterflies, small mammals
yg-Sept	Warm season, clump forming, airy, fragrant flowers/orange in fall	Birds
'g-Oct	Warm season, clump forming, drooping, airy flowers	Host *Cercyonis pegala* (Common wood nymph), *Polites origenes* (Crossline skipper), *Pompeius verna* (Little glassywing), *Poanes viator* (Broad-winged skipper) butterflies, birds

aecrista fasciculate

Sorghastrum nutans

Gaillardia aristata

MEADOW AND PRAIRIE FLOWERS

Native to these regions	Zone	Scientific Name	Common Name	Sun	Height	Color
(minus PA, WV; plus CT)	4–8	*Eryngium yuccifolium*	Rattlesnake master	S, PS	3-5'	White
(minus NM; plus ND, SD)	3–9	*Eupatorium perfoliatum*	Common boneset	S, PS	3-5'	White
(minus OH, IN; plus NY, IA)	1–5	*Geum triflorum*	Prairie smoke	S, PS	6-8"	Pink
(minus MI, WI, MN; plus NY, MO)	6–10	*Helianthus angustifolius*	Swamp sunflower	S	5-7'	Yellow
(minus TN, AR plus Texas)	8–11	*Helianthus debilis*	Dune sunflower	S	2-4'	Bright yellow
(plus CO, WA)	4–9	*Heliopsis helianthoides*	False sunflower	S, PS	4-6'	Gold
(plus NY, WV, ND, SD)	4–9	*Liatris aspera*	Rough blazingstar	S, PS	3-5'	Purple/Pi
(plus AR, LA, MS, MA, NY, NJ, PA, KY, ND, SD, OK, TX)	4–9	*Liatris pycnostachya*	Prairie blazingstar	S, PS	3-5'	Purple/Pi
(minus VT, FL, MS, KY, MN; plus MO)	5–9	*Liatris scariosa*	Northern blazing star	S, PS	2-4'	Reddish-P
	5–9	*Lilium columbianum*	Oregon lily	PS	3-6'	Orange-R
(minus FL)	3–9	*Monarda fistulosa*	Wild bergamot	S, PS	2-4'	Lavender
(minus NJ, FL, IA; plus NY, MA, CT	4–8	*Parthenium integrifolium*	Wild quinine	S	3-5'	White
(minus FL; plus SD)	2–8	*Penstemon digitalis*	Smooth penstemon	S, PS, SH	2-3'	White
(plus NY, CT, ND, SD)	4–9	*Phlox pilosa*	Downy phlox	S, PS	1-2'	Pink
(minus ID; plus NV)	3–9	*Ranunculus occidentalis*	Western buttercup	S, PS	1-2'	Yellow
(minus NH, ME, RI, MD, NC, TX; plus SD)	3–10	*Ratibida pinnata*	Yellow coneflower	S, PS	3-6'	Yellow
(minus AR, NV)	3–7	*Rudbeckia hirta*	Black-eyed Susan	S, PS	1-3'	Yellow
(minus AR, NM; plus UT, CO)	4–7	*Rudbeckia triloba*	Brown-eyed Susan	S, PS	2-5'	Yellow
(minus NJ, DE, SC, DC)	3–9	*Ruellia humilis*	Hairy wild petunia	S, PS	1'	Lavender
OH, IN, IL, KY, TN, AL, GA, FL, MO, KS, OK, AR	5–8	*Silene regia*	Royal catchfly	S, PS	2-4'	Red

Bloom	Feature	Wildlife
e-Aug	Thistle like flower heads, spiny leaves	Butterflies, moths, honeybees
e-Sept	Tiny white flowers in fuzzy clusters	Butterflies, birds
ril-June	Cup shaped flowers	Butterflies
t-Oct	Daisy like flower heads, yellow with purple center	Butterflies, birds
r round	Blooms repeatedly, winter interest, may be aggressive	Butterflies, bees, birds
e-Sept	Adaptable, very long bloom time	Hummingbirds, butterflies, birds
g-Sept	Dense spikes	Hummingbirds, butterflies
y-Sept	Fuzzy flower heads open from the top down	Butterflies, bees, beneficial insects
g-Sept	Less dense spikes, interrupted clusters	Butterflies
e-Sept	Popular wild flower, only grows 6½" in higher elevations, orange speckled, fragrant flowers.	Hummingbirds, butterflies
y-Sept	Bright blooms, fragrant foliage	Hummingbirds, butterflies, birds
e-Sept	Fragrant leaves, good cut flower	Butterflies
e-July	Tolerates high heat & humidity	Hummingbirds, bees
y-June	Saucer shaped flowers	Hummingbirds, butterflies
ril-June	1st bloom of spring, often found in moist, well drained areas	Butterflies
y-Sept	Yellow rays droop downward	Butterflies, birds
e-Sept	Daisy-like flower heads	Host *Chlosyne gorgone* (Gorgone checkerspot), *Chlosyne lacinia* (Bordered patch), deer resistant, butterflies birds, bees
y-Oct	Tolerates several hours of shade, short lived	Birds
e-Aug	Low Profile Meadow, leafy, bushy appearance	Hummingbirds, butterflies
y-Aug	Needs excellent drainage	Hummingbirds

MESIC/MEDIUM SOILS (WELL-DRAINED LOAM, SILT LOAM, SANDY LOAM, ETC.)

MEADOW AND PRAIRIE FLOWERS

Native to these regions	Zone	Scientific Name	Common Name	Sun	Height	Color
■ ■ ■ ■ ■ (minus NC, SC, GA, FL, MT, WY, UT; plus NY, PA, VA)	5–9	Silphium laciniatum	Compass plant	S, PS	5-10'	Yellow
■ ■ ■ ■ ■ (minus VT, NH, TN, NC, SC)	3–9	Solidago rigida	Stiff goldenrod	S, PS	3-5'	Yellow
■ ■ ■ ■ ■ ■ (minus ME, FL, AL, MT, VT)	3–8	Solidago speciosa	Showy goldenrod	S, PS	1-4'	Yellow
VT, MA, MI, IL, WI, MN, IA, MO, ND, SD, NE, KS, OK, MT, WI	4–9	Tradescantia bracteata	Prairie spiderwort	S	1-2'	Blue
■ ■ ■ ■ ■ (minus VT, AR, NM)	5–8	Tradescantia ohiensis	Ohio spiderwort	S, PS	2-3'	Blue
■ ■ ■ (minus WY, UT, NW; plus NY, MA, KY, MS, OK, AR)	5–9	Vernonia fasciculata	Common ironweed	S, PS	4-6'	Red Pink
■ ■ ■ ■ (minus NC, SC, GA, AL, WS, MN, AR; plus MA, KY)	5–9	Vernonia missurica	Missouri ironweed	S, PS	3-6'	Purple
■ ■ ■ (minus VT, ME, MS; plus OH)	5–9	Vernonia noveboracensis	New York ironweed	S, PS	7'	Purple
■ ■ ■ ■ ■ (minus VT, FL)	4–8	Viola pedata	Birdsfoot violet	S, PS	4"	Blue

MEADOW AND PRAIRIE GRASSES

Native to these regions	Zone	Scientific Name	Common Name	Sun	Height	Color
■ ■ ■ ■ ■ ■ (plus AZ)	4–9	Andropogon gerardii	Big bluestem	S, PS	5-8'	Purplish-r
■ ■ ■ ■ ■ (minus VT, RI, ME, MN, NE; plus TX, OK)	3–8	Andropogon virginicus	Broom-sedge	S, PS	2-3'	Yellow
■ ■ ■ ■ ■ ■ ■ ■ (minus VT, NH, MA, RI, NC, NV)	4–8	Bouteloua curtipendula	Side-oats grama	S, PS	2-3'	Straw
■ ■ ■ ■ ■ (minus MN, NE)	5–8	Chasmanthium latifolium	Northern sea oats	S, PS, SH	3'	Gold
■ ■ ■ ■ ■ ■ ■ ■ (minus GA, FL, AL, MS, LA)	3–8	Elymus canadensis	Canada wild rye	S, PS	5'	Yellow, Green, Brown
■ ■ (minus ID; plus MT)	7–11	Festuca califonica	California fescue	S, PS	3-6'	Yellow
■ ■ ■ ■ ■ ■ ■ ■ (minus FL, MS, LA, AR, OK, KS, SD)	4–9	Festuca rubra	Creeping red fescue	S, PS	1-3'	Yellow
■ ■ ■ ■ ■ ■ (plus NY, VT, ME, PA, MD, DE, KY, AL, MS, LA, AR)	4–9	Koeleria macrantha	Prairie junegrass	S, PS	1-2'	Lt. Green Buff

Bloom	Feature	Wildlife
-Sept	Showy Flowers	Butterflies, birds, small mammals
-Sept	Good showy fall flower	Butterflies, bees
-Sept	Showy flowers-threatened	Numerous pollinators
e-July	Showy flowers last one day	Unknown
e-Sept	Showy clusters of blue, three-petaled flowers	Unknown
-Sept	Takes water inundation, densely clustered flowers	Host *Vanessa virginiensis* (American painted lady), butterflies
-Sept	One of the best late flowering plants for attracting butterflies	Host *Vanessa virginiensis* (American painted lady), butterflies
-Oct	Tall, upright form adds structure to meadow	Butterflies
y-June	Large pansy-like flowers	Host *Speyeria idalia* (Regal fritillary), birds, butterflies, small mammals
-Sept	Warm season clump forming, very tolerant of conditions	Host *Anatrytone logan* (Delaware skipper), *Atrytonopsis hianna* (Dusted skipper), deer resistant, birds, small mammals
t-Nov	Warm season, clump forming, very adaptable to conditions, fall seed heads radiant in sunlight	Host *Poanes zabulon* (Zabulon skipper), butterflies, birds, cover, nesting, food
-Sept	Warm seaso, clump forming, flowers purple turning to straw	Host *Hesperia viridis* (Green skipper), *Hesperia attalus* (Dotted skipper), deer resistant, birds, butterflies
-Oct	Warm season, clump forming & rhizomatous, self sows in moist conditions	Host *Amblyscirtes hegon* (Pepper & salt skipper), *Amblyscirtes belli* (Bells roadside skipper), *Amblyscirtes aenus* (Bronzed roadside skipper), deer resistant, birds, butterflies, small mammals
rch-June	Cool season, clump forming, self sows, fast growing, nurse crop	Host Zabulon skipper butterfly, deer resistant, butterflies, birds, small mammals
il-June	Cool season, clump forming, elegant, blue-green foliage	Deer resistant
ril-Sept	Cool season, rhizomatous, wide spread, flowering time varies	Birds
y-June	Cool season, clump forminggoes dormant in summer in hot, humid conditions	Birds

MEADOW AND PRAIRIE GRASSES

Native to these regions	Zone	Scientific Name	Common Name	Sun	Height	Color
▪▪▪▪▪▪▪ (plus ID)	2–9	*Panicum virgatum*	Switchgrass	S, PS	3-6'	Straw
▪▪▪▪▪▪▪▪ (minus OR, NV)	3–8	*Schizachyrium scoparium*	Little bluestem	S, PS	2-3'	Bluish
▪▪▪▪▪▪▪	3–9	*Sorghastrum nutans*	Indiangrass	S, PS	3-7'	Gold
▪▪▪▪▪ (plus OK, TX)	3–8	*Sporobolus heterolepis*	Prairie dropseed	S, PS	2-4'	Gold/Orange
▪▪▪▪▪▪ (minus AR)	5–10	*Tridens flavus*	Purpletop	S, PS	2-5'	Purple

Agastache foeniculum

Asclepias tuberosa

Panicum virgatum

Bloom	Feature	Wildlife
-Nov	Warm season, clump forming and rhizomatous, aggressive, airy, purple seed heads	Host *Anatrytone logan* (Delaware skipper), birds, butterflies
-Sept	Warm season, clump forming, turns red in fall	Host *Hesperia ottoe* (Ottoe skipper), *Hesperia sassacus* (Indian skipper), *Polites origenes* (Crossline skipper), *Atrytonopsis hianna* (Dusted skipper), *Hesperia meskei* (Dixie skipper), *Hesperia metea* (Cobweb butterfly), deer resistant, birds, butterflies
-Sept	Warm season, clump forming and some rhizamatous spread, adaptable	Host *Amblyscirtes hegon* (Pepper & salt skipper), deer resistant, birds, butterflies, small mammals
-Sept	Warm season, clump forming, airy, fragrant flowers	Birds
-Oct	Warm season, clump forming, drooping, airy flowers	Host *Cercyonis pegala* (Common wood nymph), *Polites origenes* (Crossline skipper), *Pompeius verna* (Little glassywing), *Poanes viator* (Broad-winged skipper), butterflies, birds

Echinacea purpurea

Lilium columbianum

Eileen Stark

MEADOW AND PRAIRIE FLOWERS

Native to these regions	Zone	Scientific Name	Common Name	Sun	Height	Color
■ ■ ■ ■ (minus MA, CT, RI; plus MI, WI, MN, NM, AZ)	3–8	Geum macrophyllum	Large leafed avens	PS	1-2'	Yellow
■ ■ ■ ■ (minus MI, WI, MN; plus NY, MO)	6–9	Helianthus angustifolius	Swamp sunflower	S	5-7'	Yellow
■ ■ ■ ■ ■ ■ ■ ■ (minus NH)	3–8	Helenium autumnale	Sneezeweed	S	4'	Yellow
■ (plus OR, AZ)	7–8	Helenium bigelovii	Tall sneezeweed	S	2'	Yellow
■ ■ ■ ■ ■ ■ (minus AZ; plus CO, WA)	4–9	Heliopsis helianthoides	False sunflower	S, PS	4-6'	Gold
■ ■ ■ ■ ■ (minus AR, AZ, ME, MN, NH, VT; plus KS, MO, UT)	5–10	Hibiscus moscheutos	Crimson-eyed rose mallow	S, PS	3-6'	Creamy white
■ ■ ■ ■ (minus DE, NJ, GA, FL; plus NY, OK, TX)	6–9	Iris virginica var. shrevei	Wild iris, Southern blue flag	S	1-3'	Blue/Viol•
■ ■ ■ ■ (minus ME, VT, NH, RI, MN; plus MO, AR, LA)	4–9	Liatris spicata	Dense blazingstar	S, PS	3-6'	Purple/Pi•
■ ■ ■ ■ ■ ■ ■ (plus CO, UT)	3–8	Lobelia cardinalis	Cardinal flower	PS, SH	2-5'	Red
■ ■ ■ ■ ■ (minus FL; plus OK, TX, ND, SD, WY, CO)	4–8	Lobelia siphilitica	Great blue lobelia	S, PS	1-4'	Blue
■ ■	4–9	Lupinus rivularis	Riverbank lupine	S, PS	1-3.5'	Blue or Violet
■ ■ ■ ■ (minus FL, AL, MS, AR, LA, ID; plus IA, MO)	4-9	Monarda didyma	Scarlet bee balm	S, PS	3-6'	Red
■ ■ ■ (minus DC, MN, NC, TN)	4-9	Monarda media	Purple bergamot	S, PS	2-3'	Reddish Purple
■ ■ ■ (plus NY, CT, PA, DE, MI, NE)	6–9	Mimulus guttatus	Golden monkey-flower	S, PS	2-3'	Yellow
AK, CA, NV, OR, WY	3–8	Nemophila menziesii	Baby blue eyes	PS	6"-1'	Blue whit•
■ ■ ■ ■ ■ ■ ■ (minus ID, KY, NE; plus OK, TX)	4–8	Nuttallanthus canadensis	Blue toadflax, Canada toadflax	S, PS	1-2'	Blue
■ ■ ■ (minus PA, NJ, DE, DC, MN; plus MO, OK)	3–8	Phlox glaberrima	Marsh phlox, Smooth phlox	S, PS	2-4'	Red/Purpl•
■ ■ ■ ■ (minus ME, VT, NH, RI, MN, LA; plus TX, OK, MO)	3–9	Rudbeckia fulgida	Orange coneflower	S, PS	2-4'	Yellow/ Orange
■ ■ ■ ■ ■ ■ ■ ■ (minus AR, NV)	3–7	Rudbeckia hirta	Black-eyed Susan	S, PS	1-3'	Yellow

Bloom	Feature	Wildlife
oril-Aug	Long bloom time, good in shadier, wet meadow sites in high to low elevations	Butterflies
ept-Oct	Purple disk florets	Butterflies, birds
ug-Oct	Wedge shaped ray florets	Butterflies, deer resistant
ne-Aug	Could bloom May through October	Butterflies
ne-Sept	Adaptable, very long bloom time	Butterflies, birds, hummingbirds
ly-Sept	Showy flowers have a crimson band of red at flower throat	Hummingbirds, bees
ay	Perfers very wet soils, fragrant	Deer resistant
ug-Sept	Long lasting flowers	Hummingbirds, deer resistant, butterflies, birds
ly-Sept	Showy red blooms, relies on hummingbirds for pollination	Hummingbirds, butterflies
ly-Sept	More sun tolerant than L.cardinalis	Butterflies
ay-June	Grows in sandy soils near wet marshes and streams, coastal	Larval host butterflies, butterflies
ne-Oct	Blooms longer in northern climates, fragrant leaves	Hummingbirds, butterflies, birds
ly-Aug	Fragrant, not as widespread as *Monarda fistulosa*	Butterflies, bees, hummingbirds
arch-Sept	Annual, reseeds freely	Hummingbirds
eb-June	Annual, spring wildflower	Bees, butterflies, birds
ay-Sept	Annual, reseeds freely	Butterflies, bees, birds
ne-Sept	Fragrant, showy flowers	Hummingbirds, butterflies
ly-Sept	Variable species with numerous varieties.	Butterflies
ne-Sept	Daisy-like flowerheads	Host *Chlosyne gorgone* (Gorgone checkerspot), *Chlosyne lacinia* (Bordered patch), deer resistant, butterflies birds, bees

MEADOW AND PRAIRIE FLOWERS

Native to these regions	Zone	Scientific Name	Common Name	Sun	Height	Color
AR, CT, IA, IL, IN, KS, KY, LA, MA, MI, MO, MS, NC, NY, OK, TN, TX, WI	4–8	Rudbeckia subtomentosa	Sweet Black-eyed Susan	S, PS	3-6'	Yellow
WA, OR, CA	5–9	Sidalcea malviflora	Dwarf checkermallow	S, PS	3-4'	Pink/Mauv
(minus FL, MN; plus DC, VA, WV, IA, MO, AR)	4–8	Silphium terebinthinaceum	Prairie dock	S, PS	3-8'	Yellow
(minus DC, KY, MD, MO, WV; plus ID, NC, NJ, NM, PA, TX, VA)	3–9	Sisyrinchium montanum	Strict blue-eyed grass	S, PS, S	8-15"	Violet-Blue
NY, MI, OH, IN, IL, WI	3–9	Solidago ohioensis	Ohio goldenrod	S	3-4'	Yellow
(minus FL, AL; plus KS, MO, AR, LA, WA, OR)	3–9	Spiraea tomentosa	Steeplebush	S, PS, SH	2-4'	Peach Pink
(minus VT)	5–8	Tradescantia ohiensis	Ohio spiderwort	S, PS	2-3'	Blue
(minus NJ, WI, MN, NE; plus NY)	5–9	Vernonia altissima	Tall ironweed	S	5-8'	Red/Pink
(minus WY, UT, NW; plus NY, MA, KY, MS, OK, AR)	5–9	Vernonia fasciculata	Common ironweed	S, PS	4-6'	Red Pink
(minus NC, SC, GA, AL, WS, MN, AR; plus MA, KY)	5–9	Vernonia missurica	Missouri ironweed	S, PS	3-6'	Purple
(minus VT, ME, MS; plus OH)	5–9	Vernonia noveboracensis	New York ironweed	S, PS	7'	Purple
(minus NH; plus SD, ND, OK, TX)	3–8	Veronicastrum virginicum	Culver's root	S, PS	3-6'	White

MEADOW AND PRAIRIE GRASSES

(minus VT, RI, ME, MN, NE; plus TX, OK)	3–9	Andropogon virginicus	Broom-sedge	S, PS	2-3'	Yellow
(minus SC, FL)	3–9	Calamagrostis canadensis	Bluejoint reed grass	S, PS	3-5'	Purplish-Ta
(minus OK, KS; plus ND, MT)	3–9	Carex comosa	Longhair sedge	S	2-4'	Green
(minus FL; plus OK, TX)	3–8	Carex crinita	Fringed sedge	PS, SH	1-3'	Green
(minus NE; plus KY, TN, OK, AR)	3–8	Carex muskingumensis	Palm sedge	S, PS	2-3'	Green
(minus UT)	3–8	Carex vulpinoidea	Fox sedge	S, PS	1-3'	Gold

Bloom	Feature	Wildlife
ly-Sept	Mildly fragrant, long bloom time	Butterflies
ay-June	High coastal meadows-will bloom all summer if moist	Host *Vanessa annabella* (West coast lady), *Vanessa cardui* (Painted lady), *Pyrgus communis* (Common checkered skipper), *Strymon melinus* (Gray hairstreak) butterflies.
ly-Sept	May not flower until 2nd or 3rd year	Birds
ay-July	Wildflower that has grasslike appearance but is really a member of the iris family	Hummingbirds, butterflies, bees, beneficial insects
ıg-Sept	Largest & showiest blooms of any goldenrod	Butterflies, birds, beneficial insects
ıg-Sept	Small and thickly clustered in a pyramidal spike	Host *Hyalophora columbia* (Columbia silkmoth), butterflies, birds
ne-Sept	Showy clusters of blue, three-petaled flowers	Unknown
ıg-Sept	Dark red stems, saucer shaped terminal flowers	Butterflies
ly-Sept	Takes water inundation, densely clustered flowers	Butterflies
ıg-Sept	One of the best late flowering plants for attracting butterflies	Host *Vanessa virginiensis* (American painted lady), butterflies, bees
ıg-Oct	Tall, upright form adds structure to meadow	Butterflies
ly-Aug	Good along woodland edge, upright, dense terminal flowers	Butterflies, bees
ept-Nov	Warm season, clump forming, very adaptable to conditions, fall seed heads radiant in sunlight	Host *Poanes zabulon* (Zabulon skipper), butterflies, birds, cover, nesting, food
ıne-Aug	Cool season, rhizomatous, self sows	Birds
ay-June	Cool season, clump forming, flower has three bristly spikelets	Birds
ay-June	Cool season, clump forming	Birds, waterfowl
ay-June	Cool season, rhizomatous, insignificant flowers	Birds
ay-June	Cool season, rhizomatous, seed heads short lived	Birds, waterfowl

MEADOW AND PRAIRIE GRASSES

Native to these regions	Zone	Scientific Name	Common Name	Sun	Height	Color
▣▣▣▣▣ (minus MN, NE)	5–8	*Chasmanthium latifolium*	Northern sea oats	S, PS, SH	3'	Gold
▣▣▣▣▣▣ (plus NC)	4–9	*Deschampsia cespitosa*	Tufted hair grass	PS	2-4'	Purplish-green
▣▣▣▣▣ (minus FL, AL, MS, LA, TX; plus ND, SD, OK, NM)	3–8	*Elymus hystrix*	Bottle-brush grass	S, PS	3-4'	Green
▣▣▣▣▣▣▣▣ (minus Fl, MS, LA, AR, OK, KS, SD)	4–9	*Festuca rubra*	Creeping red fescue	S, PS	1-3'	Yellow
▣	3–7	*Hierochloe odorata*	Vanilla sweet grass	S, PS	1-2'	Straw
▣▣▣▣ (minus VT, NH, ME, NM, AZ, IA, NE; plus OH, IN, IL)	3–9	*Muhlenbergia capillaris*	Hairawn muhly	S	1-3'	Pink Purple
▣▣▣▣▣▣ (plus ID)	3–9	*Panicum virgatum*	Switchgrass	S, PS	3-8'	Straw
▣ (minus TN; plus TX)	7–8	*Rhynchospora colorata*	White-topped sedge	S, PS	1-2'	White
▣▣▣▣▣▣▣ (minus NV, AR; plus NC, TN, AR, LA)	4–9	*Spartina pectinata*	Prairie cordgrass	S	5-6'	Yellow

Monarda media

Bruce Jones

Hibiscus moscheutos

Bloom	Feature	Wildlife
g-Oct	Warm season, clump forming & rhizomatous, self sows in moist conditions	Host *Amblyscirtes hegon* (Pepper & salt skipper), *Amblyscirtes belli* (Bells roadside skipper), *Amblyscirtes aenus* (Bronzed roadside skipper), deer resistant, birds, butterflies, small mammals
ne	Cool season, clump forming, fine textured flowers turn buff color in fall	Host *Poanes melane* (Umber skipper), birds
ne-Aug	Cool season, clump forming, bristly spikelets turn buff color in fall	Host *Enodia anthedon* (Northern pearly eye), butterflies
ril-Sept	Cool season, rhizomatous, wide spread, flowering time varies	Birds
y-Aug	Cool season, rhizomatous, fragrant flowers & foliage, bronze colored spikelets	Birds
t	Warm season-clump forming, grows in a variety of habitats & soils	Deer resistant
g-Nov	Warm season, clump forming & rhizomatous, aggressive, airy, purple seed heads	Host *Anatrytone logan* (Delaware skipper), birds, butterflies
ne-Aug	Cool season, rhizomatous, showy, white bracts have daisy-like appearance	Insect pollinators, deer resistant
g-Oct	Warm season, rhizomatous, native to fresh water marshes and wet prairies	Birds, small mammals

nthus angustifolius

Lobelia cardinalis

Bruce Jones

Eupatorium fistulosum

Homebuyers were attracted to this development in Middleton, Wisconsin because of the prairie planted throughout the permanent green space. In addition to the year round beauty and wildlife, prairie plants mitigate potential erosion, caused by roof runoff. The homeowners' association maintenance costs are greatly reduced with yearly prairie burn management versus the weekly mowing required for turf.

Encourage change by example. Plant wildflower meadows and other natural landscapes and include your neighbors in the process. Show them what your plan is and explain the benefits gained, such as storm water control, wildlife habitat and elimination of pesticides. Start small. You can plant islands of native plants in your lawn and expand the beds as your neighbors become more accepting of a natural look. To aid in a comfortable transition from lawn to meadow and to blend with adjacent landscapes, maintain a mowed strip of grass along roads and in front yards. As more people choose to plant natural landscapes, the more mainstream these diverse, sustainable settings become and the sooner our ecosystems will be rebuilt.

This curving, mowed border lends a natural, yet tended, feel to this prairie planting in a suburban Wisconsin neighborhood. Michael Healy, Biologic Environmental Consulting.

We can transform the lawn culture through beautiful, natural landscape models and educational community outreach. Penn State Cooperative Extension staff and the local Conservation District in York, Pennsylvania are doing just that. They have formed MAEscapes (Mid-Atlantic Ecological Landscapes) to help educate the public about "the importance of restoring and preserving Mid-Atlantic ecological landscapes, native plants and their communities by demonstrating landscaping principles, processes and practices that are beneficial, responsible and sustainable" (from Mission statement *Mid-Atlantic Ecological Landscapes*, www.maescapes.org).

Originally, their own facility grounds were a perfect example of a non-native grass landscape with little plant or animal diversity. The area was difficult to maintain and mow. Heavy foot traffic caused soil compaction that then created serious water runoff into the parking area. Additionally, the single species turf grass could not support wildlife needs such as food or cover.

To demonstrate the use of native plants to create wildlife habitat and conserve water, they removed the turf and installed demonstration gardens, including a meadow strip. Now the native plant gardens support many butterflies, beneficial insects and birds, and reduce maintenance and water use.

To help visitors to the gardens have a better understanding of the benefits of native plants, MAEscapes has signage explaining the important aspects of meadow creation, including site conditions, plant communities and meadow establishment. Although these signs are very detailed, simple home made signs might also work well to help explain to neighbors your own natural landscape. There are a number of organizations like the Audubon Society and the National Wildlife Federation, with programs that offer tools to create healthy habitats for wild life. When you register your native habitat, you receive a sign. A small donation may be required.

With efforts like these, we can work with our neighbors, homeowner associations and local government officials to improve restrictive weed laws and create enlightened natural landscaping ordinances. See the general resource section, pg. 231, for links to publications, fact sheets and sample ordinances to use as tools to help win over skeptics and convert outdated landscape and weed laws and establish your own natural habitat.

Mid-Atlantic Ecological Landscapes

MEADOW GARDEN

Creating a Place for the Good Guys

What is Integrated Pest Management (IPM)?

Integrated Pest Management is the sustainable practice of using a variety of cultural, biological and chemical techniques to manage insects and plant diseases. One goal of IPM is to reduce any harmful impact chemicals may have on wildlife and on soil and water quality.

IPM methods include proper plant selection, biological pest controls, using traps for monitoring insect populations and regularly examining plants for signs of trouble. Pesticides should be used as a last resort and applied at the most vulnerable time in an insect's life cycle.

Meadows naturally occur in sunny spots throughout the Mid-Atlantic region. This MAEscapes meadow garden is designed to mimic a natural meadow, but uses more flowers and fewer grasses. This type of garden can be designed to complement any landscape. Once established, perennial meadows provide year-round interest and economic benefits. Less lawn to mow means lower equipment and fuel costs, as well as improved air quality. Planting a meadow garden in your yard will help restore important native vegetation and vital wildlife habitat that has been lost to urban sprawl.

Conserve Natural Enemies

Insects are an important part of a meadow garden. Many do important pest management work for you. These useful insects, mites and spiders are referred to as "natural enemies" or "beneficial insects". In a diverse landscape, there are usually plenty of beneficials already at work, quietly keeping pest populations at tolerable levels. To encourage natural enemies in the landscape, maintain a habitat that allows beneficials to survive and reproduce.

Above: The native meadow grass *Schizachyrium scoparium*, Little Bluestem, is beautiful in the winter. Aphids are a favorite food of the Convergent Lady Beetle. The Wheel Bug, with its bizarre appearance and deadly beak, is one of the largest assassin bugs. Wheel bugs are beneficial insects and should be considered valuable allies. Do not handle them, however, as they can inflict a painful and lasting "bite" with their beak.

Benefits

The native plants chosen for this site require no fertilizer. In fact, native meadow plants often do best in infertile soils. Once established, the close spacing of plants crowds out most weeds.

Diverse garden plants host a variety of insects including predators and parasites. These beneficial insects are a natural control that prevents destructive insects from overpopulating the environment, eliminating the need for pesticides.

The deep roots of meadow grasses and flowers trap, clean and filter rainwater and runoff. Meadows are vital links to cleaner and healthier watersheds.

Meadow gardens increase biodiversity. Native vegetation provides seasonal food, nesting sites and cover for a host of wildlife, particularly ground dwelling birds.

Establishment and Maintenance

Meadows require considerably less care than a traditional lawn. A newly planted meadow garden will require water and some hand weeding until established. This MAEscapes garden is cut back once a year in early spring. The cuttings are removed and composted off site. Removing the plant material prevents the soil from becoming too rich for the meadow plants. The use of pesticides is not necessary.

Site Conditions

The Meadow Garden receives full sun. It is very dry due to sloped conditions. The soil has been severely disturbed by development and land use. Heavy foot traffic has contributed to the densely compacted soil.

Left: The summer meadow shows beautiful colors and textures. Mixed with the grasses is *Baptisia australis*, Wild False Indigo. Above: Eastern bluebirds are primarily insect eaters who shift towards seeds and berries in colder months when insects are not available. Bluebirds find most of their food close to or on the ground.

Plant Communities

Plants do best and require less maintenance when combined with other plants that have similar soil, sun and moisture needs. Meadows are generally made up of grasses and herbaceous perennials and contain few shrubs or trees. Grouping plants that might grow together in a natural community is ideal.

Plants for this garden were chosen for their ability to withstand heat, drought, salt and drying winds. *Asclepias verticillata*, Whorled Milkweed, and *Sporobolus heterolepsis*, Prairie Dropseed grass, combine with herbaceous perennials such as *Asclepias tuberosa*, Butterfly Weed, and *Allium cernuum*, Nodding Onion, to create a striking, yet durable, garden.

Degraded ecosystem before wetland restoration as shown below.

RESTORED ECOSYSTEMS

More and more cities, communities, corporations and individuals are realizing the importance of reclaiming the ecosystems that existed before human development of an area and the subsequent introduction of harmful, invasive species. The rebuilding of natural areas such as meadows, prairies, wetlands, savannas and forests, translates to sustainability, wildlife habitat, storm water management and lower maintenance costs.

This Illinois retention pond was restored to wetland habitat at half the cost of adjusting the storm water pipes to drain the water. The water remains 6-8" deep. The wetland was successfully planted with seed and plugs in a drought year and is now home to Great Egrets, Great Blue Herons, Mallards, and Green Herons.

Great Egret at home in the restored wetland.

Jack Pizzo

left, Wetland plants *Sagittaria latifolia* (Arrowhead), *Peltandra virginica* (Arrow arum), and *Scirpus validus v. creber* (Great bulrush). In the upland *Ratibida pinnata* (Yellow coneflower), *Monarda fistulosa* (Bee balm), *Schizachyrium scoparium* (Little bluestem), *Desmodium canadense* (Showy tick trefoil), *Veronicastrum virginicus* (Culver's root), and *Verbena hastata* (Blue vervain). Jack Pizzo and Associates.

Invasive plants and woody growth had overtaken and smothered the native species in the degraded oak savanna adjacent to this community. Oak savannas are an intermediate zone between forests and prairies. These are endangered ecosystems that still may be saved by our intervention. A restoration team removed the unwanted vegetation and did a controlled burn of the area. Once the understory was opened up, within months, the savanna was reborn with a stunning display of spring blooming, native plants, *Mertensia virginica* (Virginia blue bells) and *Podophyllum peltatum* (Mayapple).

In New York City, Friends of the High Line rescued the long abandoned, elevated railroad structure and its existing ecosystem from demolition. The High Line has been transformed into an urban meadow in the sky. The original plant species that existed in the railway ecosystem were inventoried and have been incorporated into the landscape plan. Over 160 of the reestablished grasses and perennial flowers are native to the state of New York.

Restoration work, Jack Pizzo and Associates.

Iwan Baan

Iwan Baan

This is perhaps, the ultimate urban meadow!
Design, Piet Oudolf.

FUTURE STEWARDS

Often, it is useful to examine the past. I think about the model my Dad created when he gave my brothers, sisters and me each our own patch of garden to plant whatever we wanted. He was teaching something that is very fundamental, something that has been largely lost in recent history. He was teaching us that it is vital to know how to do things and to understand why things work. He gave us ownership, not of the earth, but of the process and the outcome.

When we create meadows or prairies with our children, we make available important knowledge tools. Not only do they learn how to plant and care for the landscape, but children get inside the meadow, exploring it for themselves, which allows them to make connections to the natural world and learn the value of all living creatures. They learn that soil isn't just dirt, it's full of tiny, unseen, living organisms, whose roles are just as critical and connected to the balance of an ecosystem as are the roles of birds, butterflies and plants.

Hollin Meadows Elementary School, in Fairfax County Virginia, scrapped the notion of a traditional front lawn when students, parents and teachers, planted a meadow instead. Students in science classes regularly explore the meadow, look for pollinators and collect specimens of flower parts, insect eggs, seedpods and chewed leaves for examination and identification. Science teacher Jason Pittman feels that one of the reasons the meadow is such a productive learning tool is that the experiences are so memorable to the students. "As a teacher I can follow down every question and every interesting tidbit

that comes up and allow them to just let their exploration lead learning. We then take those things back in the classroom and use them to meet our curriculum objectives."

Children begin to recognize that human beings can easily tip the balance in an ecosystem by their actions. With this hands-on, learn-by-doing approach, children are more apt to develop co-existence skills and become protecting stewards rather than reckless consumers of the environment. And as kids grow up, surrounded by natural landscapes, non-native lawns will be seen as an unenlightened, landscaping choice of the past. Meadows, prairies and other natural landscapes will become the new landscaping norm.

All over the globe, like-minded groups and individuals are working to save and restore ecosystems. Size is not an issue. We want to take back every inch of earth possible, especially in cities and suburbs. In this reclamation effort, we can each make a difference by restoring the ecosystems in our own little patches of garden.

Student maintenance crew loads up wheelbarrow with dead winter grasses for a trip to the school's compost pile.

above: With the aid of Shawn Akard, Outdoor Education Coordinator, students tend to the meadow throughout the school year and cut it back in late winter for spring renewal.

left: Exploration leads to learning and understanding the natural world.

Minnesota homeowners wanted to replace a chaotic mix of evergreens and ornamental grasses in their north facing, sloping front yard. EnergyScapes, Inc. designed and installed this simple, calming prairie garden with a mix of native flowers and grasses.

regional resources
for creating meadows

Finding local resources, such as nurseries, providing plants native to your area, is a key element in the successful outcome of your meadow or prairie planting.

The following sections are broken into nine broad regions. Within those regions, resources are listed in alphabetical order by state. The regional resource categories are comprised of:

• Web Resources

• Native Plant and Mail Order Nurseries

• Landscape Designers and Restoration Specialists

• Native Plant Societies

• Universities, Extension Services, Soil Testing Labs and Educational Organizations

• Gardens and Arboretums Preserving Natural Landscapes

More general resources follow the regional sections. In the general resource section you can find relevant books, plant databases and tools for bringing natural landscaping to your garden and community.

The regional resources lists are provided as a starting point in the creation of your meadow or prairie.[1] The lists are by no means complete. The need for these resources is growing and the industry is responding. New native plant vendors, consultants and programs are constantly being established. As part of this development, there is a growing understanding that the "right plant for the right place" is not only a native plant compatible with the site conditions, but also a plant native to your ecoregion. What exactly is an ecoregion? As the map on page 234 shows, an ecoregion (otherwise known as a bioregion) is a geographic area constituting a natural ecological community with characteristic flora, fauna, and environmental conditions and bounded by natural rather than man made borders.

For example, in Oregon, areas west of the Cascade Mountains, in the Willamette Valley, have higher rainfall, rich soils and temperate conditions. In the region east of the mountains, dry conditions persist and there are greater extremes in temperature. The plant pallet is vastly different in these ecoregions, located within the same state. Truthfully, it is rare that any state consist of a single ecoregion.

On the map, you can find your ecoregion. To learn about the topography, soils, vegetation and climate conditions in the ecoregion, use the corresponding number and locate the description. The description list starts on page 235, following the general resource section.

Understanding your ecoregion, doing a site analysis and working with local native plant nurseries and professionals will help further fine tune your quest to create a flourishing, truly native meadow or prairie.

[1]Vendor listings do not constitute endorsement of these businesses or individuals.

central plains region

WEB RESOURCES

Grow Native
www.grownative.org

Center for Plant Conservation (CPC)
Conserving and restoring America's
native plants
P.O. Box 299
St. Louis, MO 63166
314-577-9450
www.mobot.org/CPC

Missouri Prairie Foundation
abenson@bensonlaw.com
www.moprairie.org

Nebraska Statewide Arboretum
University of Nebraska
Lincoln, NE 68583-0715
402-472-2971
www.arboretum.unl.edu

U.S. Environmental Protection Agency
Central Plains Region: Resource Conservation
Challenge (RCC) Program
US EPA Region 7
901 N. 5th Street
Kansas City, KS 66101
913-551-7003 or 800-223-0425
www.epa.gov/region07
www.epa.gov/greenkit/landscap.htm

Wildlife Habitat Council
www.wildlifehc.org

SEEDS, NATIVE PLANTS AND
MAIL ORDER NURSERIES

Iowa
Allendan Seed Company
1966 - 175th Lane
Winterset, IA 50273
515-462-1241

Conservation Seeding & Restoration, Inc
506 Center Street West
Kimberly , ID 83341
208-423-4835
www.csr-inc.com

Diversity Farms
25494 320th
Dedham, IA 51440
712-683-5555

Heyne Custom Seed Service
26420 510th St. R.R. I, Box 78
Walnut, IA 51577-9745
712-784-3454

Ion Exchange, Inc.
1878 Old Mission Drive
Harpers Ferry, IA 52146-7533
800-291-2143
www.ionxchange.com

Central Plains prairie in July. Jon Wingo, DJM Ecological Services.

McGinnis Tree and Seed Co.
309 E Florence
Glenwood, IA 51534
712-527-4308

Rose Hill Nursery
2282 Teller Ave
Rose Hill, IA 52586
515-632-8308

WildDesigns Landscaping
12220 580th Street
Centerville, IA 52544
641-895-4846

Kansas
Kaw River Restoration Nurseries
1904 Elm Street, P.O. Box 470
Eudora, KS 66025
785-542-3090
www.appliedeco.com

De Lange Seed, Inc.
P.O. Box 7
Girard, KS 66743
620-724-6223
www.delangeseed.com

Sharp Bros. Seed Co.
202 S. Sycamore
Healy, KS 67850
800-462-8483 620-398-2231
buffalo@sharpseed.com

Missouri
Easyliving Wildflowers
P.O. Box 522
Willow Springs, MO 65793
417-469-2611
john@easywildflowers.com

Environmental Repair Services / The Native Grass Manager
P.O.Box 152
Clinton, MO 64735
660-885-6127
www.prairiesource.com

Hamilton Seeds and Wildflowers
HC Rt. 9, Box 138
Elk Creek, MO 65464
417-967-2190
www.hamiltonseed.com

Missouri Wildflowers Nursery
9814 Pleasant Hill Road
Jefferson City, MO 65109
573-496-3492
mowldflrs@sockets.net
sharpbro@iland.net

Osage Prairie Mercantile
P.O. Box 152
Clinton, MO 64735
660-885-6127
www.Prairiesource.com

Rock Post Wildflowers Nursery
5798 Windy Meadows Lane
Fulton, MO 65251
573-642-6927
mike-ann@sockets.net

Prairie Hill Farm
877 CR 263
Auxvasse, MO 65231
573-387-4680

Pure Air Native Seed Company
Frank & Judy Oberle
24882 Prairie Grove Trail
Novinger, MO 63559
660-488-6849
www.PureAirSeed.com

Sharp Bros. Seed Co.
396 SW Davis-Ladue
Clinton, MO 64735
660-885-7551
sales@sharpbro.com

Nebraska
Habitat Management Solutions, LLC
1011 Alexander Avenue
Elba, NE 68835
308-754-5338

Stock Seed Farms
28008 Mill Road
Murdock, NE 68407-2350
402-867-3771
www.stockseed.com

LANDSCAPE DESIGNERS AND RESTORATION SPECIALISTS

Iowa
Wild Designs Landscaping
12220 580th St
Centerville, IA 52544
641-895-4846

Kansas
Applied Ecological Services
701 E. 22nd Street
Lawrence, KS 66046
785-842-3300
www.AppliedEco.com

Missouri
Barker Horticultural Services
barkerplants2@aol.com
573-242-3300

DJM Ecological Services
Jon Wingo
1001 Pratt Place
Florissant, MO 63031
314-974-4282
www.djmecological.com

Ecological Design Solutions
11 Pinehurst Trail Ct.
Maryland Heights, MO 63043
314-220-3267
www.ecological-design.com

Native Scape Landscaping
871 W. Paddington Dr
Nixa, MO 65714
417-379-3786
www.nativescapelandscaping.com

Rock Post Wildflowers
Fulton, MO
573-642-6927
mike-ann@socket.net

NATIVE PLANT SOCIETIES

Iowa Native Plant Society
Brian Hazlett
Sioux City, IA
Brian.Hazlett@briarcliff.edu
www.public.iastate.edu/~herbarium/inps/
index.php

Iowa- Prairie Coalition Action Network
(Iowa, Texas, Missouri)
leeprairie@austin.rr.com or
Grantridge@aol.com

Kansas Wildflower Society
University of Kansas, R.L. McGregor
Herbarium
2045 Constant Avenue
Lawrence, KS 66047-3729
www.kansasnativeplantsociety.org/index.
htm

Missouri Native Plant Society
P.O. Box 20073,
St. Louis, MO 63144-0073
www.web.missouri.edu/~umo_herb/monps

Nebraska Native Plant Society
www.unl.edu/nebnps/NNPSindex.html

UNIVERSITIES, EXTENSION SERVICES, SOIL TESTING LABS AND EDUCATIONAL ORGANIZATIONS

University of Iowa Extension
www.extension.iastate.edu

A&L Heartland Laboratory, Inc.
111 Linn Street, P.O. Box 455
Atlantic, IA 50022
800-434-0109
www.al-labs.com

Iowa State University Soil and Plant Analysis Lab
G501 Agronomy Hall
Ames, IA 50011-1010
515-294-3076
www.agron.iastate.edu/soiltesting

Kansas State University Research and Extension
www.ksre.ksu.edu/DesktopDefault.aspx

Kansas State University Soil Testing Laboratory
2308 Throckmorton Hall
Manhattan, KS 66506
785-532-7897
www.agronomy.ksu.edu/soiltesting/
DesktopDefault.aspx

University of Missouri Extension
www.extension.missouri.edu/index.aspx

Kinsey's Agricultural Services
297 County Highway 357
Charleston, MO 63834
573-683-3880
www.kinseyag.com

University of Missouri, Delta Soil Testing Lab
P.O. Box 160
Portageville, MO 63873
573-379-5431
http://soilplantlab.missouri.edu

University of Missouri Soil and Plant Testing Laboratory
23 Mumford Hall
Columbia, MO 65211
573-882-3250
www.soiltest.psu.missouri.edu

University of Nebraska Extension
www.extension.unl.edu/home

Midwest Laboratories, Inc
13611 B St.
Omaha, NE 68144-3693
402-334-7770
www.midwestlabs.com

University of Nebraska Soil and Plant Analytical Laboratory
139 Keim Hall
Lincoln, NE 68583
402-472-1571
http://lancaster.unl.edu/ag/crops/soils.shtml

Ward Laboratories
P.O. Box 788, 4007 Cherry Avenue
Kearney, NE 68848
800-887-7645
www.wardlab.com

GARDENS AND ARBORETUMS PRESERVING NATURAL LANDSCAPES

Brenton Arboretum
25141 260th St
Dallas Center, IA 50063-8336
515-992-4211
www.thebrentonarboretum.org

Dyck Arboretum of the Plains
177 West Hickory Street
Box 3000
Hesston, KS 67062
620-327-8127
www.dyckarboretum.org

Kansas Landscape Arboretum
488 Utah Road
Wakefield, KS 67487-9294
785-461-5760
www.naturalkansas.org/kansas.htm

Overland Park Arboretum and Botanical Gardens
8909 W. 179th Street
Overland Park, KS 66085
913-685-3604
www.opkansas.org

Powell Gardens
1609 N.W. U.S. Highway 50
Kingsville, MO 64061
816-697-2600
www.powellgardens.org

Shaw Nature Reserve
Division of Missouri Botanical Garden
Hwy. 100 & I-44 P.O. Box 38
Gray Summit, MO 63039
636-451-3512
www.shawnature.org

great lakes region

WEB RESOURCES

US Environmental Protection Agency Great Lakes Region Green Landscaping: Greenacres US EPA Region 5
77 W. Jackson Blvd.
Chicago, IL 60604
312-353-2000 | 800-621-8431
www.epa.gov/greenacres

SEEDS, NATIVE PLANT AND MAIL ORDER NURSERIES

Illinois
Blazing Star Nursery
2107 Edgewood Drive
Woodstock,Il 60098
815-338-4716 www.blazing-star.com

Bluestem Prairie Nursery
13197 E. 13th Road
Hillsboro, IL 62049
217-532-6344 bluestemnursery@yahoo.com

Earthskin Nursery
9331 NCR 3800E
Mason City, IL 62664
217-482-3524 www.earthskinnursery.com

Enders Greenhouse
104 Enders Drive
Cherry Valley, IL 61016
815-332-5255
www.endersgreenhouse.com

Gerard & Greene
26225 S. Woodlawn Avenue
Crete, IL 60417
708-672-1201 www.gerardandgreene.com

The Natural Garden, Inc.
38 W 443 Hwy. 64,
St. Charles, IL 60175
630-584-0150
www.thenaturalgardeninc.com

Pizzo & Associates
10729 Pine Road
Leland, Il 60531
815-495-2300 www.pizzo.info

Possibility Place Nursery
7548 W. Monee-Manhattan Road
Monee, IL 60449
708-534-3988 www.possibilityplace.com

Wilson Seed Farms
Chris Wilson, 10872 1400 E. Street
Tiskilwa, IL 61368
815-878-8572 www.wilsonseed.com

Simply Native Nursery
681 State Hwy 135
Alexis, IL 61412
309-371-9598
www.simplynativenursery.com

Warm evening light baths home and prairie grass, *Schizachyrium scoparium* (Little bluestem), in Great Lakes region. Jack Pizzo & Associates, Ltd.

Indiana
Earthly Goods, Ltd.
620 E. Main St
New Albany, IN 47150
812-944-3283 www.earthlygoods.com

Earth Source, Inc. &
Heartland Restoration Services
14921 Hand Road
Fort Wayne, IN 46818
260-489-8511 www.earthsourceinc.net

Edge of the Prairie Wildflowers
1641 W. Oak Hill Road
Crawfordsville, IN 47933
765-362-0915

JFNew Native Plant Nursery
128 Sunset Drive
Walkerton, IN 46574
586-2412 www.jfnew.com

Native Plants Unlimited, LLC
13600 Connor Knoll Parkway
Fishers, IN 46038. Tel.
317-506-5456
www.nativeplantsunlimited.com

Spence Restoration Nursery (wholesale)
2220 East Fuson Road
Muncie, IN 47302
765-286-7154 www.spencenursery.com

Winterhaven Wildflowers & Native Plant Preserve
5724 S 900 W
West Point, IN 47992
765-714-4288 www.winterhavenfarm.us

Michigan
Michigan Wildflower Farm
11770 Cutler Road
Portland, MI 48875
517-647-6010
www.michiganwildflowerfarm.com

Native Connections
17080 Hoshel Road
Three Rivers, MI 49093
269-580-4765 www.nativeconnections.net

The Native Plant Nursery, Inc
Ann Arbor, MI 48107
734-677-3260 www.nativeplant.com

Spring Lake Restoration Nurseries
21938 Mushtown Road
Prior Lake, MN 55372
952-447-1919 www.appliedeco.com

WILDTYPE Design
Native Plants & Seed
900 North Every Road
Mason, MI 48854
517-244-1140 www.wildtypeplants.com

Minnesota
Boreal Natives
3943 Munger Shaw Road
Cloquet, MN 55720
218-729-7001 www.prairieresto.com

Carlson Prairie Seed Farm, Inc.
2077 360th Avenue
Lake Bronson, MN 56734
218-794-2693

Feder Prairie Seed Co.
1740 Industrial Drive
Blue Earth, MN 56013
507-526-3049 www.federprairieseed.com

Kaste Seed, Inc.
11779 410th St. SE
Fertile, MN 56540
218-945-6738
www.mnnwgpa.org/kaste.htm

Minnesota Native Landscapes
8740 77th St NE
Otsego, MN 55362
763-295-0010
www.mnnativelandscapes.com

Morning Sky Greenery
44804 East Highway 28
Morris, MN 56267
320-795-6234
www.morningskygreenery.com

Out Back Nursery
15280 110th Street South
Hastings, MN. 55033
651-438-2771 www.outbacknursery.com

Natural Shore Technologies, Inc.
6275 Pagenkopf Rd
Maple Plain, MN 55359
612-703-7581 www.naturalshore.com

Prairie Hill Wildflowers
8955 Lemond Road
Ellendale, MN 56026
507-451-7791 seedman@myclearwave.net

Prairie Moon Nursery
32115 Prairie Lane
Winona, MN 55987
866-417-8156 www.prairiemoon.com

Prairie Restorations, Inc.
Princeton, MN 55327
763-389-4342 www.prairieresto.com

Prairie Wild Enterprises Inc.
275 E 4th St South
Cottonwood, MN 56229
507-423-5575 www.prairiewild.com

Shooting Star Native Seeds
20740 County Road 1
Spring Grove, MN 55974
507-498-3944
www.shootingstarnativeseed.com

Ohio
Envirotech Consultants / Nursery
5380 Twp. Road 143 NE
Somerset, OH 43783
740-743-1669 www.envirotechcon.com

Naturally Native Nursery
13737 St. Rt. 582 (Middleton Pike)
Bowling Green, OH 43402
419-833-2020 www.naturallynative.net

Ohio Prairie Nursery
Hiram, Ohio 44234
330-569-3380 www.ohioprairienursery.com

The Ohio Seed Co.
8888 Parson Road
Croton, OH 43013
614-879-8366
dougwittman@agribiotech.com.

Seeds of the Tall Grasses
1961 Buttermilk Hill Road
Delaware, OH 43015
740-369-5625

University of Minnesota, Soil Testing Laboratory
1902 Dudley Avenue
St. Paul, MN 55108
612-625-3101 www.soiltest.coafes.umn.edu

Ohio State University Cooperative Extension Service
www.ag.ohio-state.edu/~intranet

Brookside Laboratories, Inc.
308 S. Main Street
New Knoxville, OH 45871
419-753-2448 www.blinc.com

Spectrum Analytic, Inc.
P.O. Box 639 1087 Jamison Road
Washington Court House, OH 43160
800-321-1562 www.spectrumanalytic.com

University of Wisconsin Extension
www.uwex.edu/ces

K-Ag Laboratories International, Inc.
2323 Jackson St.
Oshkosh, WI 54901
920-233-5641 www.kaglab.com

Midwestern Bio-Ag
10955 Blackhawk Drive, Box 160
Blue Mounds, WI 53517
800-327-6012 www.midwesternbioag.com

University of Wisconsin
Soil and Plant Analysis Lab
8452 Mineral Point Road
Verona, WI 53593-8696
608-262-4364 www.uwlab.soils.wisc.edu

GARDENS AND ARBORETUMS
PRESERVING NATURAL LANDSCAPES

Chicago Botanical Garden
1000 Lake Cook Road
Glencoe, IL
847-835-5440 www.chicagobotanic.org

Lincoln Memorial Garden & Nature Center
2301 East Lake Shore Drive
Springfield, IL 62712-8908
217-529-1111 www.lmgnc.org

The Morton Arboretum
4100 Illinois Route 53
Lisle, IL
630-968-0074 www.mortonarb.org

Clegg Botanical Gardens
1782 N. 400 E.
Lafayette, IN 47905
765-423-1325

Taltree Arboretum & Gardens
450 West 100 North
Valparaiso, IN 46385
219-462-0025 www.taltree.org

Fernwood Botanical Garden & Nature Preserve
13988 Range Line Road
Niles, MI 49120
269-695-6491 www.fernwoodbotanical.org

Matthaei Botanical Gardens
1800 North Dixboro Road
Ann Arbor, MI 48105-9741
734-647-7600 www.mbgna.umich.edu

Carleton College Cowling Arboretum
Carleton College (located adjacent to campus)
Northfield, MN
507-222-4543
www.apps.carleton.edu/campus/arb

Saint John's Arboretum
Saint John's University
New Science 104
Collegeville, MN 56321-3000
320-363-3163 www.csbsju.edu/arboretum

Stillwater Prairie Reserve
2645 E. St Route 41
Troy, OH 45373
937-335-6273
www.miamicountyparks.com/stillwater.html

Stranahan Arboretum
University of Toledo
4131 Tantara Drive
Toledo, OH 43623
419-841-1007
www.utoledo.edu/as/arboretum

Cofrin Memorial Arboretum
Cofrin Center for Biodiversity
University of Wisconsin-Green Bay
Dept. of Natural and Applied Sciences
Green Bay, WI 54311-7001
920-465-5032
www.uwgb.edu/biodiversity/arboretum

Ledge View Nature Center
W2348 Short Road
Chilton, WI 53014
920-849-7094
www.co.calumet.wi.us/departments2.
iml?dept_id=70

University of Wisconsin-Stevens Point: Schmeeckle Reserve
2419 North Point Drive
Stevens Point, WI 54481-1209
715-346-4992
www.uwsp.edu/cnr/Schmeeckle

University of Wisconsin–Madison Arboretum
1207 Seminole Highway
Madison, WI 53711-3726
608-263-7888 www.uwarboretum.org

Schizachyrium scoparium (Little bluestem) in winter. Prairie Restorations, Inc.

mid-atlantic region

WEB RESOURCES

Alliance for the Chesapeake Bay

A regional nonprofit organization that
builds and fosters partnerships to protect
and to restore the Bay and its rivers. Guides,
publications, resources, plant lists, restoration
tools and training.
DC: 202-466-4633 | MD: 410-377-6270
PA: 717-737-8622 | VA: 804-775-0951
www.alliancechesbay.org

Chesapeake Conservation Landscaping Council

info@chesapeakelandscape.org
www.chesapeakelandscape.org

Environmental Assessment and Innovation Division

US Environmental Protection Agency
Mid-Atlantic Region Green Landscaping
US EPA Region 3
1650 Arch Street
Philadelphia, PA 19103-2029
215-814-2717 | 215-814-3215
www.epa.gov/reg3esd1/garden

U.S. Fish and Wildlife Service

Chesapeake Bay Filed Office
www.fws.gov/chesapeakebay

SEEDS, NATIVE PLANTS AND MAIL ORDER NURSERIES

Delaware

Delaware Native Plant Society

P.O. Box 369,
Dover, DE 19901
302-735-8918
www.delawarenativeplants.org

Gateway Garden Center

7277 Lancaster Pike
Hockessin, DE 19707
302-239-2727
www.gatewaygardens.com

Shelterwood Farm

179 Tuxward Road,
Hartly, DE 19953
302-492-8071

Kentucky

Dropseed Native Nursery

1205 S. Buckeye Lane
Goshen, KY 40026
502-439-9033
www.dropseednursery.com

Habitats Native Plant Nursery, LLC

Jacob Bartley, P.O. Box 265
Silver Grove, KY 41085
859-442-9414
www.habitatsnursery.org

Soft mounds of powder blue *Aster oblongifolius* (Fragrant aster) predominate entry meadow in
October. Fringetree Design Studios, LLC.

John P. Rhody Nursery
Kentucky Division of Forestry
P.O. Box 97
Gilbertsville, KY 42044
800-866-0803 | 270-362-8331

M&M Native Grass Seed Co.
Rt. 1 Box 18
Stephensport, KY 40170
270-547-6855

Morgan County Nursery
438 Tree Nursery Road
West Liberty, KY 41472
606-743-3511

Nolin River Nut Tree Nursery
797 Port Wooden Road
Upton, KY 42784
270-369-8551
www.nolinnursery.com

Shooting Star Nursery
160 Soards Rd
Georgetown, KY 40324
502-867-7979
www.shootingstarnursery.com

Maryland
American Native Plants
4812 E. Joppa Road
Perry Hall, MD 21236
410-634-2847
www.americannativeplants.net

American Plant Food
7405 River Road
Bethesda, MD 20817
301-469-7690
www.americanplant.net

Behnke's Nursery
11300 Baltimore Avenue (US Rte 1)
Beltsville, MD 20705: 301-937 1100
Potomac, MD: 301-983-9200
www.behnke.com

Cavano's Perennials (Wholesale)
6845 Sunshine Avenue
Kingsville, MD 21087
410-592-8077   www.cavanos.com

Clear Ridge Nursery, Inc.
217 Clear Ridge Road
Union Bridge, MD 21791
888-226-9226 | 410-775-7700
www.gonative.us

Earthly Pursuits, Inc.
2901 Kuntz Road
Windsor Mill, MD 21244
410-96-252
www.earthlypursuits.net

Environmental Concern Inc.
201 Boundary Lane
St. Michaels, MD 21663
410-745-9620   www.wetland.org

Homestead Gardens
743 W. Central Avenue
Davidsonville, MD 21035
800-300-5631
Retail 410-798 5000
Wholesale 410-798 1873
www.homesteadgardens.com

Kurt Bluemel, Inc. (Wholesale)
2740 Green Lane
Baldwin, MD 21013
410-557-7229
www.kurtbluemel.com

New Jersey
New Moon Nursery (wholesale)
James and Kimberly Brown
Bridgeton, NJ
888-998-1951
Info@newmoonnursery.com

Pinelands Nursery, Inc.
323 Island Road
Columbus, NJ 08022
609-291-9486 | 800-667-2729
www.pinelandsnursery.com

Toadshade Wildflower Farm
53 Everittstown Road
Frenchtown, NJ 08825
908-996-7500
www.toadshade.com

Wild Earth Native Plant Nursery
1005 Farmingdale Road
Freehold, NJ 07728
732-308-9777
wildearthnpn@compuserve.com

Pennsylvania
Doyle Farm Nursery
158 Norris Road
Delta, PA 17314
717-862-3134
jld@doylefarm.com

Edge of the Woods Native Plant Nursery, LLC
2415 Route 100
Orefield, PA 18069
610-395-2570
www.edgeofthewoodsnursery.com

Ernst Seeds
9006 Mercer Pike
Meadville, PA 16335
800-837-3321 | 814-336-2404
www.ernstseed.com

Meadowood Nursery
24 Meadowood Drive
Hummelstown, PA 17036
717-566-9875
www.meadowoodnursery.com

Mid Atlantic Natives
12506 Susquehanna Trail South
New Freedom, PA 17349
717-227-0924
www.midatlanticnatives.com

North Creek Nurseries (Wholesale)
388 North Creek Road
Landenburg, PA 19350
877-326-7584
www.northcreeknurseries.com

Northeast Natives & Perennials
1716 E. Sawmill Road
Quakertown, PA 18951
215-901-5552
www.nenativesandperennials.com

Redbud Native Plant Nursery
1214 N Middletown Road
Glen Mills, PA 19342
610-358-4300
www.redbudnativeplantnursery.com

Sugarbush Nursery
4272 Morgantown Road
Mohnton, PA 19540
610-856-0998
www.sugarbushnursery.com

Sylva Native Nursery & Seed Co., Inc (wholesale)
3815 Roser Road
Glen Rock, PA 17327
717-227-0486
www.sylvanative.com

Yellow Springs Farm
1165 Yellow Springs Road
Chester Springs, PA 19425
610-827-9204
www.yellowspringsfarm.com

Virginia
Native Seeds
7327 Haefork Lane
Gloucester Point, VA 23062
804-642-0736

Nature By Design
300 Calvert Avenue
Alexandria, VA 22301
703-683-4769
www.nature-by-design.com

Pinelands Nursery
8877 Richmond Road
Toano, VA 23168
757-667-2729 | 800-667-2729
www.pinelandsnursery.com

Sassafras Farm
7029 Bray Road
Hayes, VA 23072
804-642-0923
sassafrasfarm@verizon.net

Southern Exposure Seed Exchange
P.O. Box 460
Mineral, VA 23117
540-894-9480
www.southernexposure.com

West Virginia
Enchanter's Garden
HC 77 Box 108
Hinton, WV 25951
304-466-3154
www.enchantersgarden.com

Grounds For Nature-Terra DeMedici
P.O. Box 1211
Hedgesville, WV 25427
304-258-3687
www.groundsfornature.com

Sunshine Farm & Garden
HC67 Box 539B
Renick, WV 24966
304-497 2208
www.sunfarm.com

LANDSCAPE DESIGNERS AND RESTORATION SPECIALISTS

Delaware
Verde Works LLC
Christopher Canning RLA, MSLA, ASLA
911 W. Church Rd
Newark DE, 19711
302-650-8411
www.verdeworks.com

District of Columbia

DC Greenworks
1341 H Street NE
Washington, DC 20002
202-518-6195
www.dcgreenworks.org

Maryland

Bay Smart Gardening
Alice N. Mutch, Master Gardener
1754 Birdbrook Trail
Annapolis, MD 21401
410-353-3861
www.baysmartgardening.com

Gardens of the Three Graces
Catherine Zimmerman
10211 Lorain Ave
Silver Spring, MD 20901
301-754-1414
www.themeadowproject.com

Good Earth Gardeners, LLC
Kara Bowne Crissey
410-212-7014
www.GoodEarthGardeners.com

Heal Earth Gardens
Carole Barth
Silver Spring, MD 20901
301-593-7863
www.healearthgardens.com

Natural Resources Design, Inc.
Lauren Wheeler
402 Boyd Avenue
Takoma Park MD 20912
DC Office 202-489-6214
MD Office 301-891-1569
www.naturalresourcesdesign.com

Pax Garden Design
Chris Pax
Central MD
301-271-1971
www.paxgardens.com

Sylvan Green Earth Consulting
10805 River Road
Denton, MD 21629
410-310-0160
www.sylvangreenearth.com/consulting.html

Washington Landscapes, LLC.
Peter C. Dickens
17210 Manning Road, East
Accokeek, MD 20607
301-283-3999
www.washingtonlandscapes.com

Pennsylvania

Andropogon Associates
10 Shurs Lane
Philadelphia, PA 19127-2186
215-487-0700
www.andropogon.com

Cotswold Gardens
James Hollis
176 Woodview Road
West Grove PA 19390
610-345-1076
www.cotswoldgardensinc.com

ECOdesign and Management
Harriet Wentz
P.O. Box 546
West Chester, PA 19381
610-659-6737 | 866-496-9882
www.ecodesignmanage.com

Fringetree Design Studios, LLC
David Hughes
P.O. Box 156
Upper Black Eddy PA 18972
610-847-0915
fringetree@epix.net

Green Man Enviroscaping LLC
Everett A. Warren
440 Acorn Drive
Lehighton, PA 18235
610-442-7964
www.greenmanenvy.com

KMS Design Group, LLC
206 Bridge St.
Phoenixville, PA 19460
610-726-1324
www.kmsdesigngroup.com

Larry Weaner, Larry Weaner Landscape Design Associates
43 Limekiln Pike, Suite 100
Glenside, PA 19038
215-886-9740
www.lweanerdesign.com

Taproot Native Design
Jessie Laurel Benjamin, Landscape Designer
1062 Glen Hall Road
Kennett Square, PA 19348
484-887-8612
www.taprootdesign.com

Virginia
Peggy Bowers
Horticulturist Consultant
Northern Virginia
sundogpeg@cox.net

Cole Burrell
Native Landscape Design and Restoration
University of Virginia
Charlottesville, VA 22904
434-975-2859   ccb9d@virginia.edu

Claudia Thompson-Deahl
12250 Sunset Hills Road
Reston, VA 20190
703-435-6547
Claudia@reston.org

Jeff Wolinski
Consulting Ecologist
38643 Morrisonville Road
Lovettsville, VA 20180
540-882-4947

NATIVE PLANT SOCIETIES

Delaware Native Plant Society
P.O. Box 369
Dover, DE 19903
302-674-5187
www.delawarenativeplants.org

District of Columbia
Botanical Society of Washington
Dept. of Botany, NHB
166 Smithsonian Institution
Washington, D.C. 20560
www.botsoc.org

Kentucky Native Plant Society
c/o Dept. of Biological Sciences, Moore 235
Eastern Kentucky University
521 Lancaster Avenue
Richmond, KY 40475-3102
www.knps.org

Maryland Native Plant Society
P.O. Box 4877
Silver Spring, MD 20914
www.mdflora.org

The Native Plant Society of New Jersey
Office of Continuing Professional Education
Cook College
102 Ryders Lane
New Brunswick, NJ 08901-8519
www.npsnj.org

Botanical Society of Western Pennsylvania
5837 Nicholson St.,
Pittsburgh, PA 15217
www2.carlow.edu/sites/botanical/about.
html

Delaware Valley Fern & Wildflower Society
263 Hillcrest Road,
Wayne, PA 19087
www.dvfws.org

Pennsylvania Native Plant Society
1001 E. College Avenue,
State College, PA 16801
www.pawildflower.org

Virginia Native Plant Society
400 Blandy Farm Lane #2
Boyce, VA 22620
540-837-1600
www.vnps.org

West Virginia Native Plant Society
P.O. Box 808,
New Haven, WV 25265-0808
www.wvnps.org

University of Delaware Cooperative Extension
www.ag.udel.edu/extension

University of Delaware Soil Testing Program
152 Townsend Hall
531 S College Avenue
Newark, DE 19717-1303
302-831-1392
ag.udel.edu/other_websites/DSTP

University of the District of Columbia Cooperative Extension Services
www.udc.edu/cooperative_extension/coop_ext.htm

University of Kentucky Cooperative Extension Service
www.ces.ca.uky.edu/ces

University of Kentucky Soil Testing Laboratory
103 Regulatory Service Bldg.
Lexington, KY 40546-0275
859-257-2785
www.soils.rs.uky.edu

Waters Agricultural Laboratories, Inc.
2101 Calhoun Road
Owensboro, KY 42301
270-685-4039
www.watersag.com

University of Maryland Extension
www.extension.umd.edu

Rutgers New Jersey Cooperative Extension
www.njaes.rutgers.edu/county

Rutgers Cooperative Extension, Soil Testing Laboratory
P.O. Box 902
Milltown, NJ 08850
732-932-9295
www.rce.rutgers.edu/soiltestinglab/default.asp

Pennsylvania State Cooperative Extension
www.extension.psu.edu

Pennsylvania State University
Agricultural Analytic Services University Laboratory
Tower Road
University Park, PA 16802
814-863-0841
www.aasl.psu.edu

A&L Eastern Agricultural Laboratories, Inc.
7621 Whitepine Road
Richmond, VA 23237
804-743-9401
www.al-labs-eastern.com

Virginia Cooperative Extension, Virginia Tech
www.ext.vt.edu

Virginia Tech Soil Testing Laboratory
145 Smyth Hall (0465)
Blacksburg, VA 24061
540-231-6893
www.soiltest.vt.edu

West Virginia University Extension Service
www.wvu.edu/~exten

Soil Testing Laboratory
Ag. Sciences Building
West Virginia University
Morgantown, WV 26506
304-293-6256
www.caf.wvu.edu/~forage/3201.htm

Delaware Nature Society
3511 Barley Mill Road
Hockessin, DE 19707
302-239 2334
www.delawarenaturesociety.org

Irvine Nature Center
11201 Garrison Forest Road
Owings Mills, MD 21117
443-738-9200
www.explorenature.org

MAEscapes
Mid-Atlantic Ecological Landscapes Partnership
Penn State Cooperative Extension
112 Pleasant Acres Road
York, PA 17402
717-840-7408
www.maescapes.org

The Nature Conservancy—Maryland
5410 Grosvenor Lane, Suite 100
Bethesda, MD 20814
301-897 8570
amishra@tnc.org

The Nature Conservancy—Virginia
490 Westfield Road
Charlottesville, VA 22901
434-295 6106
dwhite@tnc.org

GARDENS AND ARBORETUMS PRESERVING NATURAL LANDSCAPES

Mt Cuba Center
P.O. Box 3570,
Greenville, DE 19807
302 329-4244
www.mtcubacenter.org

United States National Arboretum
3501 New York Avenue, NE
Washington, DC 20002-1958
202-245-2726
www.usna.usda.gov

Bernheim Arboretum & Research Forest
State Highway 245
P. O. Box 130
Clermont, KY 40110-0130
502-955-8512
www.bernheim.org

Adkins Arboretum
12610 Eveland Road
P.O. Box 100
Ridgely, MD 21660
410-634-2847
www.adkinsarboretum.org

Lewis W. Barton Arboretum
Meadford Leas
One Medford Leas Way
Medford, NJ 08055
609-654-3000
www.medfordleas.org/arboretum.htm

Bowman's Hill Wildflower Preserve
1635 River Road (PA Route 32)
New Hope, PA 18938
215-862-2924
www.bhwp.org

Brandywine River Museum
U.S. Route 1, P.O. Box 141
Chadds Ford, PA 19317
610-388-2700
www.brandywinemuseum.org/gardens.html

Longwood Gardens
1001 Longwood Road
Kennett Square, PA 19348
610-388-1000
www.longwoodgardens.org

American Horticultural Society, River Farm
7931 East Boulevard Drive
Alexandria, VA 22308
703-768-5700 800-777-7931
www.ahs.org

Blandy Experimental Farm & The State Arboretum of Virginia
400 Blandy Farm Lane
Boyce VA 22620
540-837-1758
www.virginia.edu/blandy

West Virginia Botanic Garden
714 Venture Drive
Morgantown, WV 26508-7308
304-376-2717
www.wvbg.org

Rippling Waters Organic Farm
55 River Road
Steep Falls, ME 04085
207-642-5161 www.ripplingwaters.org

Union Agway
2179 Heald Highway
Union, ME 04862
207-785-4385 www.unionagway.com

Massachusetts
New England Wild Flower Society
Nasami Farm and Sanctuary
128 North Street
Whately, MA 01093
413-397-9922
www.newfs.org/visit/nasami-farm

Project Native
342 North Plain Road
Housatonic, MA 01236
413-274-3433 www.projectnative.org

New Hampshire
Found Well Farm
730 Borough Road
Pembroke, NH 03275
603-228-1421 www.foundwellfarm.com

New Hampshire State Forest Nursery
405 Daniel Webster Hwy.
Boscawen, NH 03303
603-796-2323 www.nhnursery.com

Oakridge Nurseries
East Kingston, NH 03872
603-642-7339

Van Berkum Nursery (Wholesale)
4 James Road
Deerfield, NH 03037
603-463-7663 www.vanberkumnursery.com

New York
Amanda's Garden
8410 Harpers Ferry Road
Springwater, NY 14560
585-669-2275 www.amandagarden.com

Catskill Native Nursery
607 Samsonville Road
Kerhonkson, NY 12446-1543
845-626-2758
www.catskillnativenursery.com

Fiddlehead Creek Farm and Native Plant Nursery
7381 State Route 40
Fort Ann, NY 12827
518-632-5505 www.fiddleheadcreek.com

Fort Pond Native Plants, Inc.
26 S Embassy Street
Montauk, NY 11954
631-668-6452 www.nativeplants.net

Native Landscapes Garden Center
991 Rt. 22
Pawling, NY 12564
845-855-7050 www.nativelandscaping.net

The Plantsmen Nursery, LLC
482 Peruville Road
Groton, NY 13073
607-533-7193 www.plantsmen.com

Vermont
Vermont Wildflower Farm
R.R.7, Box 5
Charlotte, VT 05445
800-424-1165 | 802-985-9455

LANDSCAPE DESIGNERS AND RESTORATION SPECIALISTS

Arrowwood Gardens
10 Virginia Street
Niantic, CT 06357
860-460-1398
www.arrowwoodgardens.com

Camilla Worden Garden Design LLC
Camilla Worden
78 Deer Hill Avenue
Danbury, CT 06810-7938
203-790-9809 www.camillaworden.com

Ecologic Consulting
Troy Shirt Factory Building
Glens Falls, NY 12804
518-792-9557 www.ecologicconsulting.net

The Horticultural Intuitive
209 East Pond Rd
Nobleboro, ME 04555
207-441-7045 www.thilandscapes.com

Larry Weaner Landscape Design Associates
43 Limekiln Pike, Suite 100
Glenside, PA 19038
215-886-9740
Connecticut Office 203-834-0174
www.lweanerdesign.com

Muse Design
3 Locust Drive
Sag Harbor, NY 11963
631-725-8725 www.musedesign.net

Northeast Organic Farmers Association
NOFA Organic Land Care Program (CT & MA)
Stevenson CT 06491 203-888-5146
www.organiclandcare.net/aolcp
(Directory of Organic Land Care Professionals)

Plantscapes, Inc.
Mike Nadeau
Fairfield, CT 06825
203-382-0335
www.plantscapesorganics.com

Risa Edelstein Designs AOLCP, MCA
36 Tanager Street
Arlington, MA 02476
617-710-8157
www.gardenandthegoodlife.typepad.com

Southern Tier Consulting and Nursery, Inc.
2701-A Rt. 305, P.O. Box 30
West Clarksville, NY 14786
800-848-7614 | 585-968-3120
www.southerntierconsulting.com

The Underground
(Directory of landscape professionals)
Framingham, MA 01703-2440
508-872-3792
theunderground.pbworks.com

NATIVE PLANT SOCIETIES

Connecticut Botanical Society
New Haven, CT 06532-0004
www.ct-botanical-society.org

Connecticut Chapter—NEWFS
25 Lanz Lane
Ellington, CT 06029-2310
860-871-8085 ctnewfs@att.net

Maine Chapter—NEWFS
RR 1, Box 79 Sawyers Island
Boothbay, ME 04537
207-633-4327 gccarr@clinic.net

New England Wild Flower Society
180 Hemenway Road
Framingham, MA 01701-2699
www.newfs.org

Cape Cod Chapter—NEWFS
508-432-4188

New York Flora Association
New York State Museum 3132 CEC,
Albany, NY 12230
www.nyflora.org

The Finger Lakes Native Plant
Society of Ithaca
532 Cayuga Heights Road
Ithaca, NY 14850
607-257-4853
www.fingerlakesnativeplantsociety.org

Niagara Frontier Botanical Society
Buffalo Museum of Science
1020 Humboldt Parkway
Buffalo, NY 14211
www.acsu.buffalo.edu/~insrisg/botany

Rhode Island Wild Plant Society
Peace Dale, RI 02883-0114
www.riwps.org

Vermont Chapter—NEWFS
New London, NH 03257
603-763-0045 tkhewitt@aol.com

UNIVERSITIES, EXTENSION SERVICES, SOIL TESTING LABS AND EDUCATIONAL ORGANIZATIONS

Connecticut Cooperative Extension System
www.extension.uconn.edu

Soil Nutrient Analysis Laboratory
6 Sherman Place, U-5102
University of Connecticut
Storrs, CT 06269-5102
860-486-4274
www.soiltest.uconn.edu

University of Maine Cooperative Extension
www.extension.umaine.edu

University of Maine Analytical Lab
Maine Soil Testing Service
5722 Deering Hall
Orono, ME 04469
207-581-2945 www.anlab.umesci.maine.edu

Woods End Research Laboratory
Mt. Vernon, ME 04352
207-293-2457 www.woodsend.org

University of Massachusetts Extension
www.umassextension.org

University of Massachusetts Soil Testing Laboratory
West Experiment Station
North Pleasant Street
Amherst, MA 01003
413-545-2311
www.umass.edu/plsoils/soiltest

Cornell University Cooperative Extension Service
www.cce.cornell.edu/Pages/Default.aspx

New Hampshire Cooperative Extension Service
www.extension.unh.edu

UNH Soil Testing Lab
Spaulding Life Sciences
38 College Road
Durham, NH 03824
603-862-3210 soil.testing@unh.edu

Cornell University, Nutrient Analysis Laboratories
804 Bradfield Hall
Ithaca, NY 14853
607-255-4540
www.css.cornell.edu/soiltest

University of Rhode Island Cooperative Extension Service
www.uri.edu/ce/index1.html

University of Vermont Extension System
www.uvm.edu/extension

UVM Agricultural & Environmental Testing Laboratory
219 Hills Building
Burlington, VT 05405-0082
800-244-6402
www.uvm.edu/pss/ag_testing

Northeast Organic Farmers Association, (NOFA)
NOFA Organic Land Care Program (CT & MA)
Stevenson CT 06491
203-888-5146 www.organiclandcare.net

GARDENS AND ARBORETUMS PRESERVING NATURAL LANDSCAPES

Connecticut College Arboretum
270 Mohegan Avenue
New London, CT 06320
860-439-5020
www.conncoll.edu/green/arbo

Coastal Maine Botanical Gardens
Boothbay, ME 04537
207-633-4333
www.mainegardens.org

Cornell Plantations
1 Plantations Road
Ithaca, NY, 14850
607-255-2400
www.cornellplantations.org

Denison Pequotsepos Nature Center
109 Pequotsepos Road
Mystic, CT 06355
860-536-1216 www.dpnc.org

Garden in the Woods
(New England Wild Flower Society)
180 Hemenway Road
North Framingham, MA 01701-2699
508-877-7630
www.newfs.org/visit/Garden-in-the-Woods

northwest region

WEB RESOURCES

US Environmental Protection Agency
Northwest Region Greenscapes Program
www.epa.gov/greenscapes
www.epa.gov/greenacres

U.S. EPA, Region 10
1200 Sixth Avenue Suite 900
Seattle, WA 98101
800-424-4372 or 206-553-1200

Naturescaping: Oregon Department of Fish & Wildlife
Information & Education
P.O. Box 59
2501 SW 1st
Portland, OR 97201
503-872-5274
www.dfw.state.or.us/NS

King Conservation District
1107 SW Grady Way, Suite 130
Renton, WA 98057
425-282-1897
www.kingcd.org

Guidelines for planting native seed
Pacific Northwest Natives
1525 Laurel Heights Drive NW
Albany, OR 97321
541-928-8239
www.pacificnwnatives.com

NATIVE PLANT AND MAIL ORDER NURSERIES

Idaho
Buffalo-berry Farm
5 I East Lake Fork Road
McCall, ID 83638
208-634-3062

Conservation Seeding & Restoration, Inc
506 Center Street West
Kimberly, ID 83341
208-423-4835
www.csr-inc.com

Native Seed Foundation
7312 Perkins Lake Road
Moyie Springs, ID 83845
208-267-1477
www.nativeseedfoundation.com

Native wildflowers *Aquilegia chrysantha* (Golden columbine), *Penstemon strictus* (Rocky mountain penstemon), *Gaillardia aristata* (Blanket flower), and *Linum lewisii* (Lewis blue flax) combine with drought tolerant non-natives and native grasses; *Festuca idahoensis* (Idaho fescue), *Koeleria macrantha* (Prairie junegrass), *Leymus cinereus* (Great Basin wildrye) and *Pseudoroegneria spicata* (Bluebunch wheatgrass).

Drought and cold tolerant sub alpine prairie planting. Ketchum, Idaho. Design, Kelley Weston and Karen Sherrerd ASLA, Native Landscapes Inc.

Natives West Nursery and Landscaping
155 Falcon Ridge Rd
Kooskia, ID 83539
208-926-7707
www.nativeswest.com

Palouse-Clearwater Environmental Institute (PCEI) Learning Nursery
P.O. Box 8596, 1040 Rodeo Drive
Moscow, ID 83843
208-882-1444
www.pcei.org/water/nursery.htm

Seeds Trust-High Altitude Gardens
P.O. Box 596
Cornville, AZ 86325
928-649-3315
www.seedstrust.com
(Seeds collected in mts. of central ID)

Sun Mountain Natives
1406 East F Street
Moscow, ID 83843
208-883-7611
www.sunmountainnatives.net

Oregon
Aurora Nursery, Inc. (wholesale)
22821 Boones Ferry Road
N.E. Aurora, OR 97002
503-678-7903
www.auroranursery.com

Bosky Dell Natives
23311 SW Bosky Dell Lane
West Linn, OR 97068
503-638-5945
www.boskydellnatives.com

Confederated Tribes of the Umatilla Indian Reservation
Tribal Native Plant Nursery
Pendleton, OR 97801
541-310-1071
www.tribalnativeplants.com

Deschutes Native Seed Resources LLC
Spring Alaska Olson
1490 NW Newport Ave
Bend, OR 97701
541-647-9604
springalaska@hotmail.com

Echo Valley Natives
18883 S. Ferguson Road
Oregon City, OR 97045
503-631-2451
www.echovalleynatives.com

Humble Roots Farm and Nursery, LLC
Mosier, OR 97040
503-449-3694
web.mac.com/humbleroots/Site/
HumbleHome.html

Heritage Seedlings, Inc. (wholesale)
Lynda Boyer, Restoration Biologist and Native Plant Manager
4194 71st Ave SE
Salem OR 97317
503-585-9835 x103
www.heritageseedlings.com

Hobbs & Hopkins, Ltd. (seed)
1712 SE Ankeny
Portland, OR 97214
800-345-3295

La Ferme Noire
39621 Almen Drive
Lebanon, OR 97355
541-258-8990

Livingscape Nursery
3926 N. Vancouver
Portland, OR 97227
503-248-0104
www.livingscapenursery.com

Native Plant Nursery
73820 HWY 331
Pendleton, OR 97801
541-310-1071
www.tribalnativeplants.com

Oregon Native Plant Nursery
Woodburn, OR 97071-0886
503-981-2353
oregonnativeplant@yahoo.com

Pacific Northwest Natives
1525 Laurel Heights Drive NW
Albany, OR 97321
541-928-8239
www.pacificnwnatives.com

Portland Nursery
5050 SE Stark
Portland, OR 97215
503-231-5050 or 503-788-9000
www.portlandnursery.com

Rugged Country Plants
53671 W. Crockett Rd
Milton-Freewater, OR 97862
541-938-3970
www.ruggedcountryplants.com

Willamette Gardens
3290 SW Willamette Avenue
Corvallis, OR 97333
541-754-0893
www.willamettegardens.com

Washington
BFI Native Seeds, LLC
1145 S Jefferson Ave
Moses Lake, WA 98837
509-765-6348
www.bfinativeseeds.com

Derby Canyon Natives
9750 Derby Canyon Road
Peshastin, WA 98847
509-548-9404
www.derbycanyonnatives.com

Inside Passage Seeds
Port Townsend, WA 98368
800-361-9657
www.insidepassageseeds.com

Friendly Natives Plants and Design
Bainbridge Island WA 98110
206-387-5943
www.friendlynatives.net/Welcome.html

Frosty Hollow Ecological Restoration
Langley, WA 98260
360-579-2332

Garden Treasures Nursery & Organic Farm
3328 State Route 530
Arlington WA 98223
360-435-9272
www.arlingtongardentreasures.com

Methow Natives
19 Aspen Lane
Winthrop, WA 98862
509-996-3562
www.methownatives.com

Milestone Nursery
7th and State Street (Highway 14)
Lyle, WA
509-365-5222
milestone@gorge.net

Nothing But Northwest Natives
14836 NE 249th ST
Battle Ground, WA 98604
360-666-3023
www.nothingbutnwnatives.com

Plantas Nativa LLC
628 Old Samish Rd
Bellingham, WA 98226
360-715-9655
www.plantasnativa.com

Plants of the Wild
Tekoa, WA 99033
509-284-2848
www.plantsofthewild.com

Sound Native Plants, Inc.
Olympia, WA 98507-7505
360-352-4122
www.soundnativeplants.com

Tree Frog Farm, Inc.
3679 Sunrise Road
Lummi Island, WA 98262
360-758-7260
www.treefrogfarm.com/nativeplants

Wildlands Nursery
1941 Saint St
Richland, WA 99320
509-948-5864
www.wildlandsnursery.com

Woodbrook Nursery
5919 78th Ave NW
Gig Harbor, WA 98335-7568
253-265-6271
www.woodbrooknativeplantnursery.com

LANDSCAPE DESIGNERS AND RESTORATION SPECIALISTS

Idaho
Conservation Seeding & Restoration, Inc
506 Center Street West
Kimberly, ID 83341
208-423-4835
www.csr-inc.com

Native Landscapes Inc.
Kelley Weston
810 South Main
Hailey ID
208-578-2200
www.native-landscapes.com

Natives West Nursery and Landscaping
155 Falcon Ridge
Kooskia, ID 83539
208-926-7707
www.nativeswest.com

Oregon
Eastern Oregon Stewardship Services
Prineville, OR
541-447-8166
byoutie@crestviewcable.com

Michele Eccleston
503-358-8588
www.thepurplegarden.com

The Garden Angels Landscape Design, Project Management & Contracting, LLC
910 Madrona Avenue SE
Salem, OR 97302
503-581-5356
www.TheGardenAngels.com

Gretchen Vadnais Landscape Architects, LLC
12115 NW Old Quarry Road
Portland, OR 97229
503-646-3517
gretchen@gvla.net | kathleen@gvla.net

Donna Giguere, APLD
Landscape Design & Consultation
503-777-1177
www.giguerelandscapedesign.com

Mark Griswold Wilson
Restoration Ecologist
1123 SE Harney Street
Portland, OR 97202
mgwilson@teleport.com

Innovative Landscapes
Bart Johnson
Eugene, OR 97405
541-510-7346
bartj77@gmail.com

Dennis Lueck
2755 Potter Street
Eugene, OR 97405
541-684-8716

Deschutes Native Seed Resources LLC
Spring Alaska Olson
1490 NW Newport Ave
Bend, OR 97701
541-647-9604
springalaska@hotmail.com

Madrona Consulting, Aryana Ferguson
Eugene, OR 97405
541-729-8339
madronaconsulting@comcast.net

MIG
Dean Apostol
815 SW 2nd Avenue
Portland, OR 97204
503-297-1005
www.migcom.com

Native Plant Nursery
73820 HWY 331 P.o. Box 638
Pendleton, OR 97801
541-310-1071
www.tribalnativeplants.com

Plan-It Earth Design
1725 SE 34th Avenue
Portland, OR 97214
503-239-0105
www.plan-it-earthdesign.com

Second Nature Garden Design
Eileen Stark
Portland, OR 97212
503-467-8545
www.sngdesign.net

Urban Renaissance, LLC
4908 SW Barnes Road
Portland, OR 97221
503-2232426
www.landscapedesigninaday.googlepages.com

Visionscapes Northwest
17605 NW Lone Rock Drive
Portland, OR 97229
503-531-3947
www.visionscapesnorthwest.com

Washington
BFI Native Seeds, LLC
1145 S Jefferson Ave
Moses Lake, WA 98837
509-765-6348
www.bfinativeseeds.com

Derby Canyon Natives
9750 Derby Canyon Road
Peshastin, WA 98847
509-548-9404
www.derbycanyonnatives.com

Frosty Hollow Ecological Restoration
Langley, WA 98260
360-579-2332

Greenbelt Consulting
Clinton, WA 98236
360-341-3433
www.greenbeltconsulting.com

Mariposa Naturescapes
Seattle, WA
206-419-1836
www.MariposaNaturescapes.com

Plantas Nativa East, LLC
303 Twisp River Road
Twisp, WA 98856
509-341-4133
www.pneast.com

Seasons Garden Design
Vancouver, WA
360-546-2746
www.SeasonsGardenDesign.com

Sound Native Plants, Inc.
Olympia, WA 98507
360-352-4122
www.soundnativeplants.com

Wildlands Nursery
1941 Saint St
Richland, WA 99320
509-948-5864
www.wildlandsnursery.com

NATIVE PLANT SOCIETIES

Idaho Native Plant Society
P.O. Box 9451
Boise, ID 83707-3451

Native Plant Society of Oregon
P.O. Box 902, Eugene, OR 97440
www.NPSOregon.org
www.idahonativeplants.org

Washington Native Plant Society
6310 NE 74th Street, Suite 215E
Seattle, WA 98115
206-527-3210
www.wnps.org

UNIVERSITIES, EXTENSION SERVICES, SOIL TESTING LABS AND EDUCATIONAL ORGANIZATIONS

University of Idaho Extension
www.extension.uidaho.edu

University of Idaho, Analytical Sciences Laboratory
Helm Research Center 222 W. Sixth Street
Moscow, ID 83843-2203
208-885-7081
www.agls.uidaho.edu/asl

Oregon State University Extension Service
www.extension.oregonstate.edu

Soil Foodweb, Inc.
728 S.W. Wake Rubin Avenue
Corvallis, OR 97333
541-752-5066
www.soilfoodweb.com

Washington State University Extension
www.ext.wsu.edu

Soiltest Farm Consultants, Inc.
2925 Driggs Drive
Moses Lake, WA 98837
800-764-1622 | 509-765-1622
www.soiltestlab.com/index.html

Center for Urban Horticulture
University of Washington
3501 NE 41st Street
University of Washington
P.O. Box 354115
Seattle, WA 98195-4115
206-543-8616
www.weber.u.washington.edu/~urbhort

Washington State University, Cooperative Extension, King County
506-Second Avenue, Suite 612
Seattle, WA 98104
Community Horticulture Education
206-205-1438 | 541-729-8339
www.gardening.wsu.edu/text/nwnative

GARDENS AND ARBORETUMS PRESERVING NATURAL LANDSCAPES

Idaho Botanical Garden
2355 Old Penitentiary Road
Boise, ID 83712
208-343-8649
www.idahobotanicalgarden.org

Mount Pisgah Arboretum
34901 Frank Parrish Road
Eugene, OR 97405
541-747-3817
www.mountpisgaharboretum.org

The Oregon Garden
879 West Main Street
Silverton, OR 97381
503-874-8100
www.oregongarden.org

Bellevue Botanical Garden Society
12001 Main Street
Bellevue, WA 98005-3522
425-452-2750
www.bellevuebotanical.org

Washington Park Arboretum
University of Washington
Box 358010
Seattle, WA 98195-8010
206-543-8800
www.depts.washington.edu/wpa

pacific region

WEB RESOURCES

US Environmental Protection Agency Pacific Region Greenscapes
U.S. EPA Environmental Information Center
75 Hawthorne Street, 13th Floor
San Francisco, CA 94105
415-947-8000 | 866-372-9378
r9.info@epa.gov

EPA Southern California
213-244-1800

San Diego Border Liaison Office
610 West Ash Street, Suite 905
San Diego, CA 92101
619-235-4765 | 800-334-0741
www.epa.gov/region09/waste/organics/
greenscapes

Calflora
(information on wild California plants)
www.calflora.org

SEEDS, NATIVE PLANT AND MAIL ORDER NURSERIES

Albright Seed Company
Carpinteria, CA 93014-1275
805-684-0436 www.albrightseed.com

Central Coast Wilds
336 Golf Club Drive
Santa Cruz, CA 95060
831-459-0656 www.CentralCoastWilds.com

Freshwater Farms/North Coast Native Seed Bank
5851 Myrtle Avenue
Eureka, CA 95503
707-444-8261 www.freshwaterfarms.com

Golden State Growers
San Luis Obispo, CA 93406
805-234-3751

Las Pilitas Nursery
3232 Las Pilitas Road
Santa Margarita, Ca 93453
805-438-5992 www.laspilitas.com

Las Pilitas Nursery
8331 Nelson Way
Escondido, CA 92026
760-749-5930 www.laspilitas.com

Native Revival Nursery
2600 Mar Vista Dr
Aptos, CA 95003
831-684-1811 www.nativerevival.com

North Coast Native Nursery
Petaluma, CA 94953
707-769-1213
www.northcoastnativenursery.com

Sierra Seed Supply
358 Williams Valley Road
Greenville, CA 95947
530-284-7926 www.sierraseedsupply.com

California natives *Layia platyglossa* (Tidy tips), *Nemophila menziesii* (Baby blue-eyes) and *Festuca rubra* (Creeping red fescue) flank flagstone path. Jenny Fleming meadow garden.

Theodore Payne Foundation for Wild Flowers and Native Plants, Inc.
10459 Tuxford Street
Sun Valley, CA 91352
818-768-1802 www.theodorepayne.org

The Reveg Edge
Redwood City, CA 94064
650-325-7333
www.ecoseeds.com/standards.html

Sierra Seed Supply
358 Williams Valley Road
Greenville, CA 95947
530-284-7926 www.sierraseedsupply.com

The Watershed Nursery
601 A Canal Blvd.
Richmond, CA 94804
510-234-2222 www.reconnativeplants.com

LANDSCAPE DESIGNERS AND RESTORATION SPECIALISTS

Argia Designs
Native Landscape Design and Consultation
San Diego, CA
760-420-2411 www.argiadesigns.com

AY Sustainable Design
1821 Stratton Circle
Walnut Creek, CA 94598
424-298-7315 www.aysustainabledesign.com

California's Own Native Landscape Design
Greg Rubin, Contracting and Restoration
www.calown.com

Central Coast Wilds
336 Golf Club Drive
Santa Cruz, CA 95060
831-459 0656 www.CentralCoastWilds.com

East Bay Wilds
1972 A 36th Avenue
Oakland, CA 94601
510-409-5858 www.eastbaywilds.com

Freshwater Farms/North Coast Native Seed Bank
5851 Myrtle Avenue
Eureka, CA 95503
707-444-8261 www.freshwaterfarms.com

Paul Furman
San Francisco, CA
415-722-6037 www.edgehill.net

Indig Design
Peigi Duvall
Woodside, CA 94062-0146
650-704-3926 www.indigdesign.com

Late Afternoon Design
310 North School Street
Ukiah, CA 95482
707-462-5133 www.lateafternoon.com

Native Here Nursery
101 Golf Course Drive
Berkeley, CA 94708
510-549-0211 www.ebcnps.org

NativeScape Development Inc.
10849 Ralston Avenue
Pacoima, CA 91331
818-899-1541 www.gogreennsd.com

Second Nature Design
Alma Hecht
415-586-6578 www.secondnature.bz

Tierra Seca Landscape Design
Dr. Brian Swope
415-947-0228 www.tierraseca.com

Three Ravens Ranch
Cedarville, CA 96104
530-279-6361 www.3ravensranch.com

NATIVE PLANT SOCIETIES

California Native Plant Society
1722 J Street, Suite 17
Sacramento, CA 95814
916-447-2677 www.cnps.org

UNIVERSITIES, EXTENSION SERVICES, SOIL TESTING LABS AND EDUCATIONAL ORGANIZATIONS

University of California Cooperative Extension
www.ucanr.org

ABC ORGANICS Crop Research Foundation
P.O. Box 967
Camarillo, CA 93011
805-675-8747 www.abcorganics.com

Soil Control Lab, Inc.
42 Hangar Way
Watsonville, CA 95076
831-724-5422 www.compostlab.com

Soil and Plant Lab
352 Mathew Street
Santa Clara, CA 95050-0153
408-727-0330
www.soilandplantlaboratory.com

Timberleaf Soil Testing
39648 Old Spring Rd.
Murrieta, CA 92563-5566
951-677-7510
www.timberleafsoiltesting.com

Wallace Laboratories
365 Coral Circle
El Segundo, CA 90245
310-615-0116 www.bettersoils.com

GARDENS AND ARBORETUMS PRESERVING NATURAL LANDSCAPES

Conejo Valley Botanic Garden
Thousand Oaks, CA www.conejogarden.org

Mc Connell Arboretum & Gardens
840 Auditorium Drive
Redding, CA 96001
530-243-8850 www.turtlebay.org

Rancho Santa Ana Botanic Garden
1500 North College Avenue
Claremont, CA 91711-3157
909-625-8767 www.rsabg.org

Regional Parks Botanic Garden
Native Plants of California
Berkeley, CA 94708-2396
510-544-3169 www.nativeplants.org

John Rodman Arboretum
Pitzer College
1050 North Mills Avenue
Claremont CA 91711
www.pitzer.edu/offices/arboretum

Santa Barbara Botanic Garden
1212 Mission Canyon Road
Santa Barbara, CA 93105
805-682-4726 www.sbbg.org

The Wrigley Memorial & Botanical Gardens
Catalina Island Conservancy
Avalon Canyon Road
Avalon, CA 90704
310-510-2595 www.catalina.com/memorial.html

rocky mountain region

WEB RESOURCES

**U.S. Environmental Protection Agency
Greenscapes Program**
www.epa.gov/greenscapes

U.S. Environmental Protection Agency
1595 Wynkoop Street
Denver, CO 80202-1129
303-312-6312 | 800-227-8917
r8eisc@epa.gov

EPA Montana Operations Office
Federal Office Building
10 West 15th Street, Suite 3200
Helena, MT 59626
406-457-5000 | 866-457-5000
www.epa.gov/region8

**SEED, NATIVE PLANTS AND
MAIL ORDER NURSERIES**

Colorado
Arkansas Valley Seed
Longmont, CO: 877-907-3337
Denver, CO: 877-957-3337
Monte Vista, CO: 719-852-3505
www.avseeds.com

Beauty Beyond Belief Wildflower Seed
3307 S. College Avenue #104
Fort Collins, CO 80525
970-204-0596
www.bbbseed.com

Pleasant Avenue Nursery, Inc.
506 S. Pleasant Avenue
Buena Vista, CO 81211-1669
719-395-6955
www.pleasantavenuenursery.com

Sharp Bros. Seed Co.
104 East 4th Street Road
Greeley, CO 80631
800-421-4234 | 970-356-4710
buffalo.gxy@sharpseed.com

Sun Chaser Seeds
1566 Fillmore Court
Louisville, CO 80027
www.sun-chaser.com

Western Native Seed
Coaldale, CO 81222
719-942-3935
www.westernnativeseed.com

Montana homeowners wanted the landscape surrounding their home to blend with the native landscape beyond. Natural landscape designer, Linda Iverson, worked with the disturbed, infertile soils and combined a diverse mix of Montana native grasses, forbes and a handful of shrubs into a beautiful, sustainable prairie landscape. Plants pictured; *Elymus trachycaulus* (Slender wheatgrass) *Pseudoroegneria spicata* (Bluebunch wheatgrass), *Solidago missouriensis* (Missouri goldenrod), *Echinacea angustifolia* (Pale purple coneflower), *Monarda fistulosa* (Horsemint) and *Ratibida columnifera* (Prairie coneflower). Linda Iverson, Linda Iverson Landscape Design.

Montana
Blackfoot Native Plants
Kathy Settevendemie
P.O. Box 761
Bonner, MT 59823
406-244-5800
www.blackfootnativeplants.com

Circle S Seed Company
14990 Madison Frontage Rd
Three Forks, MT 59752-9451
406-285-3269
www.circlesseeds.com

Native Ideals Seed Company, LLC.
31046 Jocko Road
Arlee, MT 59821
www.nativeideals.com

Southwest Montana Native Landscapes
Catherine Cain
15000 Hwy 91 North
Glen MT 59732
406-498-6198
www.nativeplantsmontana.com

Westscape Wholesale Nursery
110 Progressive Drive
Belgrade, MT
406-388-1116
www.westscapenursery.net

Windflower Native Plant Nursery
West Glacier, MT 59936
406-387-5527
www.windflowernativeplants.com

Nevada
Blue Diamond Nursery
Blue Diamond, NV 89004
702-875-1968
www.cactuscactus.com

North Dakota
Heimbuch Seed Farm
9748 122nd Avenue SE
Cogswell, ND 58017
888-428-6741
www.hsfgrownative.com

Towner State Nursery
878 Nursery Road
Towner, ND 58788-9500
701-537-5636
tnursery@ndak.net

South Dakota
Fuller Native Seeds (wetland seeds)
401 E. Sioux Avenue
Pierre, SD 57501
605-224-6994

Seed Exchange
36787 SD Hwy 44
Platte, SD 57369
605-337-9882
www.avseeds.com

Seeds of the Plains
HC 76, Box 21
Belvidere, SD 57521
605-344-2265
lehman@gwtc.net

Utah
Grable's Alpine and Rock Garden Plant Nursery
2166 Wellington
Salt Lake City, UT 84106
801-466-2445
www.grablesalpines.com

Granite Seed
P.O. Box 117
Lehi, UT 84043
801-768-4422

Great Basin Natives
75 West 300 South
Holden, UT 84636
435-795-2303
www.greatbasinnatives.com

Stevenson Intermountain Seed, Inc.
Ephrim, UT 84627
435-283-6639
www.stevensonintermountainseed.com

Water Wise Gardens
45 N Main Street
Lewiston, UT 84320
435-258-2145
www.waterwisegardens.org

Wildland Nursery
370 E 600 North
Joseph, UT 84739
435-527-1234
www.wildlandnursery.com

Wyoming
Little Goose Native Plants & Wildflowers
226 Main Street, Box 445,
Bighorn, WY 82833
307-672-5340
www.helpfulgardener.com

Wind River Seed Company
3075 Lane 51 1/2
Manderson, WY 82432-9506
307-568-3361
www.windriverseed.com

LANDSCAPE DESIGNERS AND RESTORATION SPECIALISTS

Colorado
Aquatic and Wetland Company
9999 Weld County Road 25
Fort Lupton, CO 80621
303-442-4766
www.aquaticandwetland.com

Design Workshop
953 S Frontage Road West, #102
Vail, CO 81657
970-476-8408

Montana
Beth MacFawn Landscape Design, Inc.
Bozeman, MT 59771
406-587-5211
www.montanalandscapedesigner.com

Great Bear Restoration
Tim W. Meikle, Restoration Ecologist
Hamilton Carriage House
310 North 4th Street
Hamilton, MT 59840
406-363-5410, ext. 117
www.great-bear.biz

Linda Iverson Landscape Design
1270 Lower Sweet Grass Road
Big Timber, MT 59011
406-932-5840
lilandscape@mtintouch.net

Montana Native Landscapes
Madeline Mazurski
5278 Elk Ridge Road
Missoula, MT 59802
406-542-0262

Native Landscapes and Reclamation
5132 Highway 89 South
Livingston MT 59047
406-222-0457

South Dakota
Cindy Reed, Consultant
P.O. Box 461
Hot Springs, SD 57747
605-745-3397

Little Goose Native Plants & Wildflowers
226 Main Street, Box 445
Bighorn, WY 82833
307-672-5340
www.helpfulgardener.com

NATIVE PLANT SOCIETIES

Colorado Native Plant Society
P.O.Box 200
Fort Collins, CO 80522-0200
www.conps.org

Montana Native Plant Society
P.O. Box 8783
Missoula, MT 59807-8782
www.mtnativeplants.org/1

Missoula Restoration Volunteers
www.groups.google.com/group/missoula-restoration

Northern Nevada Native Plant Society
P.O. Box 8965
Reno, NV 89507-8965
www.heritage.nv.gov/nnps.htm

South Dakota Great Plains Native Plant Society
P.O. Box 461
Hot Springs, SD 57747

Utah Native Plant Society
P.O. Box 520041
Salt Lake City, UT 84152-0041
www.unps.org / www.gpnps.org

Wyoming Native Plant Society
P.O. Box 2500
Laramie, WY 82073
http://www.uwyo.edu/wyndd/wnps/wnps_home.htm

UNIVERSITIES, EXTENSION SERVICES, SOIL TESTING LABS AND EDUCATIONAL ORGANIZATIONS

Colorado State Cooperative Extension
www.ext.colostate.edu

Colorado State Univ. Soil, Water and Plant Testing Laboratory
Room A-319 NESB
Fort Collins, CO 80523
970-491-5061
www.colostate.edu/Depts/SoilCrop/soillab.html

Montana State University Extension Service
www.extn.msu.montana.edu

University of Nevada Cooperative Extension
www.unce.unr.edu

North Dakota State University Extension Service
www.ag.ndsu.edu/extension

North Dakota State University Soil Testing Laboratory
Soil Science Dept., P.O. Box 5575
Fargo, ND 58105
701-231-8942
www.soilsci.ndsu.nodak.edu

Utah State University Extension
www.extension.usu.edu

Albion Laboratories, Inc.
101 N. Main Street
Clearfield, UT 84015
866-243-5283
www.AlbionMinerals.com

Utah State University Analytical Labs
166 Ag. Science Bldg, 4830 Old Main Hill
Logan, UT 84322
435-797-2217
www.usual.usu.edu

University of Wyoming, Soil Testing Laboratory
P.O. Box 3354
Laramie, WY 82071
307-766-2135
www.uwadmnweb.uwyo.edu/
RenewableResources/soil/soil_lab.htm

Prairie Wetlands Learning Center
602 State Highway 210 East
Fergus Falls, MN 56537
218-988-4480
www.fws.gov/midwest/pwlc

Betty Ford Alpine Garden
Ste 395, 183 Gore Creek Drive
Vail, CO 81657-4544
970-476-0103
www.bettyfordalpinegardens.org

Denver Botanic Gardens
1005 York Street,
Denver, CO 80206
720-865-3585
www.botanicgardens.org

The Hudson Gardens & Event Center
6115 South Santa Fe Drive
Littleton, CO 80120
303-797-8565
www.hudsongardens.org

Red Butte Garden and Arboretum
300 Wakara Way
Salt Lake City, Utah 84108.
801-585-0556
www.redbuttegarden.org

South Dakota State University's McCrory Gardens
Brookings, SD 57007
605-688-5921
www.sdstate.edu

Cheyenne Botanic Gardens
710 S. Lions Park Drive
Cheyenne, WY 82001
307-637-6458
www.botanic.org

First year meadow planting from seed. Snow Creek Landscaping, LLC, North Carolina

southeast region

WEB RESOURCES

US Environmental Protection Agency Greenscapes Program
www.epa.gov/greenscapes

United States Environmental Protection Agency Region 4
Sam Nunn Atlanta Federal Center
61 Forsyth Street, SW
Atlanta, GA 30303-8960
404-562-9900 | 800-241-1754
www.epa.gov/Region4

Association of Florida Native Nurseries
www.afnn.org

Perfect Island
Public service website with comprehensive information on native landscaping with native plants of barrier islands and bay shorelines of the mainland.
941-778-1200 | 941-779-6097
www.perfectisland.us

Tennessee Valley Authority Native Plant Search
www.tva.gov/river/landandshore/
stabilization/plantsearch.htm

SEEDS, NATIVE PLANTS AND MAIL ORDER NURSERIES

Alabama
Biophilia Native Nursery
12695 County Road 95
Elberta, AL 36530
251-987-1200 www.biophilia.net

White City Nursery, U.S. Alliance, Coosa Pines Corp.
707 Co. Road 20 West
Verbena, AL 36091
334-365-2488 kk4iz@alltel.com

Arkansas
Pine Ridge Gardens
832 Saycamore Rd.
London, AR 72847
501-293-4359

Ozark Wildflower Company
HC 70 Box 169
Jasper, AR 72641
870-446-5629

Pine Ridge Gardens
Native plants; Selected ornamentals
832 Sycamore Road
London, AR 72847
501-293-4359 www.pineridgegardens.com

Florida
Florida Native Plants, Inc.
730 Myakka Rd.
Sarasota, FL 34240
941-322-1915 www.floridanativeplants.com

Hard Scrabble Farms
P.O. Box 281
Terra Ceia Island, FL 34250
941-722-0414

Mail-order Natives
P.O. Box 9366
Lee, FL 32059
850-973-6830 www.mailordernatives.com

Native & Uncommon Plants
4157 Ortega Blvd
Jacksonville, FL 32210
904-388-9851
www.nativeanduncommonplants.com

Native Nurseries of Tallahassee, Inc.
1661 Centerville Rd.
Tallahassee, FL 32308
850-386-8882 www.nativenurseries.com

Plant Creations Inc., Nursery & Landscaping
28301 SW 172nd Avenue
Homestead, FL 33030
305-248-8147 www.plantcreations.com

Sumter Natives
P.O. Box 121
Dade City, FL 33526
352-568-8665 | 352-568-8891
ndwht@aol.com

That Native Plant Place
1112 Sanctuary Road
Naples, FL 34120
941-348-1093
www.thatnativeplantplace.com

Wildflowers of Florida, Inc.
Terry Zinn
27715 NW 107 Street
Alachua, FL 32615-3504
386-462-7827
floridawildflower@worldnet.att.net

Georgia
Clifton Nursery
P.O. Box 882
Statesboro, GA 30458
912-489-8250

Garden Delights, LLC
Garden Center
GA Hwy 27
Downtown Pine Mountain
706-663-7964 www.lazyknursery.com

Lazy K Nursery, Inc.
Wholesale and Online Nursery
705 Wright Road
Pine Mountain, GA 31822
706-663-4991 www.lazyknursery.com

Rock Spring Farm
82 Brighton Road NE
Atlanta, GA 30309
404-626-8020 www.rockspringfarm.com

Louisiana
Louisiana Forest Seed Co., Inc.
303 Forestry Rd.
Lecompte, LA 71346
504-748-5850

Maypop Hill Nursery & Publications
P.O. Box 123, 4979 Spec Garig Rd
Norwood, LA 70761
225-629-5379 maypophill@wildblue.net

Prairie Basse
217 St. Fidelis Street
Carencro, LA 70520
337-896-9187

Pushpetappa Gardens
2317 Washington Street
Franklinton, LA 70438-2504
985-839-4930

Mississippi
Natchez Trace Gardens
1113 S. Huntington Street
Kosciusko, MS 39090
662-289-4979

Delta-View Nursery (wholesale)
Rt. 1 Box 28
Leland, MS 38756
800/748-9018 hardwoods@techinfo.com

North Carolina
Carolina Greenery
375 Carthage Rd
West End, NC 27376
910-947-3150 www.carolinagreenery.com

Gardens of the Blue Ridge
9056 Pittman Gap Road
Pineola, NC 28662
828-733-2417
www.gardensoftheblueridge.com

Lamtree Farm
2323 Copeland Road
Warrensville, NC 28693
336-385-6144
www.lamtreefarmnursery.com

Niche Gardens
1111 Dawson Road
Chapel Hill, NC 27516
919-967-0078 www.nichegardens.com

South Carolina
Carolina Wild
314 Camellia Drive
Anderson, SC 29625
864-261-0659 www.carolinawild.com

Tennessee
Growild, Inc.
7190 Hill Hughes Rd
Fairview, TN 37062
615-799-1910 www.growildnursery.com

Nashville Natives, LLC
7443 Liberty Road
Fairview, TN 37062
615-579-7146 www.nashvillenatives.com

Wetland Supplies (wholesale)
12845 sr 108
Altamont, TN 37301
931-692-4252
www.wetlandsupplies.com

LANDSCAPE DESIGNERS AND RESTORATION SPECIALISTS

Florida
Anne Kramer and Associates, LLC
Landscape Architects
P.O. Box 2625
Dunedin, FL 34697-2625
727-424-9850 www.annekramer.com

Botanical Visions Inc.
Design Studio
4651 N. Dixie Highway
Boca Raton, FL 33431
561-361-6677 www.BotanicalVisions.com

Ecotone Land Design, Inc.
Mark L. Johnson, RLA, ASLA
Landscape Architectural Site Planning
501 East Oak Street, Suite A
Kissimmee, FL 34744
407-931-2225 www.ecotonelanddesign.com

Floravista, Inc.
Suzanne Kennedy
Merritt Island, FL
321-427-6649 www.floravista.net

Lewis Environmental Services Inc.
Roy R. "Robin" Lewis, III
23797 NE 189th St.
Salt Springs, FL 32134
888-889-9684 | 813-505-3999
www.lewisenv.com

M. J. Nichols & Associates, LLC
14657 93rd Street North
West Palm Beach, FL 33412
561-753-0554 | 954-629-2490
www.mjnichols.com

Native & Uncommon Plants
4157 Ortega Blvd
Jacksonville, FL 32210
904-388-9851
www.nativeanduncommonplants.com

Native Florida Consulting, Inc.
Karina Veaudry, RLA, Principal
311 S. Glenwood Avenue
Orlando, FL 32803-6259
321-388-4781
nativefloridaconsulting@earthlink.net

Oecohort, LLC
Jeffrey G. Norcini
726 Riggins Road
Tallahassee, FL 32308-6222
850-491-0910 www.OecoHort.com

Springer Environmental Services
Troy Springer
813-659-0370
www.springerenvironmental.com

Wildflower South, LLC
Parker Ranspach, RLA, CA
1724 NW Arcadia Way
Boca Raton, FL 33432
561-213-7702
pranspach@comcast.net

Louisiana
EcoUrban Sustainable Landscape Design + Services
4433 Ulloa Street
New Orleans, LA 70119
504-274-8774 www.ecourbanllc.com

North Carolina
Carolina Greenery
375 Carthage Road
West End, NC 27376
910-947-3150 www.carolinagreenery.com

Snow Creek Landscaping, LLC
226 Clayton Road
Arden, NC 28704
828-687-1677 www.snowcreekinc.com

South Carolina
Earth Design, Inc.
405 Johnson Street
Pickens, SC 29671
864-898-1221 www.earthdesignsc.com

Southern Palmetto Landscapes Inc.
Brian Hodges, Landscape Architect
5675 Lowcountry Drive
Ridgeland, SC 29936
843-726-TREE
www.southernpalmetto.com
www.brianhodgesasla.com

Tennessee

Greenman Tree Care & Landscaping
119 Sycamore Road
Dickson, TN 37055
615-390-2386 www.greenmantn.com

Growild, Inc.
7190 Hill Hughes Road
Fairview, TN 37062
615-799-1910 www.growildnursery.com

Nashville Natives, LLC
7443 Liberty Road
Fairview, TN 37062
615-579-7146 www.nashvillenatives.com

NATIVE PLANT SOCIETIES

Alabama Wildflower Society
11120 Ben Clements Road
Northport, AL 35475
www.alabamawildflower.org

Arkansas Native Plant Society
P.O. Box 250250
Little Rock, AR 72225
www.anps.org

Florida Native Plant Society
P.O. Box 690278
Vero Beach, FL 32969-0278
www.fnps.org info@fnps.org

Georgia Native Plant Society
P.O. Box 422085
Atlanta, GA 30342-2085
770-343-6000 www.gnps.org

Louisiana Native Plant Society
216 Caroline Dormon Road,
Saline, LA 71070
www.lnps.org

North Carolina Wildflower Preservation Society
North Carolina Botanical Garden
Totten Garden Center
3375 Univ. of North Carolina
Chapel Hill, NC 27599-3375

South Carolina Native PlantSociety
P.O. Box 759
Pickens, SC 29671
www.scnps.org

Tennessee Native Plant Society
c/o Department of Botany
University of Tennessee
Knoxville, TN 37996-1100

The Wildflower Society
Goldsmith Civic Garden Center
750 Cherry Road
Memphis, TN 38119-4699

Mississippi Native Plant Society
Mississippi Native Plants
attn: Bob Brzuszek, Crosby Arboretum
P.O. Box 190
Picayune, MS 39466

UNIVERSITIES, EXTENSION SERVICES, SOIL TESTING LABS AND EDUCATIONAL ORGANIZATIONS

Alabama Cooperative Extension System
www.aces.edu

AU Soil Testing Lab
ALFA Bldg., 961 S. Donahue Drive
Auburn University, AL 36849-5411
334-844-3958 www.aces.edu/anr/soillab

University of Arkansas Division of Agriculture
Cooperative Extension Service
501-671-2000 www.uaex.edu

University of Arkansas Soil Testing and Research Laboratory
P.O. Drawer 767
Marianna, AR 72360
870-295-2851 www.uark.edu/depts/soiltest

University of Florida IFAS Extension
Florida Yards & Neighborhoods
352-392-1831 x267 www.fyn.ifas.ufl.edu

University of Florida, Soil Testing Laboratory
Wallace Bldg. No. 631
P.O. Box 110740
Gainesville, FL 32611
352-392-1950 x221
www.edis.ifas.ufl.edu/ss312

University of Georgia Cooperative Extension
Connect to local agents 800-ASK-UGA1
www.caes.uga.edu/Extension

University of Georgia
College of Agricultural and Environmental Sciences
Soil Plant and Water Analysis Laboratory
2400 College Station Rd.
Athens, GA 30602
706-542-5350 www.aesl.ces.uga.edu

Waters Agricultural Laboratories, Inc.
PO Box 382, 257 Newton Highway
Camilla, GA 31730
229-336-7216 www.watersag.com

Clemson Cooperative Extension
864-656-3311 www.clemson.edu/extension

Clemson University Soil Testing
Agricultural Service Laboratory
171 Old Cherry Road
Clemson, SC 29634
864-656-2068 www.clemson.edu/agsrvlb

Louisiana State University Agricultural Center Research and Extension
Links to Parish Offices www.lsuagcenter.com

Louisiana State University, Soil Testing and Plant Analysis Lab
126 Madison B. Sturgis Hall
Baton Rouge, LA 70803
225-578-1261
www.lsuagcenter.com/en/our_offices/
departments/SPESS/Service+Labs/soil_
testing_lab

Mississippi State University Extension Service
www.msucares.com

Mississippi State University, Soil Testing Laboratory
Box 9610
Mississippi State, MS 39762
662-325-3313
www.msucares.com/crops/soils/testing.html

North Carolina State University & A&T State University
Cooperative Extension
www.ces.ncsu.edu

North Carolina Dept. of Agriculture and Consumer Services
Agronomic Division–Soil Testing Section
4300 Reedy Creek Road
Raleigh, NC 27607
919-733-2655
www.ncagr.gov/agronomi/sthome.htm

A&L Analytical Laboratories Inc.
2790 Whitten Road
Memphis, TN 38133
800-264-4522   www.al-labs.com

University of Tennessee Extension Service
www.utextension.utk.edu

University of Tennessee Soil Test Lab
5201 Marchant Drive
Nashville, TN 37211-5112
615-832-5850
www.bioengr.ag.utk.edu/soiltestlab

GARDENS AND ARBORETUMS PRESERVING NATURAL LANDSCAPES

Biophilia Native Nursery
12695 County Road 95
Elberta, AL 36530
251-987-1200   www.biophilia.net

University of Alabama Arboretum
4800 Arboretum Way
Tuscaloosa, AL 35487
205-553-3278   www.arboretum.ua.edu

University of Central Florida Arboretum
4000 Central Florida Blvd, tr 525
Orlando FL 32816   www.arboretum.ucf.edu

University of South Florida Botanical Gardens
4202 E. Fowler Avenue NES107
Tampa, FL 33620-5150
813-974-2329   www.cas.usf.edu

Georgia Perimeter College
Native Plant Botanical Garden
3251 Panthersville Rd.
Decatur, GA 30034
678-891-2668   www.gpc.edu/~decbt

The Crosby Arboretum
370 Ridge Road
Picayune, MS 39466
601-799-2311
www.crosbyarboretum.msstate.edu

North Carolina Botanical Garden
The University of North Carolina
100 Old Mason Farm Road
Chapel Hill, NC 27599
919-962-0522   www.ncbg.unc.edu

Brookgreen Gardens
P.O. Box 3368
Pawleys Island, SC 29585-3368
800-849-1931   www.brookgreen.org

South Carolina Botanical Garden
102 Garden Trail
Clemson University
Clemson, SC 29634-0174
864-656-3405
www.clemson.edu/public/scbg

Reflection Riding Arboretum & Botanical Garden
400 Garden Road
Chattanooga, TN 37419
423-821-9582   www.reflectionriding.org

New Mexico

Agua Fria Nursery, Inc.
1409 Agua Fria Street
Santa Fe, NM 87505-3507
505-983-4831

Bernardo Beach Native Plant Farm
1 Sanchez Drive
Veguita, NM 87062
505-345-6248

Curtis & Curtis Inc. (seeds)
Star Rte Box 8A
Clovis, NM 88101
505-762-4749

Earthseeds
3369 Montezuma Ave, #226
Santa Fe, NM 87501
505-471-6926
www.earthseed.com

Santa Fe Greenhouses
High Country Gardens
2902 Rufina St.
Santa Fe, NM 87507-2929
800-925-9387 | 505-473-2700
6400 San Mateo, NE
Albuquerque, NM
505-856-7641
www.highcountrygardens.com

Osuna Nursery
501 Osuna Road NE
Albuquerque, NM
505-345-6644

Plants of the Southwest
6670 4th Street, NW
Albuquerque, NM
505-344-8830
3095 Agua Fria Road, R.R. 6, Box 11A
Santa Fe, NM 87507
800-788-7333 | 505-438-8888
www.plantsofthesouthwest.com

Santa Ana Garden Center & Native Plant Nursery
157 Jemez Dam Road
Bernalillo, NM 87004
505-867-1322
www.santaana.org

Tooley's Trees
Truchas, NM 87578
505-689-2400
www.tooleystrees.com

Oklahoma

Grasslander
Rt. #1 Box 56
Hennessey, OK 73742
405-853-2607
www.grasslander.com

Johnston Seed Co.
319 West Chestnut
Enid, OK 73702
800-375-4613 | 580-233-5800
www.johnstonseed.com

Lorenz's O.K. Seeds LLC
511 W Oklahoma Avenue
Okeene, OK 73763
800-826-3655
www.lorenzseed.com

Texas

Bamert Seed Co.
1897 CR 1018
Muleshoe, TX 79347
800-262-9892 | 806-272-5506
www.bamertseed.com

Green Mama's Organic Garden Center
5324 Davis Blvd.
North Richland Hills, TX 76180
817-514-7336
www.greenmamas.com

Native American Seed
3791 N US Hwy 377
Junction, TX 76849
800-728-4043
www.seedsource.com

Native Ornamentals
Mertzon, TX 76941
325-835-2021
texican@ispwest.com

Wichita Valley Landscape
5314 Southwest Parkway
Wichita Falls, TX 76310
940-696-3082
www.wvlandscape.com

LANDSCAPE DESIGNERS AND RESTORATION SPECIALISTS

Arizona

Arizona Revegetation & Monitoring Co.
Elgin, AZ 85611
520-455-5780
www.azreveg.com

Del Sol Group
1414 W. Broadway, Suite 124
Tempe, AZ 85282
480-642-9845
www.groupdelsol.com

EnvironSystems Management, Inc.
23 East Fine Avenue
Flagstaff, AZ 86001
928-226-0236 www.esmaz.com

Gardening Insights
Tucson, AZ
520-603-2703
www.gardeninginsights.com

Greenfire Ecological Landscaping
Dennis Pepe
Tucson, AZ
520-429-7306
www.greenfireaz.com

Harris Environmental Group, Inc.
58 E. 5th Street
Tucson, AZ 85705-8362
520-628-7648
www.heg-inc.com

Palo Verde Designs
Lisa Kelk
9842 S 45th Place
Phoenix, AZ 85044-5515
602-471-7350
www.paloverdedesigns.com

C.F. Shuler, Inc
7332 E. Butherus Drive, Suite 104
Scottsdale, AZ 85260
480-483-0535
www.cfshulerinc.com

Sage Landscape Architecture
2315 E. Speedway Blvd.
Tucson AZ 85719
520-740-0950
www.sagelandscape.com

Turner Design LLC
4930 N. Calle la Vela
Tucson AZ 85718
520-405-4633
www.turner-design.com

Urban Organics Landscaping
219 S Olsen Avenue
Tucson AZ 85719
520-791-9131
www.uolandscaping.com

Zona Gardens, L.L.C.
Scott Calhoun
5331 S. Civano Blvd.
Tucson, AZ 85747
520-867-8038
www.zonagardens.com

New Mexico
Julia Berman Design
4 Vuelta De La Tusa
Santa Fe, NM
505-820-3314

Judith Phillips Design Oasis
505-343-1800
www.judithphillipsdesignoasis.com

Quercus
142 Truman St NE / E-2
Albuquerque, NM
505-275-7296
www.thequercusgroup.com

WaterWise Landscapes, Inc
Albuquerque, NM
505-344-7508
waterwiselandscapesnm.com

Oklahoma
Grasslander
RRt 1, Box 56
Hennessey, OK 73742
405-853-2607
www.grasslander.com

Lorenz's O.K. Seeds LLC
511 W Oklahoma Avenue
Okeene, OK 73763
800-826-3655
www.lorenzseed.com

Native Landscapes, Inc.
Norman, OK
405-826-0181
www.nativelandscapedesign.net

Texas
A Touch O' Green Landscape & Gardens LLC
7205 Holly Fern Cove
Austin, TX 78750
512-736-4859
www.touchogreenlandscapes.com

Down to Earth Landscape Services, Inc.
1707 Maple Vista Drive
Pflugerville, TX 78660
512-252-4545 www.dtescape.com

Bill Kennedy Landscape
800 Fulgham Rd. Suite 1
Plano, TX 75093
972-398-3782
www.bklawn.com

LKS Garden Designs
1421 Natchez Dr
Plano, TX 75023
972-423-6574

Elizabeth McGreevy
11704 Crumley Ranch Road
Austin, TX 78738
512-657-9675
www.landsteward.net

Native Cottage Gardens
710 Rocky River Road
Austin, TX 78746
512-469-0121

Michael Parkey, Landscape Architect
10308 Vinemont Street
Dallas, TX 75218
214-321-5538
www.michaelparkey.com

Sans Souci Gardens
Cathy Nordstrom Central Texas
512-346-6797
www.sans-souci-gardens.com

Warne Design, Landscape Architecture
7070 Windhave Pkwy, Suite 302
The Colony, TX 75056
214-483-3218

Dixie Watkins III & Associates
11 Lynn Batts Lane, Ste 110
San Antonio, TX 78218
210-824-7836

WildflowerHaven.com
5804 Babcock Rd #144
San Antonio, TX 78240
210-884-6135
www.wildflowerhaven.com

Wichita Valley Landscape
5314 Southwest Parkway
Wichita Falls, TX 76310
940-696-3082
www.wvlandscape.com

NATIVE PLANT SOCIETIES

Arizona Native Plant Society
P.O. Box 41206
Sun Station, Tucson, AZ 85717
www.aznps.org

Native Plant Society of New Mexico
734 North Reymont Street
Las Cruces, NM 88002
www.npsnm.unm.edu

Oklahoma Native Plant Society
Tulsa Garden Center
2435 S. Peoria
Tulsa, OK 74114-1350
www.usao.edu/~onps

Native Plant Society of Texas
P.O. Box 891
Georgetown, TX 78627-0891
www.npsot.org

UNIVERSITIES, EXTENSION SERVICES, SOIL TESTING LABS AND EDUCATIONAL ORGANIZATIONS

University of Arizona Cooperative Extension Service
www.extension.arizona.edu

BBC Laboratories, Inc.
1217 North Stadem Dr.
Tempe, AZ 85281
(480) 967-5931
www.bbclabs.com

New Mexico State University Cooperative Extension Service
www.extension.nmsu.edu

New Mexico State University Soil, Water, and Plant Testing Lab
Box 30003, Dept. 3Q
Las Cruces, NM 88003
505-646-4422
www.swatlab.nmsu.edu

Oklahoma State University Cooperative Extension Service
www.oces.okstate.edu

Oklahoma State University Cooperative Extension
Soil, Water, and Forage Analytical Lab
048 Agricultural Hall
Stillwater, OK 74078
405-744-6630
www.soiltesting.okstate.edu

Texas AgriLife Extension Service, Texas A&M System
www. texasextension.tamu.edu

Texas A&M Soil, Water, and Forage Testing Laboratory
345 Heep Center
College Station, TX 77843-2474
979-845-4816
www.soilcrop.tamu.edu/soiltest

Texas Plant & Soil Lab, Inc.
5115 W. Monte Cristo
Edinburg, TX 78541
956-383-0739
www.txplant-soillab.com

Sustainable Arizona Resource & Education Council
P. O. Box 156
Sedona, AZ 86339
www.sustainablearizona.org

GARDENS AND ARBORETUMS PRESERVING NATURAL LANDSCAPES

The Arboretum at Flagstaff
4001 South Woody Mountain Road
Flagstaff, AZ 86001-8776
928-774-1442
www.thearb.org

Tohono Chul Park Inc.
7366 N Paseo Del Norte
Tucson, AZ 85704-4415
520-742-6455
www.tohonochulpark.org

**Chihuahuan Desert Nature Center &
Botanical Gardens**
HWY 118
Ft. Davis, TX 79734
432-364- 2499
www.cdri.org/Vc

Houston Arboretum and Nature Center
4501 Woodway Drive
Houston, TX 77024-7708
713-681-8433
www.houstonarboretum.org

Ladybird Johnson Wildflower Center
4801 La Crosse Avenue
Austin, TX 78739-1702
512-292-4100
www.wildflower.org

Riverside Nature Center Association
150 Francisco Lemos Street
Kerrville, TX 78028-5211
830-257-4837
www.riversidenaturecenter.org

Charles Mann

A meadow-like lawn, designed by xeriscape expert Judith Phillips, uses *Bouteloua gracilis* (Blue gramma grass) and tall swatches of *Bouteloua curtipendula* (Side oats gramma) to compliment a small adobe house in Albuquerque, New Mexico.

general resources

BOOKS

Armitage, A., 2006 *Armitage's Native Plants for North American Gardens*, Timber Press, Inc.

Brickell, C and J. Zuk *A-Z Encyclopedia of Garden Plants, American Horticultural Society*, 1997, Dorling Kindersley Publishing

Darke, R. 2007, *The Encyclopedia of Grasses for Livable Landscapes*, Timber Press, Inc.

Diboll, N. and H. Cox, 2010 "The Gardener's Guide to Prairie Plants", University of Chicago Press

Diekelmann, J. and R. Schuster, 1982 *Natural Landscaping—Designing with Native Plant Communities*, 2nd Edition, McGraw-Hill

Harker, D, G. Libby, K. Harker, S. Evans and M. Evans. 1999, *Landscape Restoration Handbook*, Second Edition, Lewis Publishers

Kahtz, A. 2008, *Perenials for Midwestern Gardens, Proven Plants for the Heartland*, Timber Press, Inc.

Kurtz, C. 2001 *A Practical Guide to Prairie Reconstruction*, University of Iowa Press, Iowa City, IA.

Leopold, D. 2005 *Native Plants of the Northeast, A Guide for Gardening and Conservation*, Timber Press, Inc.

NOFA Organic Land Care Committee, 2007 *The NOFA Organic Lawn and Turf Handbook*, Organic Land Care Committee of the Northeast Organic Farming Association

Packard, S. and C. Mutel (editors) 1997 *The Tallgrass Restoration Handbook: For Prairies, Savannas, and Woodlands*, Island Press

Phillips, J. 1987, *Southwestern Landscaping with Native Plants*, The Museum of New Mexico Press

Pyle, R.M. 1981 *National Audubon Society, Field Guide to Butterflies*, Alfred A. Knopf, New York, NY.

Ramsey Kaufman, S. and W. Kaufman, 2007 *Invasive Plants, Guide to Identification and the Impacts and Control of Common North American Species*, Stackpole Books, Mechanicsburg, PA.

Shepherd, M., S. Buchmann, M.Vaughan and S.Hoffman Black, 2003 *Pollinator Conservation Handbook; A Guide to Understanding, Protecting, and Providing Habitat for Native Pollinator Insects*, The Xerces Society

Native wildflower meadow project serves as an outdoor classroom. Deerfield Beach Middle School in Broward County Florida.

Tallamy, D., 2007, *Bringing Nature Home, How Native Plants Sustain Wildlife in Our Gardens*, Timber Press, Inc.,

Wasowski, S. and A. Wasowski 2002, *Gardening with Prairie Plants: How to Create Beautiful Native Landscapes*

WEB BASED RESOURCES

Native Plant and Seed Databases
Lady Bird Johnson Wildflower Center plant data base
www.wildflower.org/plants

Plant Conservation Alliance
www.nps.gov/plants

USDA Natural Resource Conservation Service; Plants Data Base
www.plants.usda.gov

Center for Plant Conservation
Missouri Botanical Garden
P.O. Box 299
St. Louis, MO 63166
www.centerforplantconservation.org

PlantNative
Native plant nurseries and professional directories
www.plantnative.org

Native Seed Network
Resource for both the restoration community and the native seed industry, providing powerful search tools and information on all aspects of native seed.
www.nativeseednetwork.org

TOOLS FOR CHANGE

American Beauties Native Plants
www.abnativeplants.com

Audubon At Home Bird Habitat Program
http://pa.audubon.org/Audubon_at_home.html

EPA Greenscapes Program
Provides cost-efficient and environmentally friendly solutions for green landscaping. Links to state EPA sites.
www.epa.gov/glnpo/greenacres/nativeplants/factsht.html

EPA Western Ecology Division
Find information and research about ecoregions
200 S.W. 35 Street
Corvallis, Oregon 97333
541-754-4600
www.epa.gov/wed/pages/ecoregions.htm

Monarch Watch Waystation program
http://www.monarchwatch.org/waystations/

National Wildlife Federation Backyard Habitat
http://www.nwf.org/gardenforwildlife

Pennsylvania Wildlife 10
Neighborly Natural Landscaping: Creating Natural Environments in Residential Areas
http://pubs.cas.psu.edu/freepubs/pdfs/uh142.pdf

Society for Ecological Restoration
International association with regional chapters in the United States
www.ser.org

Wildlife Habitat Council
8737 Colesville Road, Suite 800
Silver Spring, MD 20910
301-588-8994
www. wildlifehc.org

Wild Ones Institute of Learning and Development
2285 Butte des Morts Beach Road
Neenah, Wisconsin 54956
920-730-3986 | 877-FYI-WILD
www.for-wild.org

Wild Ones
Weed Laws and Native Plant Landscaping
www.for-wild.org/weedlaws/weedlaw.html

The Xerces Society
Nonprofit organization that protects wildlife through the conservation of invertebrates and their habitat. The society is at the forefront of invertebrate protection worldwide, harnessing the knowledge of scientists and the enthusiasm of citizens to implement conservation programs.
www.xerces.org

EXTENSION SERVICE
Cooperative Extension Search
(provided by Land-Grant Institutions)
Find closest extension service:
http://search.extension.org

Prairie plants handsomely border stone path. Ketchum, Idaho. Design, Kelley Weston and Karen Sherrerd ASLA, Native Landscapes Inc.

Level III Ecoregions of the Continental United States

(Revised March 2007)
National Health and Environmental Effects Research Laboratory
U.S. Environmental Protection Agency

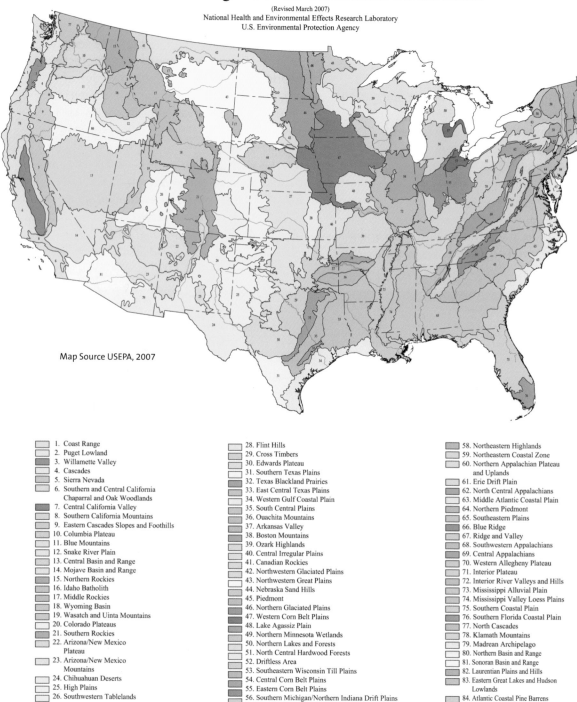

Map Source USEPA, 2007

1. Coast Range
2. Puget Lowland
3. Willamette Valley
4. Cascades
5. Sierra Nevada
6. Southern and Central California Chaparral and Oak Woodlands
7. Central California Valley
8. Southern California Mountains
9. Eastern Cascades Slopes and Foothills
10. Columbia Plateau
11. Blue Mountains
12. Snake River Plain
13. Central Basin and Range
14. Mojave Basin and Range
15. Northern Rockies
16. Idaho Batholith
17. Middle Rockies
18. Wyoming Basin
19. Wasatch and Uinta Mountains
20. Colorado Plateaus
21. Southern Rockies
22. Arizona/New Mexico Plateau
23. Arizona/New Mexico Mountains
24. Chihuahuan Deserts
25. High Plains
26. Southwestern Tablelands
27. Central Great Plains

28. Flint Hills
29. Cross Timbers
30. Edwards Plateau
31. Southern Texas Plains
32. Texas Blackland Prairies
33. East Central Texas Plains
34. Western Gulf Coastal Plain
35. South Central Plains
36. Ouachita Mountains
37. Arkansas Valley
38. Boston Mountains
39. Ozark Highlands
40. Central Irregular Plains
41. Canadian Rockies
42. Northwestern Glaciated Plains
43. Northwestern Great Plains
44. Nebraska Sand Hills
45. Piedmont
46. Northern Glaciated Plains
47. Western Corn Belt Plains
48. Lake Agassiz Plain
49. Northern Minnesota Wetlands
50. Northern Lakes and Forests
51. North Central Hardwood Forests
52. Driftless Area
53. Southeastern Wisconsin Till Plains
54. Central Corn Belt Plains
55. Eastern Corn Belt Plains
56. Southern Michigan/Northern Indiana Drift Plains
57. Huron/Erie Lake Plains

58. Northeastern Highlands
59. Northeastern Coastal Zone
60. Northern Appalachian Plateau and Uplands
61. Erie Drift Plain
62. North Central Appalachians
63. Middle Atlantic Coastal Plain
64. Northern Piedmont
65. Southeastern Plains
66. Blue Ridge
67. Ridge and Valley
68. Southwestern Appalachians
69. Central Appalachians
70. Western Allegheny Plateau
71. Interior Plateau
72. Interior River Valleys and Hills
73. Mississippi Alluvial Plain
74. Mississippi Valley Loess Plains
75. Southern Coastal Plain
76. Southern Florida Coastal Plain
77. North Cascades
78. Klamath Mountains
79. Madrean Archipelago
80. Northern Basin and Range
81. Sonoran Basin and Range
82. Laurentian Plains and Hills
83. Eastern Great Lakes and Hudson Lowlands
84. Atlantic Coastal Pine Barrens

ecoregion descriptions

Primary distinguishing characteristics of level III ecoregions of the continental United States.

1. Coast Range

The low mountains of the Coast Range are covered by highly productive, rain-drenched coniferous forests. Sitka spruce and coastal redwood forests originally dominated the fog-shrouded coast, while a mosaic of western red cedar, western hemlock, and seral Douglas-fir blanketed inland areas. Today Douglas-fir plantations are prevalent on the intensively logged and managed landscape.

2. Puget Lowlands

This broad rolling lowland is characterized by a mild maritime climate. It occupies a continental glacial trough and is composed of many islands, peninsulas, and bays in the Puget Sound area. Coniferous forest originally grew on the ecoregion's ground moraines, outwash plains, floodplains, and terraces. The distribution of forest species is affected by the rainshadow from the Olympic Mountains.

3. Willamette Valley

Rolling prairies, deciduous/coniferous forests, and extensive wetlands characterized the pre-19th century landscape of this broad, lowland valley. The Willamette Valley is distinguished from the adjacent Coast Range (1) and Cascades (4) by lower precipitation, less relief, and a different mosaic of vegetation. Landforms consist of terraces and floodplains that are interlaced and surrounded by rolling hills. Productive soils and a temperate climate make it one of the most important agricultural areas in Oregon.

4. Cascades

This mountainous ecoregion is underlain by Cenozoic volcanics and has been affected by alpine glaciations. It is characterized by steep ridges and river valleys in the west, a high plateau in the east, and both active and dormant volcanoes. Elevations range upwards to 4,390 meters. Its moist, temperate climate supports an extensive and highly productive coniferous forest. Subalpine meadows occur at high elevations.

5. Sierra Nevada

The Sierra Nevada is a deeply dissected block fault that rises sharply from the arid basin and range ecoregions on the east and slopes gently toward the Central California Valley to the west. The eastern portion has been strongly glaciated and generally contains higher mountains than are found in the Klamath Mountains to the northwest. Much of the central and southern parts of the region is underlain by granite as compared to the mostly sedimentary formations of the Klamath Mountains and volcanic rocks of the Cascades. The higher elevations of this region are largely federally owned and include several national parks. The vegetation grades from mostly ponderosa pine at the lower elevations on the west side and lodgepole pine on the east side, to fir and spruce at the higher elevations. Alpine conditions exist at the highest elevations.

15. Northern Rockies

The high, rugged Northern Rockies is mountainous and lies east of the Cascades. Despite its inland position, climate and vegetation are, typically, marine-influenced. Douglas fir, subalpine fir, Englemann spruce, and ponderosa pine and Pacific indicators such as western red cedar, western hemlock, and grand fir are found in the ecoregion. The vegetation mosaic is different from that of the Middle Rockies which is not dominated by maritime species. The Northern Rockies ecoregion is not as high nor as snow- and ice-covered as the Canadian Rockies although alpine characteristics occur at highest elevations and include numerous glacial lakes. Granitics and associated management problems are less extensive than in the Idaho Batholith.

16. Idaho Batholith

This ecoregion is a dissected, partially glaciated, mountainous plateau. Many perennial streams originate here and water quality can be high if basins are undisturbed. Deeply weathered, acidic, intrusive igneous rock is common and is far more extensive than in the Northern Rockies or the Middle Rockies. Soils are sensitive to disturbance especially when stabilizing vegetation is removed. Land uses include logging, grazing, and recreation. Mining and related damage to aquatic habitat was widespread. Grand fir, Douglas-fir and, at higher elevations, Engelmann spruce, and subalpine fir occur; ponderosa pine, shrubs, and grasses grow in very deep canyons. Maritime influence lessens toward the south and is never as strong as in the Northern Rockies.

17. Middle Rockies

The climate of the Middle Rockies lacks the strong maritime influence of the Northern Rockies. Mountains have Douglas-fir, subalpine fir, and Engelmann spruce forests and alpine areas; Pacific tree species are never dominant. Forests can be open. Foothills are partly wooded or shrub- and grass-covered. Intermontane valleys are grass- and/or shrub-covered and contain a mosaic of terrestrial and aquatic fauna that is distinct from the nearby mountains. Many mountain-fed, perennial streams occur and differentiate the intermontane valleys from the Northwestern Great Plains. Granitics and associated management problems are less extensive than in the Idaho Batholith. Recreation, logging, mining, and summer livestock grazing are common land uses.

18. Wyoming Basin

This ecoregion is a broad intermontane basin dominated by arid grasslands and shrublands and interrupted by high hills and low mountains. Nearly surrounded by forest covered mountains, the region is somewhat drier than the Northwestern Great Plains to the northeast and does not have the extensive cover of pinyon-juniper woodland found in the Colorado Plateaus to the south. Much of the region is used for livestock grazing, although many areas lack sufficient vegetation to support this activity. The region contains major producing natural gas and petroleum fields.

19. Wasatch And Uinta Mountains

This ecoregion is composed of a core area of high, precipitous mountains with narrow crests and valleys flanked in some areas by dissected plateaus and open high mountains. The elevational banding pattern of vegetation is similar to that of the Southern Rockies except that aspen, chaparral, and juniper-pinyon and oak are more common at middle elevations. This characteristic, along with a far lesser extent of lodgepole pine and greater use of the region for grazing livestock in the summer months, distinguish the Wasatch and Uinta Mountains ecoregion from the more northerly Middle Rockies.

20. Colorado Plateaus
Rugged tableland topography is typical of the Colorado Plateau ecoregion. Precipitous side-walls mark abrupt changes in local relief, often from 300 to 600 meters. The region is more elevated than the Wyoming Basin to the north and therefore contains a far greater extent of pinyon-juniper woodlands. However, the region also has large low lying areas containing saltbrush-greasewood (typical of hotter drier areas), which are generally not found in the higher Arizona/New Mexico Plateau to the south where grasslands are common.

21. Southern Rockies
The Southern Rockies are composed of high elevation, steep rugged mountains. Although coniferous forests cover much of the region, as in most of the mountainous regions in the western United States, vegetation, as well as soil and land use, follows a pattern of elevational banding. The lowest elevations are generally grass or shrub covered and heavily grazed. Low to middle elevations are also grazed and covered by a variety of vegetation types including Douglas fir, ponderosa pine, aspen, and juniper oak

woodlands. Middle to high elevations are largely covered by coniferous forests and have little grazing activity. The highest elevations have alpine characteristics.

22. Arizona/New Mexico Plateau
The Arizona/New Mexico Plateau represents a large transitional region between the semiarid grasslands and low relief tablelands of the Southwestern Tablelands ecoregion in the east, the drier shrublands and woodland covered higher relief tablelands of the Colorado Plateau in the north, and the lower, hotter, less vegetated Mojave Basin and Range in the west and Chihuahuan Deserts in the south. Higher, more forest covered, mountainous ecoregions border the region on the northeast and southwest. Local relief in the region varies from a few meters on plains and mesa tops to well over 300 meters along tableland side slopes.

23. Arizona/New Mexico Mountains
The Arizona/New Mexico Mountains are distinguished from neighboring mountainous ecoregions by their lower elevations and an associated vegetation indicative of drier, warmer environments, which is also due in part to the region's more southerly location. Forests of spruce, fir, and Douglas fir, that are common in the Southern Rockies and the Uinta and Wasatch Mountains, are only found in a few high elevation parts of this region. Chaparral is common on the lower elevations, pinyon-juniper and oak woodlands are found on lower and middle elevations, and the higher elevations are mostly covered with open to dense ponderosa pine forests.

24. Chihuahuan Deserts

This desertic ecoregion extends from the Madrean Archipelago in southeastern Arizona to the Edwards Plateau in south-central Texas. The region comprises broad basins and valleys bordered by sloping alluvial fans and terraces. Isolated mesas and mountains are located in the central and western parts of the region. Vegetative cover is predominantly arid grass and shrubland, except on the higher mountains where oak-juniper woodlands occur.

25. Western High Plains

Higher and drier than the Central Great Plains (27) to the east, and in contrast to the irregular, mostly grassland or grazing land of the Northwestern Great Plains (43) to the north, much of the Western High Plains comprises smooth to slightly irregular plains having a high percentage of cropland. Grama-buffalo grass is the potential natural vegetation in this region as compared to mostly wheatgrass-needlegrass to the north, Trans-Pecos shrub savanna to the south, and taller grasses to the east. The northern boundary of this ecological region is also the approximate northern limit of winter wheat and sorghum and the southern limit of spring wheat.

26. Southwestern Tablelands

Unlike most adjacent Great Plains ecological regions, little of the Southwestern Tablelands is in cropland. Much of this elevated tableland is in sub-humid grassland and semiarid range land. The potential natural vegetation in this region is grama-buffalo grass with some mesquite-buffalo grass in the southeast and shinnery (midgrass prairie with open low and shrubs) along the Canadian River.

27. Central Great Plains

The Central Great Plains are slightly lower, receive more precipitation, and are somewhat more irregular than the Western High Plains to the west. Once a grassland, with scattered low trees and shrubs in the south, much of this ecological region is now cropland, the eastern boundary of the region marking the eastern limits of the major winter wheat growing area of the United States.

28. Flint Hills

The Flint Hills is a region of rolling hills with relatively narrow steep valleys, and is composed of shale and cherty limestone with rocky soils. In contrast to surrounding ecological regions that are mostly in cropland, most of the Flint Hills region is grazed by beef cattle. The Flint Hills mark the western edge of the tallgrass prairie, and contain the largest remaining intact tallgrass prairie in the Great Plains.

29. Central Oklahoma/Texas Plains

The Central Oklahoma/Texas Plains ecoregion is a transition area between the once prairie, now winter wheat growing regions to the west, and the forested low mountains of eastern Oklahoma. The region does not possess the arability and suitability for crops such as corn and soybeans that are common in the Central Irregular Plains to the northeast. Transitional "cross-timbers" (little bluestem grassland with scattered blackjack oak and post oak trees) is the native vegetation, and presently rangeland and pastureland comprise the predominant land cover. Oil extraction has been a major activity in this region for over eighty years.

30. Edwards Plateau

This ecoregion is largely a dissected plateau that is hillier in the south and east where it is easily distinguished from bordering ecological regions by a sharp fault line. The region contains a sparse network of perennial streams, but they are relatively clear and cool compared to those of surrounding areas. Originally covered by juniper-oak savanna and mesquite-oak savanna, most of the region is used for grazing beef cattle, sheep, goats, and wildlife. Hunting leases are a major source of income.

31. Southern Texas Plains

This rolling to moderately dissected plain was once covered with grassland and savanna vegetation. Having been subject to long continued grazing, thorny brush is now the predominant vegetation type. This "brush country", as it is called locally, has its greatest extent in Mexico and contains a greater and more distinct diversity of animal life than that found elsewhere in Texas

32. Texas Blackland Prairies

The Texas Blackland Prairies is a disjunct ecological region distinguished from surrounding regions by its fine textured clayey soils and predominantly prairie potential natural vegetation. This region now contains a higher percent of cropland than adjacent regions, although much of the land has been recently converted to urban and industrial uses.

33. East Central Texas Plains

Also called the Claypan Area, this region of irregular plains was originally covered by a post oak savanna vegetation, in contrast to the more open prairie-type regions to the north, south and west and the piney woods to the east. The bulk of this region is now used for pasture and range.

34. Western Gulf Coastal Plain

The principal distinguishing characteristics of the Western Gulf Coastal Plain are its relatively flat coastal plain topography and mainly grassland potential natural vegetation.

Inland from this region the plains are more irregular and have mostly forest or savanna-type vegetation potentials. Largely because of these characteristics, a higher percentage of the land is in cropland than in bordering ecological regions. Recent urbanization and industrialization have become concerns in this region.

35. South Central Plains

Locally termed the "piney woods", this region of mostly irregular plains was once blanketed by oak-hickory-pine forests, but is now predominantly in loblolly and shortleaf pine. Only about one sixth of the region is in cropland, whereas about two thirds is in forests and woodland. Lumber and pulpwood production are major economic activities

36. Ouachita Moutains

The Ouachita Mountains ecological region is made up of sharply defined east-west trending ridges, formed through erosion of compressed sedimentary rock formations. Once covered by oak-hickory-pine forests, most of this region is now in loblolly and shortleaf pine. Commercial logging is the major land use in the region.

37. Arkansas Valley

A region of mostly forested valleys and ridges, the physiography of the Arkansas Valley is much less irregular than that of the Boston Mountains to the north and the Ouachita Mountains to the south, but is more irregular than the ecological regions to the west and east. About one fourth of the region is grazed and roughly one tenth is cropland. In the Arkansas Valley, even streams that have been relatively unimpacted by human activities have considerably lower dissolved oxygen levels, and hence support different biological communities, than those of most of the adjacent regions.

38. Boston Mountains

In contrast to the nearby Ouachita Mountains region which comprises folded and faulted linear ridges mostly covered by pine forests, the Boston Mountains ecological region consists of a deeply dissected sandstone and shale plateau, originally covered by oak-hickory forests. Red oak, white oak, and hickory remain the dominant vegetation types in this region, although shortleaf pine and eastern red cedar are found in many of the lower areas and on some south- and west-facing slopes. The region is sparsely populated and recreation is a principal land use.

39. Ozark Highlands

The Ozark Highlands ecoregion has a more irregular physiography and is generally more forested than adjacent regions, with the exception of the Boston Mountains (38) to the south. The majority of this dissected limestone plateau is forested; oak forests are predominant, but mixed stands of oak and pine are also common. Karst features, including caves, springs, and spring-fed streams are found throughout the Ozark Highlands. Less than one fourth of the core of this region has been cleared for pasture and cropland, but half or more of the periphery, while not as agricultural as bordering ecological regions, is in cropland and pasture.

40. Central Irregular Plains

The Central Irregular Plains have a mix of land use and are topographically more irregular than the Western Corn Belt Plains (47) to the north, where most of the land is in crops. The region, however, is less irregular and less forest covered than the ecoregions to the south and east. The potential natural vegetation of this ecological region is a grassland/forest mosaic with wider forested strips along the streams compared to Ecoregion 47 to the north. The mix of land use activities in the Central Irregular Plains also includes mining operations of high-sulfur bituminous coal. The disturbance of these coal strata in southern Iowa and northern Missouri has degraded water quality and affected aquatic biota.

41. Canadian Rockies

As its name indicates, most of this region is located in Canada. It straddles the border between Alberta and British Columbia in Canada and extends southeastward into northwestern Montana. The region is generally higher and more ice-covered than the Northern Rockies. Vegetation is mostly Douglas fir, spruce, and lodgepole pine at lower elevations and alpine fir at middle elevations. The higher elevations are treeless alpine. A large part of the region is in national parks where tourism is the major land use. Forestry and mining occur on the nonpark lands.

42. Northwestern Glaciated Plains
The Northwestern Glaciated Plains ecoregion is a transitional region between the generally more level, moister, more agricultural Northern Glaciated Plains to the east and the generally more irregular, dryer, Northwestern Great Plains to the west and southwest. The western and southwestern boundary roughly coincides with the limits of continental glaciation. Pocking this ecoregion is a moderately high concentration of semi-permanent and seasonal wetlands, locally referred to a Prairie Potholes.

43. Northwestern Great Plains
The Northwestern Great Plains ecoregion encompasses the Missouri Plateau section of the Great Plains. It is a semiarid rolling plain of shale and sandstone punctuated by occasional buttes. Native grasslands, largely replaced on level ground by spring wheat and alfalfa, persist in rangeland areas on broken topography. Agriculture is restricted by the erratic precipitation and limited opportunities for irrigation.

44. Nebraska Sandhills
The Nebraska Sandhills comprise one of the most distinct and homogenous ecoregions in North America. One of the largest areas of grass stabilized sand dunes in the world, this region is generally devoid of cropland agriculture, and except for some riparian

areas in the north and east, the region is treeless. Large portions of this ecoregion contain numerous lakes and wetlands and have a lack of streams.

45. Piedmont
Considered the nonmountainous portion of the old Appalachians Highland by physiographers, the northeast-southwest trending Piedmont ecoregion comprises a transitional area between the mostly mountainous ecoregions of the Appalachians to the northwest and the relatively flat coastal plain to the southeast. It is a complex mosaic of Precambrian and Paleozoic metamorphic and igneous rocks, with moderately dissected irregular plains and some hills. The soils tend to be finer-textured than in coastal plain regions (63, 65). Once largely cultivated, much of this region has reverted to successional pine and hardwood woodlands, with an increasing conversion to an urban and suburban land cover.

46. Northern Glaciated Plains
The Northern Glaciated Plains ecoregion is characterized by a flat to gently rolling landscape composed of glacial till. The subhumid conditions foster a transitional grassland containing tallgrass and shortgrass prairie. High concentrations of temporary and seasonal wetlands create favorable conditions for waterfowl nesting and migration. Though the till soils are very fertile, agricultural success is subject to annual climatic fluctuations.

47. Western Corn Belt Plains

Once covered with tallgrass prairie, over 75 percent of the Western Corn Belt Plains is now used for cropland agriculture and much of the remainder is in forage for livestock. A combination of nearly level to gently rolling glaciated till plains and hilly loess plains, an average annual precipitation of 63-89 cm, which occurs mainly in the growing season, and fertile, warm, moist soils make this on of the most productive areas of corn and soybeans in the world. Major environmental concerns in the region include surface and groundwater contamination from fertilizer and pesticide applications as well as impacts from concentrated livestock production.

48. Lake Agassiz Plain

Glacial Lake Agassiz was the last in a series of proglacial lakes to fill the Red River valley in the three million years since the beginning of the Pleistocene. Thick beds of lake sediments on top of glacial till create the extremely flat floor of the Lake Agassiz Plain. The historic tallgrass prairie has been replaced by intensive row crop agriculture. The preferred crops in the northern half of the region are potatoes, beans, sugar beets and wheat; soybeans, sugar beets, and corn predominate in the south.

49. Northern Minnesota Wetlands

Much of the Northern Minnesota Wetlands is a vast and nearly level marsh that is sparsely inhabited by humans and covered by swamp and boreal forest vegetation Formerly occupied by broad glacial lakes, most of the flat terrain in this ecoregion is still covered by standing water.

50. Northern Lakes And Forests

The Northern Lakes and Forests is a region of nutrient poor glacial soils, coniferous and northern hardwood forests, undulating till plains, morainal hills, broad lacustrine basins, and extensive sandy outwash plains. Soils in this ecoregion are thicker than in those to the north and generally lack the arability of soils in adjacent ecoregions to the south. The numerous lakes that dot the landscape are clearer and less productive than those in ecoregions to the south.

51. North Central Hardwood Forests

The North Central Hardwood Forests is transitional between the predominantly forested Northern Lakes and Forests to the north and the agricultural ecoregions to the south. Land use/land cover in this ecoregion consists of a mosaic forests, wetlands and lakes, cropland agriculture, pasture, and dairy operations.

52. Driftless Area

The hilly uplands of the Driftless Area easily distinguish it from surrounding ecoregions. Much of the area consists of a deeply dissected, loess-capped, bedrock dominated plateau. The region is also called the Paleozoic Plateau because the landscape's appearance is a result of erosion through rock strata of Paleozoic age. Although there is evidence of glacial drift in the region, the influence of the glacial deposits have done little to affect the landscape compared to the subduing influences in adjacent ecoregions. Livestock and dairy farming are major land uses and have had a major impact on stream quality.

53. Southeastern Wisconsin Till Plains

The Southeastern Wisconsin Till Plains supports a mosaic of vegetation types, representing a transition between the hardwood forests and oak savannas of the ecoregions to the west and the tall-grass prairies of the Central Corn Belt Plains to the south. Like the Corn Belt Plains, land use in the Southeastern Wisconsin Till Plains is mostly cropland, but the crops are largely forage and feed grains to support dairy operations, rather than corn and soybeans for cash crops.

54. Central Corn Belt Plains

Extensive prairie communities intermixed with oak-hickory forests were native to the glaciated plains of the Central Corn Belt Plains; they were a stark contrast to the hardwood forests that grew on the drift plains of ecoregions (55, 56) to the east. Ecoregions to the west (40, 47) were mostly treeless except along larger streams. Beginning in the nineteenth century, the natural vegetation was gradually replaced by agriculture. Farms are now extensive on the dark, fertile soils of the Central Corn Belt Plains and mainly produce corn and soybeans; cattle, sheep, poultry, and especially hogs are also raised, but they are not as dominant as in the drier Western Corn Belt Plains (47) to the west. Agriculture has affected stream chemistry, turbidity, and habitat.

55. Eastern Corn Belt Plains

The Eastern Corn Belt Plains is primarily a rolling till plain with local end moraines; it had more natural tree cover and has lighter colored soils than the Central Corn Belt Plains (54). The region has loamier and better drained soils than the Huron/Erie Lake Plain (57), and richer soils than the Erie Drift Plain (61). Glacial deposits of Wisconsinan age are extensive. They are not as dissected nor as leached as the pre-Wisconsinan till which is restricted to the southern part of the region. Originally, beech forests were common on Wisconsinan soils while beech forests and elm-ash swamp forests dominated the wetter pre-Wisconsinan soils. Today, extensive corn, soybean, and livestock production occurs and has affected stream chemistry and turbidity.

56. Southern Michigan/Northern Indiana Drift Plains

Bordered by Lake Michigan on the west, this ecoregion is less agricultural than those (54, 55) to the south, it is better drained and contains more lakes than the flat agricultural lake plain (57) to the east, and its soils are not as nutrient poor as Ecoregion 50 to the north. The region is characterized by many lakes and marshes as well as an assortment of landforms, soil types, soil textures, and land uses. Broad till plains with thick and complex deposits of drift, paleobeach ridges, relict dunes, morainal hills, kames, drumlins, meltwater channels, and kettles occur. Oak-hickory forests, northern swamp forests, and beech forests were typical. Feed grain, soybean, and livestock farming as well as woodlots, quarries, recreational development, and urban-industrial areas are now common.

57. Huron/Erie Lake Plain

The Huron/Erie Lake Plain is a broad, fertile, nearly flat plain punctuated by relic sand dunes, beach ridges, and end moraines. Originally, soil drainage was typically poorer than in the adjacent Eastern Corn Belt Plains (55), and elm-ash swamp and beech forests were dominant. Oak savanna was typically restricted to sandy, well-drained dunes and beach ridges. Today, most of the area has been cleared and artificially drained and contains highly productive farms producing corn, soybeans, livestock, and vegetables; urban and industrial areas are also extensive. Stream habitat and quality have been degraded by channelization, ditching, and agricultural activities.

58. Northeastern Highlands

The Northeastern Highlands comprise a relatively sparsely populated region characterized by nutrient poor soils blanketed by northern hardwood and spruce fir forests. Land-surface form in the region grades from low mountains in the southwest and central portions to open high hills in the northeast. Many of the numerous glacial lakes in this region have been acidified by sulfur depositions originating in industrialized areas upwind from the ecoregion to the west.

59. Northeastern Coastal Zone

Like the Northeastern Highlands, the Northeastern Coastal Zone contains relatively nutrient poor soils and concentrations of continental glacial lakes, some of which are sensitive to acidification; however, this ecoregion contains considerably less surface irregularity and much greater concentrations of human population. Although attempts were made to farm much of the Northeastern Coastal Zone after the region was settled by Europeans, land use now mainly consists of forests and residential development.

60. Northern Appalachian Plateau And Uplands

The Northern Appalachian Plateau and Uplands comprise a transition region between the less irregular, more agricultural and urbanized Erie/Ontario Drift and Lake Plain and Eastern Great Lakes and Hudson Lowlands ecoregions to the north and west and the more mountainous and forested, less populated North Central Appalachians and Northeastern Highlands ecoregions to the south and east. Much of this region is farmed and in pasture, with hay and grain for dairy cattle being the principal crops, but large areas are in forests of oak and northern hardwoods.

61. Erie Drift Plains

Once largely covered by a maple-beech-birch forest, much of the Erie Drift Plain is now in farms, many associated with dairy operations. The Eastern Corn Belt Plains (55), which border the region on the west, are flatter, more fertile, and therefore more agricultural. The glaciated Erie Drift Plain is characterized by low rounded hills, scattered end moraines, kettles, and areas of wetlands, in contrast to the adjacent unglaciated ecoregions (70, 62) to the south and east that are more hilly and less agricultural. Areas of urban development and industrial activity occur locally. Lake Erie's influence substantially increases the growing season, winter cloudiness, and snowfall in the northernmost areas.

62. North Central Appalachians

More forest covered than most adjacent ecoregions, the North Central Appalachians ecoregion is part of a vast, elevated plateau composed of horizontally bedded sandstone, shale, siltstone, conglomerate, and coal. It is made up of plateau surfaces, high hills, and low mountains, which unlike the ecoregions to the north and west, was largely unaffected by continental glaciation. Only a portion of the Poconos section in the east has been glaciated. Land use activities are generally tied to forestry and recreation, but some coal and gas extraction occurs in the west.

63. Middle Atlantic Coastal Plain

The Middle Atlantic Coastal Plain ecoregion consists of low elevation flat plains, with many swamps, marshes, and estuaries. Forest cover in the region, once dominated by longleaf pine in the Carolinas, is now mostly loblolly and some shortleaf pine, with patches of oak, gum, and cypress near major streams, as compared to the mainly longleaf-slash pine forests of the warmer Southern Coastal Plain (75). Its low terraces, marshes, dunes, barrier islands, and beaches are underlain by unconsolidated sediments. Poorly drained soils are common, and the region has a mix of coarse and finer textured soils compared to the mostly coarse soils in the majority of Ecoregion 75. The Middle Atlantic Coastal Plain is typically lower, flatter, and more poorly drained than Ecoregion 65. Less cropland occurs in the southern portion of the region than in the central and northern parts of 63.

64. Northern Piedmont

The Northern Piedmont is a transitional region of low rounded hills, irregular plains, and open valleys in contrast to the low mountains of Ecoregions 58, 66, and 67 to the north and west and the flatter coastal plains of Ecoregions 63 and 65 to the east. It is underlain by a mix of metamorphic, igneous, and sedimentary rocks, with soils that are mostly Alfisols and some Ultisols. Potential natural vegetation here was predominantly Appalachian oak forest as compared to the mostly oak-hickory-pine forests of the Piedmont (45) ecoregion to the southwest. The region now contains a higher proportion of cropland compared to the Piedmont.

65. Southeastern Plains

These irregular plains have a mosaic of cropland, pasture, woodland, and forest. Natural vegetation was predominantly longleaf pine, with smaller areas of oak-hickory-pine and Southern mixed forest. The Cretaceous or Tertiary-age sands, silts, and clays of the region contrast geologically with the older metamorphic and igneous rocks of the Piedmont (45), and with the Paleozoic limestone, chert, and shale found in the Interior Plateau (71). Elevations and relief are greater than in the Southern Coastal Plain (75), but generally less than in much of the Piedmont. Streams in this area are relatively low-gradient and sandy-bottomed.

66. Blue Ridge

The Blue Ridge extends from southern Pennsylvania to northern Georgia, varying from narrow ridges to hilly plateaus to more massive mountainous areas, with high peaks reaching over 2000 meters. The mostly forested slopes, high-gradient, cool, clear streams, and rugged terrain occur primarily on metamorphic rocks, with minor areas of igneous and sedimentary geology. Annual precipitation of over 200 centimeters can occur in the wettest areas. The southern Blue Ridge is one of the richest centers of biodiversity in the eastern U.S. It is one of the most floristically diverse ecoregions, and includes Appalachian oak forests, northern hardwoods, and, at the highest elevations, Southeastern spruce-fir forests. Shrub, grass, and heath balds, hemlock, cove hardwoods, and oak-pine communities are also significant.

67. Ridge And Valley

This northeast-southwest trending, relatively low-lying, but diverse ecoregion is sandwiched between generally higher, more rugged mountainous regions with greater forest cover. As a result of extreme folding and faulting events, the region's roughly parallel ridges and valleys have a variety of widths, heights, and geologic materials, including limestone, dolomite, shale, siltstone, sandstone, chert, mudstone, and marble. Springs and caves are relatively numerous. Present-day forests cover about 50% of the region. The ecoregion has a diversity of aquatic habitats and species of fish.

68. Southwestern Appalachians

Stretching from Kentucky to Alabama, these open low mountains contain a mosaic of forest and woodland with some cropland and pasture. The eastern boundary of the ecoregion, along the more abrupt escarpment

where it meets the Ridge and Valley, is relatively smooth and only slightly notched by small. eastward flowing streams. The western boundary, next to the Interior Plateau's Eastern Highland Rim, is more crenulated, with a rougher escarpment that is more deeply incised. The mixed mesophytic forest is restricted mostly to the deeper ravines and escarpment slopes, and the upland forests are dominated by mixed oaks with shortleaf pine. Ecoregion 68 has less agriculture than the adjacent Ecoregion 71. Coal mining occurs in several parts of the region.

69. Central Appalachians

The Central Appalachian ecoregion, stretching from central Pennsylvania to northern Tennessee, is primarily a high, dissected, rugged plateau composed of sandstone, shale, conglomerate, and coal. The rugged terrain, cool climate, and infertile soils limit agriculture, resulting in a mostly forested land cover. The high hills and low mountains are covered by a mixed mesophytic forest with areas of Appalachian oak and northern hardwood forest. Bituminous coal mines are common, and have caused the siltation and acidification of streams.

70. Western Allegheny Plateau

The hilly and wooded terrain of the Western Allegheny Plateau was not muted by glaciation and is more rugged than the agricultural till plains of Ecoregions 61 and 55 to the north and west, but is less rugged and not as forested as Ecoregion 69 to the east and south. Extensive mixed mesophytic forests and mixed oak forests originally grew in the Western Allegheny Plateau and, today, most of its rounded hills remain in forest;

dairy, livestock, and general farms as well as residential developments are concentrated in the valleys. Horizontally-bedded sedimentary rock underlying the region has been mined for bituminous coal.

71. Interior Plateau

The Interior Plateau is a diverse ecoregion extending from southern Indiana and Ohio to northern Alabama. Rock types are distinctly different from the coastal plain sediments and alluvial deposits to the west, and elevations are lower than the Appalachian ecoregions (66, 67, 68) to the east. Mississippian to Ordovician-age limestone, chert, sandstone, siltstone and shale compose the landforms of open hills, irregular plains, and tablelands. The natural vegetation is primarily oak-hickory forest, with some areas of bluestem prairie and cedar glades. The region has a diverse fish fauna.

72. Interior River Valleys And Hills

The Interior River Lowland is made up of many wide, flat-bottomed terraced valleys, forested valley slopes, and dissected glacial till plains. In contrast to the generally rolling to slightly irregular plains in adjacent ecological regions to the north (54), east (55) and west (40, 47), where most of the land is cultivated for corn and soybeans, a little less than half of this area is in cropland, about 30 percent is in pasture, and the remainder is in forest. Bottomland deciduous forests and swamp forests were common on wet lowland sites, with mixed oak and oak-hickory forests on uplands. Paleozoic sedimentary rock is typical and coal mining occurs in several areas.

73. Mississippi Alluvial Plain

This riverine ecoregion extends from southern Illinois, at the confluence of the Ohio River with the Mississippi River, south to the Gulf of Mexico. It is mostly a broad, flat alluvial plain with river terraces, swales, and levees providing the main elements of relief. Soils are typically finer-textured and more poorly drained than the upland soils of adjacent Ecoregion 74, although there are some areas of coarser, better-drained soils. Winters are mild and summers are hot, with temperatures and precipitation increasing from north to south. Bottomland deciduous forest vegetation covered the region before much of it was cleared for cultivation. Presently, most of the northern and central parts of the region are in cropland and receive heavy treatments of insecticides and herbicides. Soybeans, cotton, and rice are the major crops.

74. Mississippi Valley Loess Plains

This ecoregion stretches from near the Ohio River in western Kentucky to Louisiana. It consists primarily of irregular plains, some gently rolling hills, and near the Mississippi River, bluffs. Thick loess is one of the distinguishing characteristics. The bluff hills in the western portion contain soils that are deep, steep, silty, and erosive. Flatter topography is found to the east, and streams tend to have less gradient and more silty substrates than in the Southeastern Plains ecoregion (65). Oak-hickory and oak-hickory-pine forest was the natural vegetation. Agriculture is now the dominant land cover in the Kentucky and Tennessee portion of the region, while in Mississippi there is a mosaic of forest and cropland.

75. Southern Coastal Plain

The Southern Coastal Plain consists of mostly flat plains, but it is a heterogeneous region containing barrier islands, coastal lagoons, marshes, and swampy lowlands along the Gulf and Atlantic coasts. In Florida, an area of discontinuous highlands contains numerous lakes. This ecoregion is lower in elevation with less relief and wetter soils than the Southeastern Plains (65). It is warmer, more heterogeneous, and has a longer growing season and coarser textured soils than the Middle Atlantic Coastal Plain (63). Once covered by a variety of forest communities that included trees of longleaf pine, slash pine, pond pine, beech, sweetgum, southern magnolia, white oak, and laurel oak, land cover in the region is now mostly slash and loblolly pine with oak-gum-cypress forest in some low lying areas, citrus groves in Florida, pasture for beef cattle, and urban.

76. Southern Florida Coastal Plain

The frost free climate of the Southern Florida Coastal Plain makes it distinct from other ecoregions in the conterminous United States. This region is characterized by flat plains with wet soils, marshland and swamp land cover with everglades and palmetto prairie vegetation types. Relatively slight differences in elevation and landform have important consequences for vegetation and the diversity of habitat types. Although portions of this region are in parks, game refuges, and Indian reservations, a large part of the region has undergone extensive hydrological and biological alteration.

77. North Cascades

The terrain of the North Cascades is composed of high, rugged mountains. It contains the greatest concentration of active alpine glaciers in the conterminous United States and has a variety of climatic zones. A dry continental climate occurs in the east and mild, maritime, rainforest conditions are found in the west. It is underlain by sedimentary and metamorphic rock in contrast to the adjoining Cascades which are composed of volcanics.

78. Klamath Mountains

The ecoregion is physically and biologically diverse. Highly dissected, folded mountains, foothills, terraces, and floodplains occur and are underlain by igneous, sedimentary, and some metamorphic rock. The mild, subhumid climate of the Klamath Mountains is characterized by a lengthy summer drought. It supports a vegetal mix of northern Californian and Pacific Northwest conifers.

79. Madrean Archipelago

Also known as the Sky Islands in the United States, this is a region of basins and ranges with medium to high local relief, typically 1,000 to 1,500 meters. Native vegetation in the region is mostly grama-tobosa shrubsteppe in the basins and oak-juniper woodlands on the ranges, except at higher elevations where ponderosa pine is predominant. The region has ecological significance as both a barrier and bridge between two major cordilleras of North America, the Rocky Mountains and the Sierra Madre Occidental.

80. Northern Basin And Range

This ecoregion contains arid tablelands, intermontane basins, dissected lava plains, and scattered mountains. Non-mountain areas have sagebrush steppe vegetation; cool season grasses and Mollisols are more common than in the hotter-drier basins of the Central Basin and Range where Aridisols are dominated by sagebrush, shadscale, and greasewood. Ranges are generally covered in Mountain sagebrush, mountain brush, and Idaho fescue at lower and mid-elevations; Douglas-fir, and aspen are common at higher elevations. Overall, the ecoregion is drier and less suitable for agriculture than the Columbia Plateau and higher and cooler than the Snake River Plain. Rangeland is common and dryland and irrigated agriculture occur in eastern basins.

81. Sonoran Basin And Range

Similar to the Mojave Basin and Range to the north, this ecoregion contains scattered low mountains and has large tracts of federally owned land, most of which is used for military training. However, the Sonoran Basin and Range is slightly hotter than the Mojave and contains large areas of palo verde-cactus shrub and giant saguaro cactus, whereas the potential natural vegetation in the Mojave is largely creosote bush.

82. Laurentian Plains And Hills

This mostly forested region, with dense concentrations of continental glacial lakes, is less rugged than the Northeastern Highlands (58) to the west and considerably less populated than the Ecoregion 59 to the south. Vegetation here is mostly spruce-fir with some patches of maple, beech, and birch, and the soils are predominantly Spodosols. By contrast, the forests in the Northeastern Coastal Zone (59) to the south are mostly white, red, and jack pine and oak-hickory, and the soils are generally Inceptisols and Entisols.

83. Eastern Great Lakes And Hudson Lowlands

This glaciated region of irregular plains bordered by hills generally contains less surface irregularity and more agricultural activity and population density than the adjacent Northeastern Highlands (58) and Northern Appalachian Plateau and Uplands (60). Although orchards, vineyards, and vegetable farming are important locally, a large percentage of the agriculture is associated with dairy operations. The portion of this ecoregion that is in close proximity to the Great Lakes experiences an increased growing season, more winter cloudiness, and greater snowfall.

84. Atlantic Coastal Pine Barrens

This ecoregion is distinguished from the coastal ecoregion (63) to the south by its coarser-grained soils, cooler climate, and Northeastern oak-pine potential natural vegetation. The climate is milder than the coastal ecoregion (59) to the north that contains Appalachian Oak forests and some Northern hardwoods forests. The physiography of this ecoregion is not as flat as that of the Middle Atlantic Coastal Plain, but it is not as irregular as that of the Northeastern Coastal Zone (59).

Phoebis sennae (Cloudless sulphur) lays eggs on host plants in the *Cassia species* (Pea family). Two meadow plant hosts are *Cassia marilandica* (Wild senna) and *Chamaecrista fasciculata* (Partridge pea).

glossary

acid soil: soil with a pH below 7.0

alkaline soil: soil with a pH above 7.0

annual: plant living one year or less. During this time the plants grows, flowers, produces seeds, and dies.

amphibians: cold-blooded, smooth-skinned vertebrate such as a frog or salamander, that characteristically hatches as an aquatic larva with gills. The larva then transforms into an adult having air-breathing lungs.

backfire: fire that burns into or against the wind. Often used to create a firebreak for a headfire.

backpack sprayer: small 5-gallon tank with a slide action pump, shoots a stream of water up to 20 feet.

bacteria: microscopic, single celled organisms that are mostly non-photosynthetic. They include the photosynthetic cyanobacteria (formally called blue-green algae) and actinomycetes (filamentous bacteria that give healthy soil its characteristic smell).

beneficial insect: living organisms; some are used in pest control and others are used to improve the health of soils and plants

biennial: a plant that completes its life cycle within two seasons. Biennials grow vegetatively and store food the first season and in the second season flowers, bears seed and dies.

biodiversity: variation among and within plant and animal species in a given environment; often used as a measure of health of an ecosystem

biomass: the weight or amount of living matter that makes up the total plant (the leaves, the flowers, the stem, the root system, the fruit and the seeds).

blackline: burned area created by a backfire, acts as a fire break.

burn plan: an outline of what landowners want to accomplish with prescribed burning, components of the burn and how to measure the results of the fire.

clump forming: plant that has few stolons, growing in a small bunch or clump; ie: bunchgrass. Usually not invasive.

cool season: actively grows during the spring and fall when soil temperatures are cool.

compost: a mixture of organic residues and soil that has been piled, moistened, and allowed to decompose biologically.

cover: woods, underbrush, etc. serving to shelter and conceal wild animals or birds

dibble: small, hand-held, pointed implement for making holes in soil for planting seedlings and bulbs.

dissolved oxygen: microscopic bubbles of oxygen that are mixed in the water and occur between water molecules. Dissolved oxygen is necessary for healthy lakes, rivers, and estuaries. Most aquatic plants and animals need oxygen to survive. Fish will drown in water when the dissolved oxygen levels get too low. The absence of dissolved oxygen in water is a sign of possible pollution.

diversity: an ecological measure of the variety of organisms and plants present in an ecosystem.

drifts: large areas of a landscape planted with one plant species.

drip torch: a hand-held device, used to light fires, that drips flaming fuel.

ecoregion or bioregion: an area constituting a natural ecological community with characteristic flora, fauna, and environmental conditions and bounded by natural rather than man made borders.

ecosystem: the interactions and relationships between organisms and their environments.

endemic: native or limited to a particular area

environment: the air, water, minerals, organisms, and all other external factors surrounding and affecting a given organism at any time.

erosion: the process by which the surface of the earth is worn away by the action of water, glaciers, winds, waves, etc.

Sternotherus oderatus (Stinkpot turtle) and *Ch*

ethanoic acid: a weak acid produced by the oxidation of ethanol. It is one of the simplest carboxylic acids (fatty acids). It is the acid found in vinegar.

extinct: no longer in existence; species become extinct when their habitat is destroyed by expanding development.

fertilizer: any substance containing one or more recognized plant nutrients that is used for promoting plant growth.

firebreak: a pond, river, road, plowed field, low mowed grass, burned area or anything else that stops a fire and contains it within a burn area.

fireline: the advancing fire ignited along the firebreak moving across the burn area in a line or front.

Bruce Jones

(...ainted turtle) at meadow pond edge.

flank fire: a fire that moves at a 90degree angle to the wind direction.

forb: non-grass plant, flower

fungi: multi-celled, non-photosynthetic organisms that are neither plants nor animals. Fungal cells form long chains called hyphae and may form fruiting bodies such as mold or mushrooms to disperse spores. Some fungi, such as yeast, are single celled.

fungicide: a chemical substance that destroys or inhibits the growth of fungi.

germinate: the process whereby growth, i.e. a seed, emerges from a period of dormancy.

glyphosate: a synthetic, non selective, systemic herbicide found in products such as Round Up and Rodeo. Debated to pose a threat to humans and animals as an endocrine disruptor.

grasses: any plant of the family Gramineae, having jointed stems, sheathing leaves, and seed like grains.

habitat: the natural environment of an organism; place that is natural for the life and growth of an organism.

headfire: a fast moving fire that burns with the wind.

herbicide: a substance that is toxic to plants and is used to destroy unwanted vegetation.

insecticide: a substance or preparation used for killing insects.

lawn: area planted typically with one species of grass, maintained at an even height of from one to four inches. Grass species commonly used are not native to North America.

leach: to remove soluble materials from soil with water.

lean soil: soil that is not rich in organic matter; poor soil.

meadow: an eastern ecosystem in succession from bare, disturbed soil to forest. Meadows typically have plant communities that have a high proportion of cool season grasses with a wide variety of wild flowers.

mesic: an area with well drained but moist soil for much of the growing season or year.

microbes: an imprecise term referring to any microscopic organism. Generally, "microbes" includes bacteria, fungi and sometimes protozoa.

monoculture: area without diversity of plant material, where one plant species is being cultivated every season without variance, such as a lawn.

mop-up: the process of extinguishing all smoldering debris such as logs and stumps.

mulch: any material such as straw, leaves, and loose soil that is spread upon the surface of the soil to protect plant roots from the effects of rain, soil crusting, freezing or evaporation.

native plant: a species that occurs naturally in a particular place without human intervention, dating to before European development 300 years ago.

natural organic fertilizer: materials derived from either plant or animal products containing one or more elements (other than carbon, hydrogen and oxygen) that are essential for plant growth.

naturalize: the ability of some plants, when introduced to a new habitat, to reproduce and become an established part of the environment.

nematodes: Tiny, usually microscopic, unsegmented worms. Most live free in the soil. Some are parasites of animals or plants.

non-native invasive plants: non-indigenous plant species that adversely affect the habitats they invade economically, environmentally or ecologically.

organic: of strictly animal or vegetable origin.

pelargonic acid: a chemical substance that is found in almost all species of animals and plants. It is sprayed as a herbicide and decomposes rapidly and is not toxic to humans or the environment.

pesticide: any substance or mixture of substances intended for preventing, destroying, repelling, any pest. The term pesticide also applies to herbicides, fungicides, and various other substances used to control pests.

perennial: a plant that grows indefinitely from year to year and usually produces seed each year.

pH: The measure of the concentration of hydrogen ions. When soil pH is not in the proper range, nutrient uptake can be hindered

plant communities: a group of plants that naturally grow and thrive together.

plant succession: in the absence of fire or other disturbance, the gradual maturation of vegetation types such as grasslands maturing into brush, or brush land maturing into forest.

prescribed burn: fire applied to a specific area of land under selected weather conditions to accomplish predetermined, well defined management objectives.

plugs: small-sized seedlings grown in trays usually filled with a peat substrate.

prairie: a grassland with low rainfall found in the Midwest and western United States, with a high proportion of warm season grasses and a variety of wildflowers.

Pure Live Seed (PLS): the product of the percentage of germination plush the had seed and the percentage of pure live seed, divided by 100.

rhizome: a horizontal or upright stem found underground or growing across the surface of the substrate, modified for reproduction or for food storage. It is particularly apparent in the rapid underground spread of many grasses.

root ball: the ball of soil and roots of a plant growing in a pot or other container.

seed stratification: natural process such as cold and moisture or fire which stimulates seed germination.

site analysis: site planning and design including location, man-made features, natural physical features such as trees, ground texture, soil and light conditions.

smothering: to cover existing vegetation thickly with material to kill it off

specialization: adaption of a plant or animal species to a special function or environment.

species: basic category of biological classification, composed of related individuals that resemble one another, are able to breed among themselves, but are not able to breed with members of another species.

soil: a dynamic living system formed at the interface between the lithosphere and the atmosphere in responses to forces exerted by climate and organisms, acting through time on a parent material.

stolons: horizontal stem at or just below the surface of the ground that roots at the nodes and produces new plants. Also called "runners."

sustainable: continuous, enduring, permanent. The ability of an ecosystem to maintain ecological processes, functions, biodiversity and productivity into the future.

suburban: residential areas which surround the central area of urban towns or cities.

synthetic fertilizer: "man made"; common nitrogen sources such as ammonia, ammonium sulfate and urea are by-products from the oil and natural gas industry.

urban: relating to or concerned with densely populated areas.

warm season: actively grows during the summer when soil temperatures are warm.

weed: plant that requires high nitrate levels, poor soil structure & produces huge numbers of seeds that disperse far and wide.

wetline: a firebreak made by dousing an area or line with water.

wet meadow: a wetland that is inundated early in the season and dries out later in the season.

wildfire: an out of control fire.

Bombus bimaculatus (Bumble bee), a very efficient pollinator because of its long tongue, collects nectar and pollen from *Gentianopsis crinita* (Fringed gentian).

Exposure to broad-spectrum pesticides is as toxic to beneficial insects as it is to the target species.

BEYOND PESTICIDES

701 E Street, SE ▪ Washington DC 20003
202-543-5450 phone ▪ 202-543-4791 fax
info@beyondpesticides.org ▪ www.beyondpesticides.org

LAWN PESTICIDE FACTS AND FIGURES
A Beyond Pesticides Factsheet

PESTICIDE USAGE

☐ 78 million households in the U.S. use home and garden pesticides. [i]

☐ Herbicides account for the highest usage of pesticides in the home and garden sector with over 90 million pounds applied on lawns and gardens per year. [ii]

☐ Suburban lawns and gardens receive more pesticide applications per acre (3.2-9.8 lbs) than agriculture (2.7 lbs per acre on average). [iii]

☐ Pesticide sales by the chemical industry average $9.3 billion. Annual sales of the landscape industry are over $35 billion. [iv]

☐ Included in the most commonly used pesticides per pounds per year are: 2,4-D (8-11 million), Glyphosate (5-8 million), MCPP (Mecoprop) (4-6 million), Pendimethalin (3-6 million), Dicamba (2-4 million). [v]

☐ A 2004 national survey reveals that 5 million homeowners use only organic lawn practices and products and 35 million people use both toxic and non-toxic materials. [vi]

HEALTH & EXPOSURE RISKS

☐ Of 30 commonly used lawn pesticides 13 are probable or possible carcinogens, 13 are linked with birth defects, 21 with reproductive effects, 15 with neurotoxicity, 26 with liver or kidney damage, 27 are sensitizers and/or irritants, and 11 have the potential to disrupt the endocrine (hormonal) system. [vii]

☐ Pregnant women, infants and children, the aged and the chronically ill are at greatest risk from pesticide exposure and chemically induced immune-suppression, which can increase susceptibility to cancer. [viii]

☐ Scientific studies find pesticide residues such as the weedkiller 2,4-D and the insecticide carbaryl inside homes, due to drift and track-in, where they contaminate air, dust, surfaces and carpets and expose children at levels ten times higher than preapplication levels. [ix]

CHILDREN & PESTICIDES

☐ Children take in more pesticides relative to body weight than adults and have developing organ systems that make them more vulnerable and less able to detoxify toxins. [x]

☐ The National Academy of Sciences estimates 50% of lifetime pesticide exposure occurs during the first 5 years of life. [xi]

☐ A study published in the *Journal of the National Cancer Institute* finds home and garden pesticide use can increase the risk of childhood leukemia by almost seven times. [xii]

☐ Studies show low levels of exposure to actual lawn pesticide products are linked to increased rates of miscarriage, and suppression of the nervous, endocrine, and immune systems. [xiii]

☐ Exposure to home and garden pesticides can increase a child's likelihood of developing asthma. [xiv]

- Studies link pesticides with hyperactivity, developmental delays, behavioral disorders, and motor dysfunction.[xv]
- Children ages children ages 6-11 have higher levels of lawn chemicals in their blood than all other age categories. Biomonitoring studies find that pesticides pass from mother to child through umbilical cord blood and breast milk.[xvi]

WILDLIFE, PETS & PESTICIDES

- Studies find that dogs exposed to herbicide-treated lawns and gardens can double their chance of developing canine lymphoma and may increase the risk of bladder cancer in certain breeds by four to seven times.[xvii]
- Of 30 commonly used lawn pesticides: 16 are toxic to birds, 24 are toxic to fish and aquatic organisms, and 11 are deadly to bees.[xviii]
- Pesticides can be toxic to wildlife and cause food source contamination, behavioral abnormalities that interfere with survival, and death.[xix]
- Lawn and garden pesticides are deadly to non-target species and can harm beneficial insects and soil microorganisms essential to a naturally healthy lawn.[xx]

PESTICIDES IN THE WATER

- Of 30 commonly used lawn pesticides, 17 are detected in groundwater, and 23 have the potential to leach.[xxi]
- Runoff has resulted in a widespread presence of pesticides in streams and groundwater. 2,4-D, found in weed and feed and other lawn products, is the herbicide most frequently detected in streams and shallow ground water from urban lawns.[xxii]
- Of the 50 chemicals on EPA's list of unregulated drinking water contaminants, several are lawn chemicals including herbicides diazinon, diuron, naphthalene, and various triazines such as atrazine.[xxiii]
- Runoff from synthetic chemical fertilizers pollutes streams and lakes and causes algae blooms, depleted oxygen and damage to aquatic life.

THE REGISTRATION SYSTEM & PESTICIDE REGULATION

- The health data assessed by EPA for the registration of pesticides comes from the manufacturer of the pesticide. EPA is not obligated under the *Federal Insecticide Fungicide and Rodenticide Act* (FIFRA) to review peer-reviewed scientific literature.
- The U.S. GAO has told Congress on several occasions that the public is misled on pesticide safety by statements characterizing pesticides as "safe" or "harmless." EPA states that no pesticide is 100 percent safe.[xxiv]
- Pesticide testing protocol was developed before science fully understood the human immune and hormonal system. EPA still does not evaluate data for several neurological effects or disruption of the endocrine (hormonal) system.
- EPA does not evaluate the health and environmental effects of actual pesticide formulations sold on the shelf. Data submitted to the EPA also does not account for low-dose effects, synergistic effects with inerts or combined exposure to more than one pesticide at a time.
- Most states have preemption laws that prohibit localities from passing local pesticide-related ordinances that are stricter than the state policy.[xxv]

- Studies link pesticides with hyperactivity, developmental delays, behavioral disorders, and motor dysfunction.[xv]
- Children ages children ages 6-11 have higher levels of lawn chemicals in their blood than all other age categories. Biomonitoring studies find that pesticides pass from mother to child through umbilical cord blood and breast milk.[xvi]

WILDLIFE, PETS & PESTICIDES

- Studies find that dogs exposed to herbicide-treated lawns and gardens can double their chance of developing canine lymphoma and may increase the risk of bladder cancer in certain breeds by four to seven times.[xvii]
- Of 30 commonly used lawn pesticides: 16 are toxic to birds, 24 are toxic to fish and aquatic organisms, and 11 are deadly to bees.[xviii]
- Pesticides can be toxic to wildlife and cause food source contamination, behavioral abnormalities that interfere with survival, and death.[xix]
- Lawn and garden pesticides are deadly to non-target species and can harm beneficial insects and soil microorganisms essential to a naturally healthy lawn.[xx]

PESTICIDES IN THE WATER

- Of 30 commonly used lawn pesticides, 17 are detected in groundwater, and 23 have the potential to leach.[xxi]
- Runoff has resulted in a widespread presence of pesticides in streams and groundwater. 2,4-D, found in weed and feed and other lawn products, is the herbicide most frequently detected in streams and shallow ground water from urban lawns.[xxii]
- Of the 50 chemicals on EPA's list of unregulated drinking water contaminants, several are lawn chemicals including herbicides diazinon, diuron, naphthalene, and various triazines such as atrazine.[xxiii]
- Runoff from synthetic chemical fertilizers pollutes streams and lakes and causes algae blooms, depleted oxygen and damage to aquatic life.

THE REGISTRATION SYSTEM & PESTICIDE REGULATION

- The health data assessed by EPA for the registration of pesticides comes from the manufacturer of the pesticide. EPA is not obligated under the *Federal Insecticide Fungicide and Rodenticide Act* (FIFRA) to review peer-reviewed scientific literature.
- The U.S. GAO has told Congress on several occasions that the public is misled on pesticide safety by statements characterizing pesticides as "safe" or "harmless." EPA states that no pesticide is 100 percent safe.[xxiv]
- Pesticide testing protocol was developed before science fully understood the human immune and hormonal system. EPA still does not evaluate data for several neurological effects or disruption of the endocrine (hormonal) system.
- EPA does not evaluate the health and environmental effects of actual pesticide formulations sold on the shelf. Data submitted to the EPA also does not account for low-dose effects, synergistic effects with inerts or combined exposure to more than one pesticide at a time.
- Most states have preemption laws that prohibit localities from passing local pesticide-related ordinances that are stricter than the state policy.[xxv]

xi National Research Council, National Academy of Sciences. 1993. *Pesticides in the Diets of Infants and Children*. Washington, DC: National Academy Press.

xii Lowengart, R. et al., 1987. "Childhood Leukemia and Parent's Occupational and Home Exposures, " *Journal of the National Cancer Institute* 79:39.

xiii Greenlee, A. et al. 2004. "Low-Dose Agrochemicals and Lawn-Care Pesticides Induce Developmental Toxicity in Murine Preimplantation Embryos," *Environ Health Perspect* 112(6): 703-709; Cavieres, M., et al. 2002. "Developmental toxicity of a commercial herbicide mixture in mice: Effects on embryo implantation and litter size." *Environ Health Perspect* 110:1081-1085.

xiv Salam, M.T., et al. 2004. "Early Life Environmental Risk Factors for Asthma: Findings from the Children's Health Study," *Environ Health Perspectives* 112(6): 760.

xv Shettler, T., et al. 2000. "Known and Suspected Developmental Neurotoxicants," *In Harms Way: Toxic Threats to Child Development* Cambridge, MA: Greater Boston Physicians for Social Responsibility; Guillette, E.A., et al. 1998. "An Anthropological Approach to the Evaluation of Preschool Children Exposed to Pesticides in Mexico," *Environ Health Perspectives* 106(6); Porter, Warren. "Do Pesticides Affect Learning and Behavior? The neuro-endocrine-immune connection," *Pesticides And You* 21(4): 11-15. Beyond Pesticides, Washington, D.C. www.beyondpesticides.org/pesticidesandyou (Overview of Dr. Porter's findings published in *Environ Health Perspectives* and *Toxicology and Industrial Health*.)

xvi Centers for Disease Control and Prevention. 2003 Jan. Second National Report on Human Exposure to Environmental Chemicals; Pohl, HR., et al. 2000. "Breast-feeding exposure of infants to selected pesticides," *Toxicol Ind Health* 16: 65-77; Sturtz, N., et al. 2000. "Detection of 2,4-Dichlorophenoxyacetic acid residues in neonates breast-fed by 2,4-D exposed dams," *Neurotoxicology* 21(1-2): 147-54; Houlihan, J., et al. 2005. *Body Burden, The Pollution in Newborns*. Environmental Working Group, Washington, D.C.

xvii Glickman, L., et al. 2004. "Herbicide exposure and the risk of transitional cell carcinoma of the urinary bladder in Scottish Terriers," *Journal of the American Veterinary Medical Association* 224(8):1290-1297; Hayes, H. et al., 1991. "Case-control study of canine malignant lymphoma: positive association with dog owner's use of 2,4-D acid herbicides," *Journal of the National Cancer Institute*, 83(17):1226.

xviii Beyond Pesticides Factsheet. 2005. *Environmental Effects of 30 Commonly Used Lawn Pesticides*. http://www.beyondpesticides.org/lawn/factsheets/30enviro.pdf

xix Defenders of Wildlife. *The Dangers of Pesticides to Wildlife* [white paper]. 2005 April. www.pesticidefreelawns.org/resources.

xx Restmeyer, S.J. 2003. *Ecological Pest Management: Embracing the Organic Approach to Landscape Management*. *Pesticides and You* 23(1): 11-12. Beyond Pesticides, Washington, D.C.

xxi Beyond Pesticides Factsheet. 2005. *Environmental Effects of 30 Commonly Used Lawn Pesticides*. http://www.beyondpesticides.org/lawn/factsheets/30enviro.pdf

xxii U.S. Geological Survey. 1998. Pesticides in Surface and Ground Water of the United States: Summary of Results of the National Water Quality Assessment Program; Gilliom R.J. et al. 1999 April. "Testing water quality for pesticide pollution," *Environ Science and Technology News*.

xxiii EPA. "Unregulated Drinking Water Contaminants," Office of Ground Water and Drinking Water, http://www.epa.gov/safewater/dw_unregcontaminants.html (accessed 8/8/05).

xxiv U.S. General Accounting Office. 1997. *Nonagricultural Pesticides: Risks and Regulations*. GAO/RCED-86-97; EPA. 2002. Questions and Answers: Pesticides and Mosquito Control. Department of Prevention, Pesticides and Toxic Substances. http://www.epa.gov/pesticides/factsheets/pesticides4mosquitos.htm (accessed 7/2/04).

xxv Beyond Pesticides Factsheet. 2005. *State Preemption Laws*. http://www.beyondpesticides.org/lawn/factsheets/Preemption Factsheet.pdf

xxvi Spitzer, E., Attorney General of NY. 2000. *The Secret Ingredients in Pesticides: Reducing Risk*. Abrams, R., 1991. Attorney General of NY. *"The Secret Hazards of Pesticides: Inert Ingredients."*

xxvii EPA. *Inert Ingredients in Pesticide Products*. http://www.epa.gov/opprd001/inerts/lists.html (accessed 6/7/05).

xxviii Spitzer, E., 2000.

reprinted with permission from Beyond Pesticides

chemicalWATCH Factsheet

GLYPHOSATE

Despite widespread use of the weed killer glyphosate and the prevalent myth that it is harmless, this pesticide is tied to acute human health effects and linked to non-Hodgkin's lymphoma. It is found in two Monsanto products, available over the counter, Roundup™ and Rodeo™, making glyphosate one of the most widely used and well-known herbicides on the market. Due to the string consumer line and the company's genetically engineered (GE) "Roundup Ready" crops, glyphosate is the most widely used pesticide in the U.S.[1] As of 2005, 87% of U.S. soybean fields were planted with glyphosate resistant varieties.[2] If there is one pesticide that represents the "fast-food," quick-fix generation, glyphosate would likely be it – the McPesticide of toxic chemicals.

General Use

Glyphosate (N-phosphono-methyl glycine), according to the Environmental Protection Agency's (EPA) most recent data on pesticide usage, was the seventh most widely used active ingredient in agriculture, with 34 to 38 million pounds used in 1997.[3] In 1995/96, glyphosate ranked as the second most used active ingredient in non-agricultural settings, with five to seven million pounds used in the home and garden and nine to twelve million pounds used in commercial settings.[4] Glyphosate use is currently growing at a rate of about 20 percent per year, due in large part to the growing number of genetically engineered crops that are resistant to the herbicide.[5] With this growth rate, it is estimated that as much as 100 million pounds of glyphosate was applied in 2000. Of course these numbers fail to reflect the poundage of inert ingredients in the formulations that are mixed with the glyphosate.

First registered for use in 1974, there are 63 glyphosate-containing pesticide formulations registered for use in the U.S. The isopropylamine salt of glyphosate, the active ingredient in 53 of these products, is used to kill a variety of broadleaf weeds and grasses. The principal agricultural uses include corn, wheat, sorghum, citrus and stone fruits, potatoes, onions, asparagus, coffee, peanuts and pineapple.[6] There are also a good number of non-food uses including ornamental, turf, forestry, Christmas tree production and rights-of-way.[7]

Some of the most widespread uses of glyphosate that have been attracting public attention include use in invasive weed management and home gardening. The increase of glyphosate use in these areas is directly tied to the larger problem of poor land management, including over grazing, over development, soil compaction and other stressors. Glyphosate has replaced ecologically sound and sustainable cultural practices such as green-mulching, and preventive maintenance such as aeration and dethatching.

Mode of Action

Plants treated with glyphosate translocate the systemic herbicide to their roots, shoot regions and fruit, where it interferes with the plant's ability to form aromatic amino acids necessary for protein synthesis. Treated plants generally die in two to three days. Because plants absorb glyphosate it cannot be completely removed by washing or peeling produce or by milling, baking or brewing grains. It has been shown to persist in food products for up to two years.[8]

Inert Ingredients

A letter published in the Feburary 6, 1988 *Lancet* (page 299) cited a Japanese report of 56 cases of toxic exposure to Roundup™ between June, 1984 and March, 1986. The individuals had ingested the pesticide, and experienced a range of adverse effects to their respiratory, cardovascular, and central nervous systems; nine patients died. An analysis of the findings identified one of the so-called "inert ingredients" (inerts) in the formulation, polyoxyethyleneamine (POEA), as the cause of harm. POEA is a surfactant, a chemical added to help glyphosate work its way into the plant tissue. Roundup™ contains 15% POEA.

In 2009, French researchers found that one of the inert ingredients Roundup can kill human cells, particularly embryonic, placental and umbilical cord cells.[9]

All pesticide formulations are actually toxic soups, a mixture of the active ingredient (the registered pesticide) with a variety of other chemicals such as solvents, surfactants (like POEA), and emulsifiers – the inerts. Federal law classifies inerts as trade secrets and pesticide manufactures are not required to list inert ingredients on the pesticide label. Inerts, which can make up to as much as 99% of a pesticide formulation, are often highly toxic chemicals that can be more hazardous then the active ingredient.

Inerts known to be included in glyphosate products include ammonium sulfate, benziothiazolone, 3-iodo-2-propynl butylcarbamate (IPBC), isobutane, methyl pyrrolidinone, pelargonic acid, sodium sulfite, sorbic acid, and isopropylamine. All of these chemicals are associated with skin irritation, gastric and respiratory problems.[10]

Acute Exposure

While EPA considers glyphosate to be "of relatively low oral and dermal acute toxicity,"[11] the agency does classify glyphosate in toxicity class II (class I chemicals are the most toxic in a scale from I-IV). Some glyphosate products are of higher acute

Revised August 2009

BEYOND PESTICIDES
701 E Street, S.E., Suite 200 • Washington DC 20003
202-543-5450 (v) • 202-543-4791 (f)
info@beyondpesticides.org • www.beyondpesticides.org

toxicity, primarily due to eye and/or skin irritation.

A 2008 study by the National Institute for Occupational Safety and Health (NIOSH) finds the pesticide poisoning incidence rate among U.S. agricultural workers is thirty-nine times higher than the incidence rate found in all other industries combined. Glyphosate was one of 17 pesticide implicated in the study.[12] In California, 1998 data from the state's Department of Pesticide Regulation finds that glyphosate ranks first among herbicides as the highest causes of pesticide-induced illness or injury.[13]

Beyond Pesticides' own pesticide incident reporting system has received numerous reports of people poisoned by exposure to glyphosate from around the country. These victims of pesticide exposure suffered from eye soreness, headaches, diarrhea, and other flu-like symptoms.

Symptoms following exposure to glyphosate formulations include: swollen eyes, face and joints; facial numbness; burning and/or itching skin; blisters; rapid heart rate; elevated blood pressure; chest pains, congestion; coughing; headache; and nausea.[14]

In developmental toxicity studies using pregnant rats and rabbits, glyphosate caused treatment-related effects in high dose groups, including diarrhea, decreased body weight gain, nasal discharge and death.[15]

Chronic Exposure
One reproductive study using rats found kidney effects in the high dose group while another study showed digestive effects and decreased body weight gain.[16]

A cancer study looking at rats found an increase in pancreas and liver tumors in males as well as an increase in thyroid cancer in females.[17]

A 1999 study, *A Case-Control Study of Non-Hodgkin Lymphoma and Exposure to Pesticides,* (American Cancer Society, 1999), found that people exposed to glyphosate are 2.7 times more likely to contract non-Hodgkin Lymphoma.

A Finnish study shows that glyphostate decreases the defenses of enzymes of the liver and intestines.[18] RoundUp, as a mixture of all its ingredients, has been shown to shut down a powerful antioxidant in the liver that detoxifies harmful compounds so they can be excreted through bile. A paper published in August 2000 shows that RoundUp alters gene expression and inhibits necessary steroid production by disrupting a particular protein expression. In 2002, a paper shows that RoundUp can also affect early cell division processes in embryos.[19]

There has been controversy regarding whether glyphosate at high doses causes tumors of the thyroid and testes in rats. EPA has reported that technical glyphosate is contaminated with "less than 100 parts-per-billion" of N-nitroso-glyphosate (NNG), a by-product of synthesis. Many N-nitroso compounds are animal carcinogens. EPA is not, however, requiring further investigation of the toxicological effects of NNG, because it does not typically require data on N-nitroso contaminants present at levels of less than one part-per-million.

Environmental Effects
Much of the belief about glyphosate's environmental safety is based on the expectation that residues will be "immobile in soil," and therefore the chemical will not contaminate groundwater. EPA acknowledges that the material does have the potential to contaminate surface waters. If glyphosate reaches surface water, it is not broken down readily by water or sunlight.[20] The half-life of glyphosate in pond water ranges from 70 to 84 days.[21]

Glyphosate is moderately persistent in soil, with an average half-life of 47 days, although there are studies reporting field half lives of up to 174 days.[22] Residues of glyphosate have been known to persist for months in anaerobic soils deficient in microorganisms. Glyphosate residues are difficult to detect in environmental samples and most laboratories are not able to perform this service because of the lack of generally available, economically feasible methodology.

Effects on Nontarget Animals
Glyphosate use directly impacts a variety of nontarget animals including insects, earthworms, and fish, and indirectly impacts birds and small mammals.[23] A study conducted by the International Organization for Biological Control found that exposure to Roundup™ killed over 50 percent of three species of beneficial insects – a parasitoid wasp, a lacewing and a ladybug.[24] Repeated applications of glyphosate significantly affected the growth and survival of earthworms.[25] Studies have also shown that glyphosate, and in particular the inert ingredients in the formulation of Roundup™ are acutely toxic to fish.[26]

A 2005 University of Pittsburgh study finds that Roundup alone is "extremely lethal" to amphibians in concentrations found in the environment.[27]

BEYOND PESTICIDES
701 E Street, S.E., Suite 200 • Washington DC 20003
202-543-5450 (v) • 202-543-4791 (f)
info@beyondpesticides.org • www.beyondpesticides.org

Glyphosate *chemicalWATCH* Factsheet Bibliography

[1] US EPA 2000–2001 Pesticide Market Estimates Agriculture, Home and Garden
[2] National Agriculture Statistics Service (2005) in Acreage eds. Johanns, M. & Wiyatt, S. D. 6 30, (U.S. Dept. of Agriculture, Washington, DC).
[3] Environmental Protection Agency. 1999. *Pesticides Industry Sales and Usage: 1996 and 1997 Market Estimates*. EPA-733-R-99-001. p. 21, Table 8. <http://www.epa.gov/oppbead1/pestsales/97pestsales/97pestsales.pdf>
[4] Ibid. p. 22, Table 9.
[5] Northwest Coalition for Alternatives to Pesticides. 1998. *Herbicide Factsheet: Glyphosate (Roundup).* Journal of Pesticide Reform, vol. 18, no. 3, p. 4.
[6] Environmental Protection Agency. 1993. *Glyphosate Reregistration Eligibility Decision.* p. viii. <http://www.epa.gov/REDs/old_reds/glyphosate.pdf>
[7] Ibid.
[8] Pesticide Action Network, 1997. Glyphosate fact sheet. For more information about glyphosate visit <http://data.pesticideinfo.org/4DAction/GetRecord/PC33138>
[9] Benachour, Nora and Gilles-Eric Seralini. 2009. "Glyphosate Formulations Induce Apoptosis and Necrosis in Human Umbilical, Embryonic, and Placental Cells." *Chem. Res. Toxicol.* 22 (1), pp 97–105.

[10] NCAP. 1998. p. 5.
[11] EPA. 1993.
[12] Calvert, G. et al. 2008. "Acute Pesticide Poisoning Among Agricultural Workers in the United States, 1998–2005." *American Journal of Industrial Medicine.* 51:883–898.
[13] California Pesticide Illness Surveillance Program Report – 1998. Table 4. <http://www.cdpr.ca.gov/docs/dprdocs/pisp/1998pisp.htm>
[14] NCAP. 1998. p. 5, Table 1.
[15] EPA. 1993.
[16] Ibid.
[17] NCAP. 1998. Citing EPA OPPTS, 1991, Second Peer Review of Glyphosate. Memo from W. Dykstra and G.Z. Ghali, HED to R. Taylor, Registration Division and L. Rossi, Special Review and Reregistration Division.
[18] Hietanen, E., et al. 1983. "Effects of phenoxy herbicides and glyphosate on the hepatic and intestinal biotransformation activities in the rat." Acta Pharma et Toxicol 53:103-112.
[19] Porter, W. 2004. "Do Pesticides Affect Learning and Behavior? The neuro-endocrine-immune connection." *Pesticides and You.* 24 (1):11-15.
[20] EPA. 1993

[21] Extension Toxicology Network. 1996. Pesticide Information Profiles: Glyphosate. <http://ace.orst.edu/cgi-bin/mfs/01/pips/glyphosa.htm>
[22] Ibid.
[23] NCAP. 1998. pps. 11-13.
[24] Ibid. p. 11. Citing: Hassan, S.A. et al. 1988. Results of the fourth joint pesticide testing programme carried out by the IOBC/WPRS-Working Group "Pesticides and Beneficial Organisms." J. Appl. Ent. 105: 321-329.
[25] Ibid. Citing: Springett, J.A. and R.A.J. Gray. 1992. Effect of repeated low doses of biocides on the earthworm *Aporrectodea caliginosa* in laboratory culture. *Soil Biol. Biochem.* 24(12): 1739-1744.
[26] Ibid. p. 12. Citing: Folmar, L.C., H.O. Sanders, and A.M. Julin. 1979. Toxicity of the herbicide glyphosate and several of its formulations to fish and aquatic invertebrates. *Arch. Environ. Contam. Toxicol.* 8: 269-278.
[27] Relyea, Rick. 2005. "THE LETHAL IMPACT OF ROUNDUP ON AQUATIC AND TERRESTRIAL AMPHIBIANS." *Ecological Applications,* 15(4), 1118–1124.

Beyond Pesticides works with allies in protecting public health and the environment to lead the transition to a world free of toxic pesticides. In 1981, Beyond Pesticides was established as a non-profit organization. The founders felt that without the existence of such an organized, national network, local, state and national pesticide policy would become, under chemical industry pressure, increasingly unresponsive to public health and environmental concerns.

Beyond Pesticides has historically taken a two-pronged approach to the pesticide problem by identifying the risks of conventional pest management practices and promoting non-chemical and least-hazardous management alternatives. The organization's primary goal is to effect change through local action, assisting individuals and community-based organizations to stimulate discussion on the hazards of toxic pesticides, while providing information on safer alternatives. Beyond Pesticides has sought to bring to a policy forum in Washington, DC, state capitals, and local governing bodies the pesticide problem and solutions we have become aware of on a day-to-day basis. The organization publishes a wide variety of brochures, information packets, and reports including an ongoing chemicalWATCH series, tracking chemical effects and alternatives.

Fact sheet reprinted with permission from Beyond Pesticides

BEYOND PESTICIDES
701 E Street, S.E., Suite 200 • Washington DC 20003
202-543-5450 (v) • 202-543-4791 (f)
info@beyondpesticides.org • www.beyondpesticides.org

the experts

Neil Diboll, Ecologist and President, Prairie Nursery, Inc

A true pioneer in the native plant industry and recognized internationally as an expert in native community ecology, Neil Diboll has nurtured Prairie Nursery as its president since 1982. On both professional and personal levels, Neil has dedicated his life to the propagation of native plants and their promotion in the green industry as beautiful, low maintenance alternatives. He has lectured and written extensively on prairie ecology, establishment, and native plants.

Neil's work includes designs for residential, commercial and public spaces throughout the Midwest and Northeast United States. The essence of Neil's philosophy is that we, as stewards of the planet, must work to preserve and increase the diversity of native plants and animals, with which we share our world. The protection of our natural heritage and our soil and water resources is essential to maintaining a high quality of life for today, and for the children of future generations to come.

Michael Nadeau, Designer, Organic Land Care Specialist and President, Plantscapes, Inc.

Michael Nadeau is an award winning landscape designer who began working in the industry in the early 1980's. He has over two decades of experience in organic landscaping and his specialties include rain gardens, organic vegetable gardens, woodland gardens, native grass and wildflower meadows, and lawn alternatives.

Michael is a tireless advocate for organic gardening. He is a founding committee member of the Organic Land Care Program and helped author the NOFA Standards for Organic Land Care (the nation's first organic landscaping standards) and the NOFA Organic Lawn & Turf Handbook (2006). He is an annual instructor of the NOFA five-day Accreditation Courses in Organic Land Care, held in CT, MA, RI and NY. The program's goals are to maintain soil health, eliminate synthetic pesticide and fertilizer use, and increase landscape diversity.

Michael has published many additional articles and lectures regularly on organic land care. His mission is to "extend the

Silene regia (Royal catchfy) grows along prairie

vision, principles, and expertise of organic agriculture to the landscapes where people live."

Dr. Douglas W. Tallamy, Professor and Chair of the Department of Entomology and Wildlife Ecology, University of Delaware.
Douglas Tallamy has written more than 65 research articles and has taught insect taxonomy, behavioral ecology and other courses for many years. He is a sought after speaker on these subjects. His widely read book *Bringing Nature Home, How Native Plants Sustain Wildlife in Our Gardens* brings to light the destructive impact planting alien

ature Reserve, Missouri.

plants has on native ecosystems and native insect populations. Dr. Tallamy's important message is that we can reverse the loss of biodiversity in urban and suburban areas by favoring native plants over alien plants in our landscapes. Chief among his research goals is to better understand the many ways insects interact with plants and how such interactions determine the diversity of animal communities.

Larry Weaner, Designer, Educator and President, Larry Weaner Landscape Design Associates, Inc.
Larry Weaner has been practicing landscape design professionally since 1977. He founded Larry Weaner Landscape Design Associates in 1982, a firm that combines environmental science and garden design. Larry is active as a guest lecturer and instructor for numerous horticultural and environmental organizations throughout the United States and is a past Board Member and Environmental Committee Chair of the Association of Professional Landscape Designers. Larry also developed New Directions in the American Landscape (NDAL) in 1990, a conference series dedicated to the study of natural landscape design.

Larry is considered to be one of the premier meadow designers in the country. His projects, including meadows, span more than 10 states and have been featured in national and international publications. They also have been included in garden tours sponsored by the Association of Professional Landscape Designers, The American Horticulture Society and The Garden Conservancy.

acknowledgments

I have a philosophy in life: just ask. You never know unless you take that step. So I'd like to acknowledge and thank the many people I just asked to help me in writing this book and creating the companion video.

This book could never have taken shape without Diane Buric, Diane Buric Design and Illustration. She is an extraordinary art director who took my images and copy and crafted a beautiful layout and flow of information. She is passionate about the subject and spent countless hours working with me to convey this information in a straightforward, easy to understand volume. At the very least, Diane will be getting a backyard meadow garden and pond!

My experts, Neil Diboll, Michael Nadeau, Doug Tallamy and Larry Weaner helped inspire me to create this book. They have been there all the way as it has blossomed from a simple guide to a comprehensive book on all aspects of meadow and prairie site preparation, design, planting, maintenance, native plants and insects. Their dedication to restoring ecosystems is obvious in their work and efforts to help bring this book to the public.

A very large aspect of taking on a project like this is loyal support from family and friends. In particular, I'd like to thank two of my brothers, Dave and Rick Zimmerman. Dave, who allowed me the use of his back yard as a meadow demonstration site, likes to refer to it as the day we birthed a meadow. Today, his yard is an oasis in the midst of endless lawns, for gold finches, hummingbirds, bees and butterflies. Rick, along with his son Daniel, did the sweaty part, stripping the sod and planting hundreds of plugs. This is nothing new to Rick who is an organic farmer and my springboard for organic ideas. Rick and I spent many hours, late into the night, discussing the content of this book and his input has incredibly strengthened the final product.

If you weren't drafted to appear in the book and video as Rick, Daniel and my nephew Justin Crockett were, you helped in other ways. My daughter, Cassie Cummins and my uncle and aunt, Tom and Joan Cultice, were my editors. Thank you for the punctuation and rewrite expertise!

My kids, Erin, Luke and Cassie, encouraged me and patiently listened to daily updates. My sisters, Gail Zimmerman and Carol McKeever and brother Mike Zimmerman, were called upon to read every page and gave me critical feedback. On the technical side, my brother-in-law, Mike McKeever, pulled me through numerous computer malfunctions and was instrumental in formatting the cost comparison charts. I don't think any one in the family escaped participation in this endeavor!

I want to give special thanks to three dear friends, Rick Patterson, Sandy Cannon-Brown and Stephanie Turner. Rick, my steadfast soundman on the video portions of this project, gave endless hours, tramped through many meadows and humored me as I related,

The wind picks up silky strands attached to seeds of *Asclepias tuberosa* (Milkweed) and propels them to a new home. Milkweed plants are the only plant the Monarch butterfly caterpillar can eat.

blow by blow, each small triumph and, at times, steps backward. Sandy helped find grant money, helped to edit text and offered her staff, Allison Barnett, Michelle Williams and Olivia Yeo to edit the video. Master gardener, Stephanie Turner, enthusiastically joined the actor crowd and tackled the glossary section.

Many thanks to Joan Murray and the Wallace Genetic Foundation, Inc. for awarding me a generous grant to get the project started.

I travelled many miles throughout the country working with meadow and prairie makers. They were amazingly generous and took time out of their busy schedules to show me their meadow and prairie installations. Much of their expertise is reflected in the book. For example, Jack Pizzo, Jack Pizzo and Associates, shared his cost comparison chart design. From that inspiration, I was able to create a relevant chart, which translates the cost benefits of planting meadows instead of lawns.

There are countless other people I've never met face to face who contributed information, advice, photos and good will. To everyone who shared in this book, I could not have produced it without you. Please accept my heartfelt gratitude.

bibliography

Armitage, A., 2006 *Armitage's Native Plants for North American Gardens*, Timber Press, Inc.: 121-149

Brickell, C and J. ZukA-Z *Encyclopedia of Garden Plants, American Horticultural Society*, 1997, Dorling Kindersley Publishing: 126-149, 253-257

Carson, R. 1962, *Silent Spring*, Mariner, Houghton Mifflin, New York, NY: 16-17

Darke, R. 2007, *The Encyclopedia of Grasses for Livable Landscapes*, Timber Press, Inc.: 126-149

Delaney, K., L. Rodger, P. A. Woodliffe, G. Rhynard and P. Morris A Guide to E*stablishing Prairie and Meadow Communities in Southern Ontario, Planting the Seed*: 11, 13-14, 25, 58, 74

Diboll, N., *Guide to Prairie Establishment*: 54, 74, 79-80

Geist ,K., S. Pick and M. Brittingham. 2001 *Neighborly Natural Landscaping: Creating Natural Environments in Residential Areas*, Pennsylvania Wildlife no.10: 11, 149-153

Harker, D, G. Libby, K. Harker, S. Evans and M. Evans. 1999, *Landscape Restoration Handbook*, Second Edition, Lewis Publishers: 121-149

Illinois Native Plant Guide: Root Systems of Prairie Plants: 18-19

Ingram, M., G.P. Nabhan, and S.L Buchmann. *Our Forgotten Pollinators: Protecting the Birds and Bees*. Global Pesticide Campaigner, Volume 6, pg. 258 (Pesticde page

Iowa Department of Natural Resources, Prairie Resource Unit, 2009, *Prairie Roots, Seeds of Diversity*: 18, 54, 74

Jenkins, V.S. 1994, *The Lawn: A History Of An American Obsession*: 15-18, 151-153

Kurtz, C. 2001 *A Practical Guide to Prairie Reconstruction*, University of Iowa Press, Iowa City, IA: 14, 106-119

NOFA Organic Land Care Committee, 2007 *The NOFA Organic Lawn and Turf Handbook*, Organic Land Care Committee of the Northeast Organic Farming Association: 16-17, 20, 55

Pyle, R.M. 1981 *National Audubon Society, Field Guide to Butterflies*, Alfred A. Knopf, New York, NY: 126-149

Ramsey Kaufman, S. and W. Kaufman, 2007 *Invasive Plants, Guide to Identification and the Impacts and Control of Common North American Species*, Stackpole Books, Mechanicsburg, PA: 121-122

Rappaport, B. 1993, *As Natural Landscaping Takes Root We Must Weed Out the Bad Laws-How Natural Landscaping and Leopold's Land Ethic Collie With Unenlightened Weed Laws and What Must Be Done About It*. John Marshall Law Review, Volume 26 (4): 151-154